Sevenoaks School

A HISTORY

BRIAN SCRAGG

Sevenoaks School

A HISTORY

ASHGROVE PRESS, BATH

First published for Sevenoaks School by
ASHGROVE PRESS LIMITED
4 Brassmill Centre, Brassmill Lane
Bath BA1 3JN, U.K.

© Sevenoaks School 1993

ISBN 1–85398–063–3

Photoset by Ann Buchan (Typesetters), Middlesex
Printed and bound in Great Britain by
Butler & Tanner Ltd, Frome and London

CONTENTS

LIST OF PLATES

PREFACE

Sevenoaks School has a history – a lived history – over 550 years. Sadly, over the greater part of this period, there is little written and virtually no pictorial record; for the last fifty years there is too much. To look back over six centuries, therefore, and produce not just an inert and uneven catalogue of facts but a balanced biography of a living community was a tall order. To perform it the Governors turned to Brian Scragg, one of their number.

Brian Scragg came late to schoolmastering after five years in Paris book-selling, translating, working for the Canadian Embassy and broadcasting for the BBC French Services. Kim Taylor appointed him in 1955 and he became part of the Taylor revolution. When he left in 1986 a colleague, once a pupil of his, said of his early days in the French Department that, surprisingly, "it began to look as though he was interested in education, ideas, imagination, in us" and, after his period as the first Housemaster of the new International Centre, that "his sense of a world beyond our horizons, his critique of our insularity, have changed Sevenoaks School deeply and permanently." Ultimately, as Undermaster, he served four headmasters, supporting them even when they went astray, but supporting the Common Room too when he thought they were right. He detested, then and now, showmanship and humbug, but for scholarship and the things of the mind he has an austere, unquenchable passion. It was our immense good fortune that he was available and willing to bring qualities like these to the writing of this book.

The book is not intended simply for the coffee-table. It is a serious history. But perhaps because, as he is the first to tell us, he is not a professional historian his book manages to entertain as well as instruct. It finds room not only for facts but also for conjecture and it opens up tantalising puzzles. Did William Sevenoaks start his school before providing for it in his will in 1432? Did he intend the grammar schoolmaster to be a cleric or not? How on earth did the Revd Simpson let the school dwindle to four pupils in 1748? Did the peculiar topography of Sevenoaks Town, hemmed in by the great estates of the noble and landed gentry, suffocate local initiative? Were Crofts and Birkett simply failures as headmasters or were they the victims of visionless, money-pinching governing bodies? Why did they – and the high Victorian times in which they worked – achieve so little?

The fifty years from 1830 to 1880 were probably the most formative in British educational history. Education was taking off. The monopoly of the religious denominations in providing schooling was being challenged by the growing recognition that the state had its responsibilities for the education of the nation's children. Typically British, the first controversy to rage – and rage it did – was about what kind of religious instruction was to be provided. An "agreed syllabus" was proposed, legitimised in the Forster Act of 1870, confirmed in the Butler Act of 1944 and is as yet unreformed by the Bakers and Pattens of today. More importantly, Forster's Act paved the way for compulsory attendance of children at elementary schools. Between 1870 and 1880 the numbers enrolled quadrupled – from one to four millions. It was an explosive period. But it hardly rattled the windows of the Free Grammar School of Queen Elizabeth. Nobody seems to have worried about the growth, in numbers, size and popularity, of the great public schools in the 1840s, 50s and 60s, nor about either the competition for affluent pupils that they would exert, however marginally, or the competition for poor pupils from Forster's compulsory attendances at local elementary schools. The School just muddled on. Its explosive renaissance was to be in the 1950s, not the 1850s. Is this because Taylor, Tammadge and Barker were there rather than Simpson, Crofts or Birkett? Or is it because in the nineteenth century there were no benefactors, no revenue surpluses and no capital reserves for development, whereas in this century there have been the munificent donations of Swanzy, the Johnsons and the Aishers? Did these Medici create our renaissance or did our incipient growth and success attract such benefactors?

A book that provokes questions like these is more than an official history. It is a good read. Because it is essentially about people it lets us listen over the centuries to the heart-beat of the place, sometimes weak and struggling, more recently pounding with energy and excitement. It can be commended to all who are part of the school, pupils, parents, staff and governors – past, present and to come. But not just to "insiders"; it should appeal to anyone who is interested in the birth, growth and fate of human institutions made by men – and in our case now, at last, by men and women.

William Pile

ACKNOWLEDGEMENTS

To J.T. Lennox, author in 1932 of the School's first History, which I have shamelessly and gratefully plundered; to Sir William Pile, my senior co-editor, for his constant advice, help and encouragement, and for all his labours in assembling the illustrations; to Kim Taylor (editor in 1957 of *At Honour's Game,* a rich source of material) for the fruits of his own research, and for his invaluable memories of life at Sevenoaks as a schoolboy and, later, as a Headmaster; to our President, Lord Sackville, for permission to reproduce paintings from Knole; to Ian Walker for kind guidance from a practising historian and to Professor Robin du Boulay for wise counsels on some of the mysteries of our early history; to Robert Wilkinson, Alan Tammadge and John Guyatt for proof-reading and for many helpful corrections and suggestions; to Robert Froy, Richard Barker, Gwen Robinson, Tom Mason, Claude Kempton, Kenneth Kevis, Harry Talbot, Diana Day and the late Jack Marriot for patiently submitting to tape-recorded interviews; to the many Old Sennockians who responded to my appeal for photographs, anecdotes and other memorabilia, in particular to Paul Clark, Don Brealey, Gordon Anckorn, John Brasier, Norman Prince, Richard Gunner, Peter Ware, David Handley, George Gatling, Charles Cavell, Jack Cooper and Victor Froud; to David Green of Knocker and Foskett; to School Librarians David Johnson and Rosemary Metcalfe; to the staff of Sevenoaks Public Library, the Kent Centre for Local Studies, the Corporation of London Record Office, the Guildhall Library, and the Library of the Department for Education; to William Curry for his pen sketches; to Jo Bradbury and Susie Goodson for many of the recent photographs; to David, Nicole and Catharine Press for invaluable help with the index; to the School Bursar Julian Patrick for finding me a corner to work in at School, and for patiently allowing me to monopolise so much of the time, skill and unfailing good will of Jackie Bradforth.

Brian Scragg

CHAPTER ONE

Our Founder

T he history of an old school can be told in many ways. There is the way of dates and statistics: when it was founded, how it grew, thanks to which Benefactors' gifts and legacies, what was built and when, how many children were educated, how many matches won, how many Awards. There is the way of social significance: how it related to local and national affairs, how it resisted or adapted to political change, and to religious or intellectual fashion. There is the way of rightful pride, the resounding roll-call of distinguished Old Boys or Girls. Then there is the way of amusing or edifying anecdotes, culled from contemporary accounts or correspondence, concerning the exploits and foibles of Headmasters, Governors, Staff, Pupils and Parents.

Most school histories opt for a combination of all these approaches, tending to lean more heavily towards one or the other according to the nature and importance of the school, and we would hardly wish to do otherwise. There are, however, certain difficulties in our case. First, the school archives are sadly deficient. There are long periods when, if we are lucky enough to know who the Headmaster was, we do not know how many boys were in the school, nor whether he had any staff to help him teach them. We do not know with any certainty what the school looked like before the eighteenth century – indeed, we do not always know *where* it was, for when repairs or rebuilding were in

11

train it apparently decamped to other premises, on one occasion even outside the town! Then there is the unavoidable fact that until the very end of the nineteenth century the school remained so small that its affairs attracted little local comment of eventual use to the historian.

Where then to begin? The rhetorical cry is all too familiar, but in the case of Sevenoaks the question is a real one: we are not quite sure. We know that our Founder, William Sevenoaks, died in 1432 and that his last will, made shortly before his death, included provisions for endowing in perpetuity "a Grammar School within some convenient House within the said town". Until very recently it had been assumed that the school was started then or shortly thereafter, but diligent research and persuasive arguments by a former Head-master, Kim Taylor, have suggested an earlier date – even as early as 1418, the year our Founder became Mayor of London. We shall return to this debate.

Let us start with William Sevenoaks, or Sennock, or Sevenoke, the man, or rather the abandoned child found by William Rumstead probably in 1373, according to William Lambarde, members of whose family were to play such a large part in the school's affairs over three centuries. In his *Perambulations of Kent*, printed in 1576, we read:

> About the latter ende of the reigne of King Edwarde the thirde, there was found (lying in the streetes at Sennocke) a poore childe, whose parents were unknowne, and he (for the same cause) named after the place where he was taken up, William Sennocke.
> This Orphan, was by the helpe of some charitable persons, brought up and nourtured, in such wise, that being made an Apprentice to a Grocer in London, he arose by degrees (in the course of time) to be Maior, and chiefe magistrate of that Citie.

We can put a little flesh on the bare bones of that romantic story, though unfortunately we know nothing of the orphan's early years. Stow's *Survey of London* names his finder and protector as Sir William de Romschedde, in whose manor house near Riverhill he probably lived. Since he is often referred to as "son of William Rumschedde" it is probable that he was given some tuition at home, for such rudiments of education as were normally provided by the parish priest were unlikely to have been deemed adequate for a boy destined to be apprenticed to a London livery company. In 1394, probably aged 21, he completed a seven year period of apprenticeship in London to Hugh de Bois, described as a "ferrer" (ironmonger) though he seems also to have traded as a grocer, in consequence of which William Sevenoaks was admitted to the Freedom of the Grocers' Company in that year. Now began his steady rise to a position of wealth and influence amid the intrigue and violence of a city which only a few years earlier had been briefly captured by the peasants and seen Wat Tyler slain at Smithfield before the mob he led.

12

A Grocer and a City Man

The Grocers' Company, the second oldest of London's livery companies, had been formed in 1345 from earlier fraternities of "Pepperers of Soper's Lane and Spicerers of the Ward of Cheap". In Ravenhill's "Short Account of the Grocers" we learn that "the word Grocer was a term distinguishing merchants of this society, in opposition to inferior retailers, for that they usually sold in gross quantities, by great weights. And in some of our old books the word signifies merchants that in their merchandising dealt for the *whole* of any kind". However, Sevenoaks would have been no office-bound wholesale importer and exporter in the modern sense. Much of a medieval grocer's trade was direct and personal: he owned or hired a ship, went wherever the goods were grown or traded (perhaps to Baltic or Mediterranean ports), struck his bargain, loaded his cargo, sailed home and set about selling it. We can get some impression of the risks taken by a medieval Grocer from a contemporary document, *Les Pointz de la Chartre d'Olyron,* written in 1344 in Norman French but given in an English translation as an Appendix to Baron Heath's *History of the Grocers' Company*. A typical Rule runs:

> If a ship departs for Bordeaux or elsewhere with a freight, and is overtaken at sea by a storm, and it cannot escape without casting out the goods on board, the master is bound to say to the merchants and owners, Sirs, we cannot escape without throwing overboard the wines or goods; and if there be any merchants there who will answer that their will is contrary to the reasons of the master for casting out the goods, and will not agree, the master nevertheless ought not to leave them on board but cast over so much as he shall see needful; he and the third part of his companions making oath upon the Holy Evangelists, when they have come to safety to the land, that he did it only to save the body of the ship.

Storms were not the only danger encountered by those who went to sea: there were also the privateers. There was no royal fleet in those days, and the French, with their Breton and Spanish allies, were threatening our ships and even our coastal towns. In 1403, William Sevenoaks was one of the representatives of London authorised to "take men at arms and archers and mariners for the defence of the ships which the men of town are sending to Bordeaux and other places for wine and other merchandise, and to made war on the men of Brittany and others who may do anything contrary to the truce". The experience he acquired in dealing with ships and their masters, at sea and in port, and in protecting those ships, was to be put to use at a critical moment in his public career. That career is chiefly recorded in documents in the Guildhall, handwritten by clerks, sometimes in medieval English, sometimes in Latin, sometimes in Norman French. Fortunately, in Riley's nineteenth century

Charters, ordinances, proclamations, deeds etc. of the City of London, 13th–15th Century, the French and Latin documents are translated into stately English.

In 1399, Sevenoaks was appointed to help audit the accounts of the Chamberlain and Wardens of London Bridge. By 1404 he was himself the senior of those two Wardens, and in the same year was elected by his fellow merchants one of the two Wardens who governed the Grocers' Company. In 1408, when London and the south were threatened with near-famine, he it was who arranged for large quantities of wheat to be bought in the northern counties and shipped to the city. In 1411 he was elected an Alderman – a post of considerable importance, conferring upon its holders the right to be buried with baronial honours – and was thereafter re-elected continuously for fifteen years.

It is perhaps revealing, in view of his own uncertain origins, that Sevenoaks took an unusually active interest in the "wardship" of under-age children whose fathers had died. The City of London claimed the right and responsibility to ensure that their estates were properly administered by suitable guardians, that appropriate sureties were provided, and that in due course the heirs could claim their estates from the Court of Common Council. The Calendar of the Guildhall Letter-book records three occasions when he himself provided the surety: in one case the guardian defaulted, and Sevenoaks promptly paid over his surety of £30. In 1419, when he was Mayor and chief magistrate, some relatives of a ward claimed wardship. Instead of trying the case, Sevenoaks stepped down and, acting as a witness, put before the court a long statement establishing the City's own rights and responsibilities. In a proud, self-governing city with no police force, one duty laid upon aldermen was that of conducting enquiries and interrogating wrong-doers. The few cases that we know about suggest that, as a magistrate, Sevenoaks – though a man of principle, capable of decisive action – was unfashionably merciful even when personally attacked. One offender, an attorney, John Askewythe, was called to appear before him as Sheriff, to be questioned about his part in the escape of a priest imprisoned for adultery. The examination took place at Sevenoaks' private dwelling in St. Dunstan's in the East. At one point, angered by the questioning, Askewythe "maliciously went up to the said William, and violently laid hands upon him by the breast", yet his sentence was comparatively mild: the removal of his Freedom of the City, and imprisonment in Newgate for a year and a day. In a later case, one Thomas Meynelle, a fellow grocer, said menacingly that Sevenoaks deserved to suffer the fate of Nicholas Brembre, "a man lately of as high dignity in the City, and even higher than he was, who was afterwards drawn and hanged". Though a long term of imprisonment seemed inevitable, and was at first imposed, Sevenoaks successfully pleaded with the Mayor to "remit such imprisonment on condition of his future good behaviour".

☆ ☆ ☆

In 1412 the old king, Henry IV, died. Sevenoaks, for that year one of the two sheriffs of London Middlesex, doubtless joined the great procession accompanying the son to Westminster for his coronation; he was to play a significant part in Henry V's nine extraordinary years as king of England. When Henry invaded Normandy in 1415 and gained the astonishing victory of Agincourt, Sevenoaks is named among those going with the Mayor to the Abbey to give thanks. Two years later, war broke out again: money was urgently needed, parliament was again assembled. That year Sevenoaks was elected one of four members of parliament for London, and must have helped vote the necessary taxes and subsidies. The army crossed to France, took Caen, and in 1418 began the long and costly siege of Rouen. Henry sent to London urging that "in all the haste that ye may, ye wille do arrive as manie smale vessels as ye may goodlie, with vitaille, and namely with drinke, for to come to Harfleu, and from thennes as fer as they may up river of Seyne. . .". London responded vigorously, and Sevenoaks was prominent in that response. A proclamation was posted everywhere, giving a date by which all those who could should bring

> . . .wyn, ale, beer, fisshe, flesshe or any other maner vitaille, to refreshing of the kynges hoost. . .; let him in halle haste between this and the forseyd Sonday come to William Sevenok, and certain Aldermaen and Comuners, that are assigned for the same thing in especial, unto the Churche of Seynt Dunstans in the Est, in Tourstrete, and there declare unto hem certaine quantite of ther vitaile, and they shal assigne and dispose him redy shippying for her passage.

Reinforcements were needed too, and a second proclamation urged "alle maner men that wil toward the costes of Normayde . . . let hem arraye and make hem redy inye best wyse that they can or may, in alle hast, and come to Seint Dunstanes in the Est, on Monday that next cometh, at eyghte of clok, to William Sevenok, Alderman, and his felawes, that are assigned therefor in especial, and they shal be assigned redy shippying and passage, and eche of him shal have a noble for to vitaile him. . .".

In that year, 1418, William Sevenoaks was elected Mayor of London. After arranging for payments to the suppliers of "vitailles", he organised a donation to meet the cost of the war. The following year, his grateful king wrote to him from Pontoise:

> Trusty and well beloved. We grete you well, and we thank you with all our hert of the good wil and service that we have always founde in you hedertoward, and spicillich of your kynde and notable profre of an ayde, the which ye han graunted unto us of your owne good motion, as our brother of Bedford and our Chancellor of England have written to us. . .

On another occasion, when Sevenoaks and other wealthy merchants made the king a substantial loan, the royal sword, described in the Close Rolls, was pledged as security:

A sword of Spain, garnished with gold and six great baleis and three other lesser baleis, 7 large sapphires and two other lesser sapphires, 99 great pearls of one sort and 26 other pearls of a lesser sort, worth in all 2000 pounds and troy weight 84.1/4 ounces.

In 1420, after the fall of Rouen, Henry was able to conclude the Treaty of Troyes, and his marriage to Catherine of Valois promised at last to unite the crown of England and France, and to end the long and wasting wars. Henceforth, William Sevenoaks was to be involved less dramatically in the affairs of state, but perhaps no less significantly. While mayor, he seems to have waged with unusual vigour the battle against profiteers: the Company of Fishmongers is urged to exercise proper control over the price of fish, and those who adulterate wine are to be put in the pillory. Officials abusing their position by accepting bribes or protection money are warned that they will be dismissed, for they are acting "to the great dishonour of their masters, and to the common loss of all the City". As Mayor and Alderman, Sevenoaks appears to have been an upright defender of the rule of law and to have done what he could – inevitably not very much – to combat political and commercial corruption in the city, and to reduce the violence and disorder of its streets. In 1426, a year before he retired from active public life, he was overseeing building work being done for Henry VI, "with power of imprisoning in cases of contumacy and of holding inquisitions should any materials . . . be taken away or purloined". His was the period of the great medieval mayors, which ended some thirty years later: the confusions of the Wars of the Roses undermined the relative stability which had allowed the rising mercantile class to flourish, and to ally themselves to a strong monarchy. Mayors and Alderman were city grandees, taxed as earls and barons respectively.

In 1432, probably aged 59, William Sevenoaks died, and he was buried in the church of St. Martin's on Ludgate Hill. There his monument was destroyed in the Great Fire of 1666. In the same flames disappeared his great coat of arms, which once hung at the end of Grocers' Hall: all we have is a rough sketch and the heraldic description: "On Azure, seven acorns, 2, 3, 2 Or".

Though Sevenoaks might seem to have a greater claim than his friend Richard Whittington to the celebrity conferred by folklore, legend and pantomime (for he genuinely did rise from rags to riches, whereas Whittington was the son of a west country baronet), it was not to be. However, his greatness was not quickly forgotten. In 1592, Richard Johnson wrote *The Nine Worthies of London*, celebrating "the honourable exercise of arms, the virtues of the valiant and the memorable attempts of magnanimous minds: pleasant for

16

Fig (i)   Sketch of Sir William Sevenoaks' coat of arms

Gentlemen, not unseemly for Magistrates and most profitable for Prentices".
One by one the ghosts of the Worthies are called forward to tell their tales.
"This pastime put the famous Sevenoaks in mind of his beginning, how Nature
first had initiated her work in misery, and ended it in miracles". He tells his
story in fifteen six line stanzas and an "envoi", and is by no means averse to
"improving" truth for dramatic effect: for instance, his great labours in support
of Henry V's French campaign are transmuted into his implausible claim to
have fought at Agincourt himself, and even to have engaged the Dauphin in
single combat, in which he

> Lent the Dolphyne such a blow
> As warmed his courage well to lay about
> Till he was breathless though he were so stout.

> At last the noble prince did ask my name,
> My birth, my calling and my fortunes past.
> With admiration he did hear the same
> And a bag of crownes to me he cast.
> And when he went, he said to mee:
> "Seavenoake, be proud, the Dolphyne fought with thee".

More to our purpose, the poem does not cling to these dizzy heights of
fantasy, and movingly concludes:

> By testament, in Kent I built a towne
> And briefly calde it Sevenaks from my name;
> A free schoole to sweet learning, to renowne,
> I placde for those that playde at honour's game;
> Both land and living to that towne I gave,
> Before I took possession of my grave.

There is no evidence that William Sevenoaks was married, but that means little. In the early fifteenth century marriage was often little more that a small practical adjustment in a man's life, and women had to be content with the specifically domestic role of housekeeper and child-bearer. As for children, it seems likely that he had at least one. In his last will, he decreed that if ever his beneficiaries in the parish of Sevenoaks should fail to observe its terms and provisions, then the income of all his lands and tenements should pass to "the next heir male of me the said William Sennocke, and to the heirs males of his body lawfully begotten, and so from heir male to heir male successively". A John Sevenoke is named as Executor in a will made in 1426, which makes him a likely candidate. We know very little about him. He is mentioned in one source as "a certain ecclesiastic of dissolute habits, by name John Sevenoke, Prior of Holy Trinity, London, from 1438–1445". This church was a beneficiary under one of William Sevenoaks' wills. In the records we read: "John Sevenok. The Court of Aldermen appointed Proctors to oppose the confirmation by the Bishop of London of Sevenok's election as Prior of Holy Trinity on the ground of immorality, but their opposition was ineffectual". Perhaps it is just as well that the terms of William's final will were observed, and that the School, not the son, inherited the task of honouring his memory! For the honours due to William Sevenoaks extend far beyond our local gratitude: he has a place among those men of vision who helped to change the course of national history.

CHAPTER TWO

The Foundations

Schools before the fifteenth century, whatever form they took, were fundamentally appendages of the Church, either of the monastic or abbatial establishments of the celibate regular clergy, or of the churches and cathedrals of the secular clergy: the latter were often married men, living and working amid the people in village, town and city. Sometimes these Church-based schools would be preparing young boys for eventual admission to the priesthood, sometimes merely teaching them to sing liturgical chants in a Latin they understood not at all, but though the position of Schoolmaster (or even more grandly, Chancellor) was sometimes mentioned alongside Abbot, Cantor or Treasurer, the education they purveyed was seldom more, and often less, than rudimentary rote instruction in the 3 Rs.

In these plague-ridden, lawless and turbulent times, men and women were – even more than the Elizabethans – much obsessed with death. Only heaven seemed to offer a refuge from Mutabilitie, and those who could afford good works sought to secure their place by contributing to church funds, or by endowing chantries charged to pray for their souls once they were dead. Grammar schools occasionally figured in wills, often linked with hospitals and almshouse (for the task of all three was to prepare their inmates for a better life), and invariably administered by an ecclesiastical institution.

It was against this background that the early years of the fifteenth century saw a new pattern emerging – that of grammar schools endowed as secular rather than religious foundations by municipal guilds, civic dignitaries or rich merchants, and committed not to the rudimentary skills of the church schools but to the idea of learning as an end in itself, and as a preparation for professional and vocational activities; at the same time they would reinforce the use of English as the medium of formal communication. They were Free Schools, for many of the benefactors had risen from humble origins, and they continued the tradition of admitting rich and poor together, but it was in the pursuit of scholarship, literacy and numeracy, for would-be undergraduates and apprentices alike, that these grammar schools strove to fulfil their truly revolutionary role. The central importance given to the teaching of Latin, as Lawson and Silver have pointed out in their *Social History of Education in England*, was particularly useful for those seeking indentured apprenticeships with masters of such trades as apothecaries, copyists, notaries, scriveners, stationers and suchlike.

Sevenoaks School and its Founder can thus take pride in being one of the precursors of this significant change. A little earlier, similar grammar schools had been founded in Oswestry (1408), Middleton in Lancashire (1412) and Durham (1414); and a little later at Newport in Shropshire (1442) and Newlands in Gloucestershire (1446). The trend was to survive the Wars of the Roses and the dissolution of the monasteries, and by 1535 there would be probably three to four hundred such schools throughout the land. Great trees indeed from acorns grow!

The acorn planted by William Sevenoaks grew from one of his wills, of which he made six between 1426 and 1432. In four of these the beneficiaries were churches: St Dunstan's in the East, St Martin-within-Ludgate, Holy Trinity-within-Algate and St Nicholas' Church in Sevenoaks. It is the last of these which concerns us. Sevenoaks had not lost touch with his home town during his busy years in the City, and had been involved in the sale or transfer of several properties in the area. And it was to Sevenoaks that his thoughts turned when making his final will, dated July 4th, 1432, shortly before his death.

Amongst his most important London properties were "Lands and Tenements with a Wharf adjoining, and the Houses and Builings thereupon built, with the Appurtenances . . . in the Street of Petty Wales in the Parish of All Saints, of Barking Church, near the Tower of London". It was this valuable property which he now bequeathed to the Rector and Wardens of "the Church of Sennocke", who with other parishioners were to act as trustees. During her lifetime the previous owner, Margaret Walton, was to receive a comfortable income of twenty marks from the property, but on her death the trustees are charged to devote as much as necessary "of the yearly Rents, profits and Emoluments whatsoever, coming and herafter to come out of all the Lands and Tenements aforesaid" to the establishment of a Free Grammar School and Almshouses.

Their task, precisely, was to "find and maintain for ever, one Master, an honest Man, sufficiently instructed in the Science of Grammar, Bachelor of Arts, but by no means in Holy Orders, which may keep a Grammar School in some convenient House within the said Town of Sennocke . . . that he may teach and instruct poor Children whatsoever coming thither to be taught, taking nothing of them, or their Parents or Friends, for the teaching and instructing them". As for the "twenty poor Men or Women . . . being in greater Want", who were to receive ten shillings a year, they were to dwell in "Mansion Houses . . . to be gotten and ordered with my Goods by the Leave of the King, or by other good and lawful Means, according to the Discretion of my Executors in Form aforesaid".

That looked clear enough, but in fact these few lines have been subjected to a considerable amount of learned scrutiny, and have caused some disagreement among historians. Did Sevenoaks really mean to insist that the Master should not be in Holy Orders? If so, this seemed to A.F. Leach, in his authoritative *The Schools of Mediaeval England*, to indicate "a distinctly anti-sacerdotal tendency", or at least a determination to avoid the appointment of a schoolmaster "wasting his time and performing masses for the dead as a chantry priest, or holding a living and neglecting the school". Other scholars have queried the English translation of the original Latin, pointing out that *in sacris ordinibus minime constitutus* might mean *at least* in Holy orders. Certainly, Sevenoaks' other Wills make any "anti-sacerdotal tendency" very unlikely; if he did indeed mean to exclude priests it was probably because, in keeping with his character as a generous but no-nonsense merchant and city administrator, he did not want his School to be run part-time by a Master largely occupied elsewhere.

Another puzzling thing about the Will has emerged from Kim Taylor's recent study of the Will made in 1437 by William Burton, a close associate of William Sevenoaks. From this we learn that at the time of Sevenoaks' death the provisions of his last will "could have . . . no effect", since the ownership of his London property was still shared among certain "co-feoffees" he had nominated during his lifetime, and who "had not released their right and title of and in the same lands and tenements". The nomination of co-feoffees or co-owners was a very common legal device to circumvent the law that forbade gifts made within a year of one's death to "undying bodies" such as monasteries or churches. The testator trusted his co-feoffees to carry out his wishes, which of course they sometimes failed to do. However, by 1437, Burton had acquired all the co-feoffies' rights in the London properties, and these he duly conveyed to the Rector of St Nicholas' Church in Sevenoaks and his colleagues.

21

THE PETTY WALES BENEFACTION

William Sevenoaks' founding benefaction to the School was the Harts Horn property in Petty Wales, the most easterly section of Thames Street in London. In Fig (ii) below the Wool Key, lying between the Custom House and the Tower, was the site of the Harts Horn property.

A contemporary report of 1715 reads "On Thursday evening fire broke out in Thames Street not far from the Custom House, occasioned by the accidental blowing up of a house where gunpowder was sold which fired two houses next to it . . ." The fire spread and so damaged the Custom House that it had to be demolished and be entirely rebuilt.

We do not know whether the Harts Horn was directly affected by this disaster but, in 1722, the Crown purchased the property from the School in preparation for the rebuilding of the Custom House. The new Custom House was designed by Thomas Ripley – Fig (iii) (opposite) shows its location.

Fig (ii)   Brown and Hogenberg's map of 1572

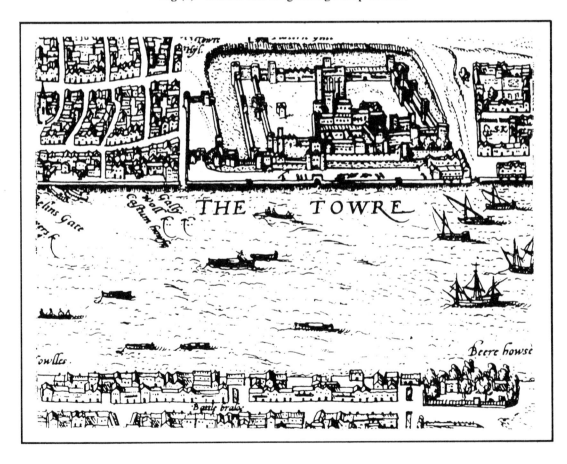

Fig (iii)   John Rocque's map of 1746

Again we do not know whether Ripley's rebuilding incorporated the Harts Horn or not. Although built on three storeys instead of Wren's two, it seems to have used the same foundations. Fig (iv) is an engraving of the riverside frontage. We can only surmise that William Sevenoaks' land, the endowment underlying the foundation of Sevenoaks School, also underlay either the east wing of Ripley's new building or the older building immediately to its east (right in picture).

Fig (iv)   Ripley's Custom House

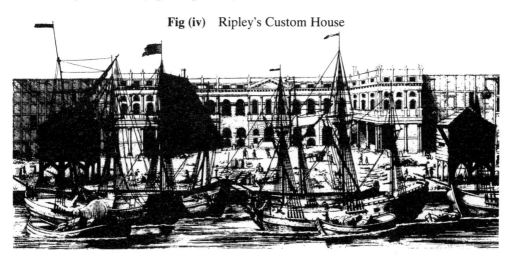

23

This does not mean that the school could not have been functioning at some time before 1438. Burton's Will, while for the most part repeating Sevenoaks' detailed instructions, makes certain surprising and significant changes. It is now stipulated that the children shall be taught, not "in some convenient house", but "in the messuage with its appurtenances which late was the said William Sevenoke's". Similarly, the poor men and women are to be housed "in those cottages with appurtenances", which a certain Stephen Browne (another eminent Grocer, Mayor of London in 1438) "and others thereof enfeoffed" (presumably by Sevenoaks) had recently conveyed for that purpose to the Rector, Vicar and two Churchwardens of St Nicholas' Church.

Since, during his lifetime, Sevenoaks already owned land and buildings suitable for use as a school and almshouses, is it not possible that they were already in use before his death? Taylor rightly reminds us that in medieval times it was not at all uncommon for schools to be functioning some years before they were endowed or incorporated. In the uniquely grand case of Winchester, for instance, the successive stages were amply documented, but in a small country town "starting a school came nearer to building a shop with living over, and trying to induce a tenant to occupy it. The need is to put up a suitable building in the hope that one of those rare birds, a Latin schoolmaster, could be induced to settle in it".

The suggestion that Sevenoaks School may have been in operation before 1432 is not prompted by any whimsical preference for the greatest possible antiquity. After all, until the early 19th century the date given for our Foundation was always 1418. Opposite this date, the year William Sevenoaks became Mayor of London, Lambarde tells us that "calling to mind the goodness of Almightie God, and the favour of the Townesmen extended towards him, he determined to make an everlasting monument of his thankfull minde for the same. And therefore of his owne charge, builded both an Hospitall for reliefe of the poore, and a free schoole for the education of youthe within this Towne: endowing the one and the other, with competent yearely living. . .". The Act of Parliament of 1597, which regularised the legal position and properties of the Foundation, declares that both school and almshouses "were at first erected by one William Sevenoke, citizen and grocer of London, in time of Henry the Sixth, and by his last Will endowed. . .". Although this would date the buildings after 1422, it again implies that they were in existence and possibly functioning before that last Will was drawn up.

However, it seems likely that we shall never know precisely when the first "poor scollers" assembled to be taught in what would one day become Sevenoaks School, nor when, in a strictly legal sense, it was founded. Perhaps it doesn't really matter very much. Many other ancient schools have been similarly uncertain about their origins. In 1432 our Founder died, and generously remembered us in his final Will, and we cannot be doing him less than honour if we gratefully celebrate certain anniversaries of that year.

24

Fig (v)   Sevenoaks School as might it have appeared in the fifteenth century

The Town and Some Early Names

What was the town of Sevenoaks like in the first quarter of the fifteenth century when William Sevenoaks was alive and the School was in its infancy? The road from Tonbridge climbed the escarpment of the Downs up Riverhill, as it does today. For a mile or so it passed through forest or woodlands that included, perhaps, the eponymous seven oak trees near the present White Hart Inn.

Where Park Grange house now stands, the road widened to form what is now Upper High Street. Here, over a century earlier, the first weekly markets had been held; here were timber-framed houses, and possibly one or two of stone; here stood St Nicholas' Church, smaller than today but with its new north aisle and its decorated windows (though as yet without its superb Perpendicular windows east and south); and here were the site and first buildings of the School and almshouses, modest structures of timber, wattle and plaster.

Some three hundred yards north of the church the road forked, exactly as it does today. One arm – the present High Street – followed fairly closely the line of Seal Hollow road to Seal, though some maps show a branch running down St John's Hill to Greatness, Otford and Dartford. The other arm – the London Road – passed through Riverhead and Knockholt via either Chipstead or Dunton Green on its way to London. Beyond this fork, continuous building may have extended no further than the Shambles with its Market Cross, though some may have straggled on as far as Bligh's. Thereafter, and as far as Riverhead, Otford and Seal, all was woodland, farmland, common land and

25

scrub – though somewhere in this area were a gallows, a vineyard and a chantry chapel.

Thus the town was hardly more than five or six hundred yards from end to end, with perhaps a hundred and fifty houses and five hundred inhabitants. To the east of the town lay the manor, farms and lawns of Knole, not yet as extensive or as magnificent as Archbishop Bourchier was to make them, but the first of several vast estates that were to come. Though timber, wattle and daub would give way to stone, brick and clay tiles, in character and appearance it would remain largely unchanged until the coming of the railway in the nineteenth century.

Between William Sevenoaks' death and 1489 – when we believe we have the name of a Master, Thomas Hales – we know nothing of the development of the school. We do know, however, that the little school survived when many others were dying, starved of good teachers of grammar by the plague and by the Universities' preoccupation with logic and philosophy. Clearly, there must have been sufficient confidence in its health and prospects to encourage local gentry and landowners to support it: the School probably owes as large a debt to these early benefactors as it does to the Swanzys, Johnsons and Aishers whose munificence in the twentieth century enabled it to grow into the great school it is today.

The earliest gift, made in 1510 by William Pett of Riverhill and others, consisted of fifteen acres of land lying east of Hollybush Lane (the site of the old Sevenoaks Recreation Ground) – subsequently always referred to as the "School Lands" (see overleaf). In 1543 a (presumably grateful) former pupil of the School, John Potkin, "of his godly Zeale towards the better Mayntenance thereof", provided an annuity of £9 from his property, the Star Inn in Bread Street, London. In 1565 John Lennard de Cheevinge granted an annuity of 10s. 8d. out of his lands at Wickhurst. In 1571 a certain Anthony Pope was moved to make a gift "unto the Scole of Sevenoke . . . towards the meyntenance of God's glory, and the eruditions and bringinge up of the Pore Scollers there in virtuouse disciplyne, godly Learninge, and good and cevill manners. . .". These edifying sentiments, however, were not all that they seemed, for Pope had somehow secured for himself an outrageously undervalued long lease on some of the School's London property. Acting under pressure, he was to all intents and purposes forced to make this "endowment", which was to take effect from the date of his death, and consisted of an interest of £7 or £8 a year from the lease of a tavern, The George in Petty Wales. We shall hear more of this establishment.

In 1578, John Porter, citizen and fishmonger of London, but born in Seal, "being moved with a godlie Zeale and charitable Mynde to further and advaunce Litterature and Learneinge, and the bringing up of Youthe in Virtue and Learneinge in the said Towne and Parish of Sevenocke, and to doe good to and amongst the Inhabitants of the said Towne of Seale. . .", promised an annual payment of £10 from his lands in the neighbourhood to augment the Master's and Usher's salaries, on condition that the children of Seal and Kemsing should be educated free at the school.

Before considering the next properly documented episode in the history of the School, one is tempted to try to imagine some of the national issues and events dominating ale-house gossip in Sevenoaks in the century or so following William's death. Or perhaps they didn't? Perhaps the talk was all of the price of land and food and marital squabbles and unpaid bills? For us, so far away, carefully arranging blocks neatly labelled Hundred Years War, Wars of the Roses, Dissolution of the Monasteries, Reformation, Murder of the Princes and so on, it is all too easy to adopt the modern global village approach, and to construct a very false picture of the lives and preoccupations of a little market town in Kent.

Nevertheless, there was one event of both national and local significance, which was indirectly to prove crucial to the development of both town and School, and that was the Battle of Solefields. In 1450 the war with France was going badly, taxes were cruelly high and the government was very unpopular. The Manor of Knole at that time was owned by James Fiennes, Lord Say and Sele, Henry VI's Treasurer and Lieutenant for Kent, upon whom local hatred was naturally focused. In late May the rebel Jack Cade assembled "the commons of Kent in great numbers" and marched on London, making camp at Blackheath and sending the king a list of fifteen grievances. The king's response was to dispatch an army to crush them. The rebels retreated into the woods around Sevenoaks, where they surprised and defeated the pursuing soldiers led by Sir Humphrey Stafford and his kinsman William Stafford: both were killed. How many of Sevenoaks School's first few pupils, one wonders, saw or heard the battle raging where today our playing fields lie?

Encouraged by success, the men from Kent marched northward again, entered London, astonishingly held it for two days, and after a violent night battle for London Bridge persuaded the King's officials at the Tower to hand over Baron Say and Sele, whom they beheaded. As Sir John Dunlop says, in *The Pleasant Town of Sevenoaks – a History*, "that axe stroke was to have far reaching consequence". Not only did the Battle of Solefields bring the town into national history, but "the decapitation of James Fiennes, Baron Say and Sele, opened the way, by the strangeness of fate, to the glories of Knole". That strange turn of fate "made Knole, for a whole century, the home of archbishops and linked the small town of Sevenoaks with the drama of the Tudor dynasty and the full tide of the Reformation".

Poor Jack Cade died in a skirmish a month after the Battle of Solefields. It is quite probable that he had unwittingly done Sevenoaks School yet another

THE "SCHOOL LANDS"

The earliest sites, (see Fig (vii) opposite), were the first school house and almshouses (A) and the 15 acres adjacent to Hollybush Lane (B) given to the School in 1510 by William Pett and others. The latter, known as the "School Lands", though also in Victorian times as School Field, remained in the School's possession until 1912. For nearly 400 years they provided a stable income from rents obtained by auction (see Fig (viii), page 30), but in the 1880s they were used as playing fields by the School Cricket Club (see below). Offered for sale in 1905 (when Walthamstow Hall purchased 3 acres), 1909 and 1912 (see Figs (ix) and (x), page 30), they were finally acquired by the local Council and became the Town's Recreation Ground. The sale proceeds (some £4000) were used in part to buy new playing fields off Solefields Road (C).

The shaded areas D and E (page 30) were given to the School by the Johnson family, Johnsons Boarding House (D) in 1927 and Park Grange (E) in 1948. Other shaded areas are post-war purchases, including the International Sixth Form Centre (F).

Fig (vi) School Field, Hollybush Lane, Sevenoaks

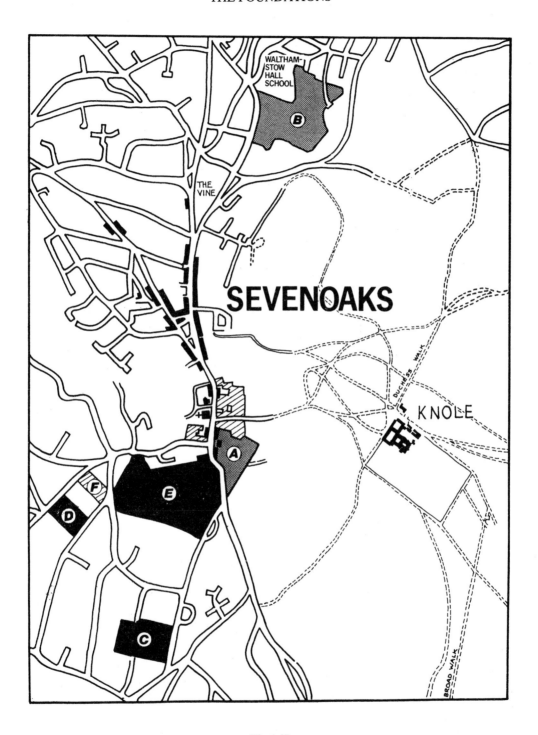

Fig (vii)

School Lands,
SEVENOAKS, KENT.

To be Let by Auction,

At the ROYAL OAK INN, SEVENOAKS;

On Thursday, the 21st of September, 1820,

In ONE or MORE LOTS;

(Subject to such Conditions, as shall be then and there produced;)

All those several Pieces or Parcels of Land, commonly called or known by the Name of the

School Lands,

Situate near the VINE, in

Sevenoaks;

and containing altogether, about

14 Acres & Half

With a convenient BARN, &c. thereon,

In a good state of Cultivation, and well calculated for a Nursery or Market Garden.

Further Particulars may be had by applying to Messrs. WILLARD and COLE, Solicitors, Sevenoaks; or to Mr. H. ROSE, of the same Place, Auctioneer.

☞ The Auction will commence precisely at Five o'Clock in the Afternoon.

CLOUT, Printer, Stationer, &c. Sevenoaks.

Fig (viii)

Local advertisements for the letting (left) and sale (below) of the School Lands.

Fig (ix)   below left

Fig (x)   below right

By the Authority of the Board of Education.

SEVENOAKS, KENT

In a very elevated and charming position, commanding beautiful views over the surrounding delightful country.

Particulars, Plan and Conditions of Sale
OF THE EXCEEDINGLY CHOICE

Freehold Building Estate,
Known as the

Sevenoaks School Lands,

Most desirably situate in HOLLY BUSH LANE, close to the Town and Vine Cricket Ground, and within ten minutes' walk of both Stations on the S.E. & C. Ry. It embraces an area of about

12a. 1r. 30p.

Possesses an Extensive Road Frontage, and from its important position, and proximity to the Town, with **Drainage, Water and Gas Facilities**, and offering

UNRIVALLED SITES
For the Erection of Superior Residences,

RIPE FOR IMMEDIATE DEVELOPMENT

And admirably adapted for **successful and profitable enterprise** by subdivision into Plots, which

MESSRS. CRONK

Have received instructions from the Governors of the Sevenoaks Grammar School Foundation to Sell by Auction at the

Auction Mart, Tokenhouse Yard, London, E.C.,

On FRIDAY, JULY 23rd, 1909,

At TWO o'clock.

May be viewed any day previous to the Sale. Particulars and Conditions of Sale may be obtained at the principal Inns and Hotels in the Neighbourhood; of

Messrs. KNOCKER, KNOCKER & Co., Solicitors, Sevenoaks, Kent; and of
Messrs. CRONK, Land Agents and Surveyors, Sevenoaks, and 12, Pall Mall, London, S.W.

J. Salmon, Steam Printer, Sevenoaks, &c.

PARTICULARS.

THE EXCEEDINGLY CHOICE

Freehold Building Estate
KNOWN AS THE

Sevenoaks School Lands

Situate in Holly Bush Lane close to the Town of Sevenoaks, the Vine Cricket Ground, and within ten minutes' walk of both Tub's Hill and Bat and Ball Stations on the S.E. & C.R. It consists of the 3 Fields with Barn and Shed thereon and embraces an area of about

15a. 1r. 30p.

and has a frontage of about 380 feet to Holly Bush Lane in which the Sewer, Water & Gas Mains are laid.

The Estate occupies

☞ A SPLENDID POSITION ☜

in the best residential part of Sevenoaks, standing high, the altitude being upwards of 500 feet above sea level,

COMMANDING LOVELY VIEWS

over Knole Park and the surrounding picturesque country, and affords

Unrivalled Sites for the Erection of Superior Residences,

which are in great demand in this delightful residential district, owing to its central position and proximity to town. It possesses EXCEPTIONAL ADVANTAGES as a Building Estate, and being

RIPE FOR BUILDING OPERATIONS

It offers a splendid opportunity of acquiring Building Land close to the Town, either with a view to building thereon or to a profitable re-sale in the near future by

SUB-DIVISION INTO PLOTS

or for the creation of Ground Rents.

The Cricket Pavilion, Flagstaff, and any other effects belonging to Sevenoaks School are not included in this sale and will be removed before completion.

favour, securing for it the distinction of being the only school to be mentioned in the works of Shakespeare. In Part 2 of *Henry VI* Cade has reached London and is accusing Lord Saye of numerous crimes. One of them is that he "has most traitorously corrupted the youth of the realm in erecting a Grammar School". In Holinshed, source of much of Shakespeare's historical material, a certain diffuse hostility towards educated men appears in the peasants' list of grievances and demands. As we shall see, by the time Shakespeare was writing the School had become quite famous, had attracted the interest of royalty and great courtiers, and its connection with Knole was already strong. It seems very likely that Shakespeare, never a stickler for historical accuracy, was simply extending that connection back to 1450. Certainly, if he did have a specific school in mind, it could have been none other than our own.

This is not the place to recount the glories of Knole in the fifteenth century and after: that has been lavishly and brilliantly done elsewhere; but the pride and prosperity in which the little town quite suddenly began to bask could not help but benefit the School. Archbishop Bourchier purchased Knole in 1456 for £266. 13s. 4d. and spent large sums extending it. He loved the house and lived in it until he died there thirty years later. In his dotage, he inadvertently connived at the illegitimate accession of Richard III, but in his prime he was a man of great culture and learning: he was almost certainly responsible for much of the important rebuilding of St Nicholas' carried out at this time. Apart from Knole, Bourchier made one other purchase of great interest to us – that of the "New Inn" opposite St Nicholas': this is the site on which the school's Manor House now stands. Bourchier's successor was Cardinal Morton, Lord Chancellor of England, Archbishop of Canterbury, Lord of the Manor of Otford, who died at Knole in 1500. Archbishop Warham, who moved into the now spacious mansion in 1502, nevertheless decided to build himself a splendid new palace at Otford. This enormous edifice, built with local bricks, brought not only employment but new glory to the neighbourhood, for in 1520 King Henry and Queen Katharine stayed there on their way to the Field of the Cloth of Gold.

Since there were no monastic establishments nearer than Tonbridge and Malling, the Dissolution of the Monasteries and Chantries had little immediate effect upon Sevenoaks, though now "it was the King who was Lord of the Manor, the great landowner, the patron of the living. His officials walked the streets of the town, lay courtiers and lawyers, not the clerks and priests of the Archbishop".

However, Sir John Dunlop has suggested that the King's appointment of John Clayton as Rector of Sevenoaks in 1540 may well have meant that those who prayed in St Nicholas', including the boys of Sevenoaks School, were given an early view of the revised version of Tyndale's Great English Bible, for Henry

VIII was much in favour of its use in churches. What lends particular poignancy to Sir John's suggestion is the fact that Tyndale's collaborator, John Frith, burned at the stake for heresy in 1533, had almost certainly been a pupil at the School.

Frith was born in Westerham in 1503, but his parents moved to Sevenoaks where his father kept an inn. He went to Eton for two years in 1520 and took his B.A. at King's College, Cambridge in 1525. It is sad that we have no school records for that time, and so cannot too loudly proclaim our part in the upbringing of our first Protestant martyr, but it is surely reasonable to surmise that he followed the quite common path from small grammar school to greater school to university.

Wolsey, impressed by the young graduate, invited him to teach at the newly founded Cardinal College (now Christ Church) in Oxford. Soon, however, he was in London helping Tyndale translate the New Testament into English. Alarmed by the young man's openly professed sympathy for the doctrines of the Reformation, Wolsey had him imprisoned for some months in a damp Oxford cellar, only releasing him on condition that he remain within ten miles of Oxford. Instead, he fled to join Tyndale at the new Protestant university of Marburg in Prussia, where Luther was active. There Frith published his *Disputacyon of Purgatorye*, a treatise in three books against Rastell, More and Fisher.

In 1532 he ventured back into England, where More, the Lord Chancellor, had him hunted down and sent to the Tower. Here he was allowed a certain amount of freedom and continued to debate with More about the Last Supper and Purgatory, which he termed "an invention of the papists". He was not without friends. Cranmer, who twenty-three years later was to burn for the same beliefs, did his best to save him, but was finally ordered by Henry VIII to bring him to trial. Convicted of denying the doctrines of purgatory and transubstantiation, he was cruelly chained in Newgate Prison. Tyndale wrote from Antwerp; "Your cause is Christ's gospel, a light that must be fed with the blood of faith". On July 4th, 1533, he was burned at the stake at Smithfield. Twenty-six years later his interpretation of the Last Supper was adopted in the Book of Common Prayer.

The School's claim to have educated William Caxton, without whose printing presses the Reformation could hardly have occurred when it did or in the form it took, is considerably less secure, though by no means outlandish. We have his own statement that he was born in the Weald of Kent. Vita Sackville-West, the late Lady Nicholson, suggested that there may be good reason for locating his birthplace more precisely:

About three miles to the south of Sevenoaks, and right down in the Weald, lies the village called Sevenoaks Weald. Half a mile from that

SCHOOL HOUSE

1. Elevation

Above and below are designs for School House and the Almshouses prepared by Lord Burlington in the 1720s. It may have been Elijah Fenton who prevailed upon the great lord to concern himself with a small country grammar school; Fenton retired from the headmastership in 1710 to become secretary to the Earl of Orrery, a relation of Lord Burlington

2. Plan

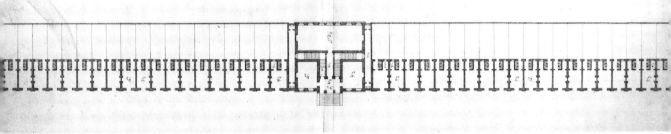

3. School House (detail)

4. A photograph of c.1875

Burlington's plans proved too grand and expensive. The governors and a local builder settled for a School House (and headmaster's residence) as below. So the building stood from 1734 to 1879 when its Palladian symmetry was unbalanced by the addition of a top floor to the right wing and a northward extension to the left (above)

5. An engraving of 1868

6. A photograph of 1932

Above, the back of School House from the garden. Below, the same view today showing the pavilions and their lanterns which caused much discussion when they were erected as part of the Site Improvement Programme

7. A photograph of 1993

8. A photograph of 1932

Above, the view until the early 1960s from School House garden looking eastwards across Knole Park. Below, the same view today with the Aisher Hall Music Centre showing above the recently planned yew hedge

9. A photograph of 1993

10. The Dining Room in 1932

11. A dormitory in 1932

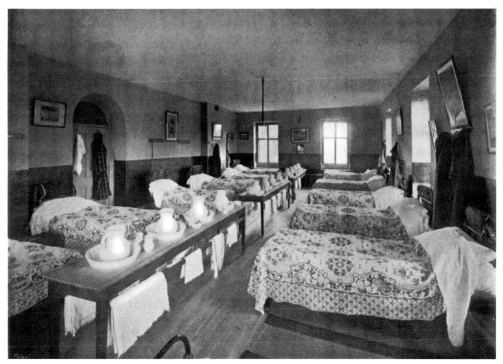

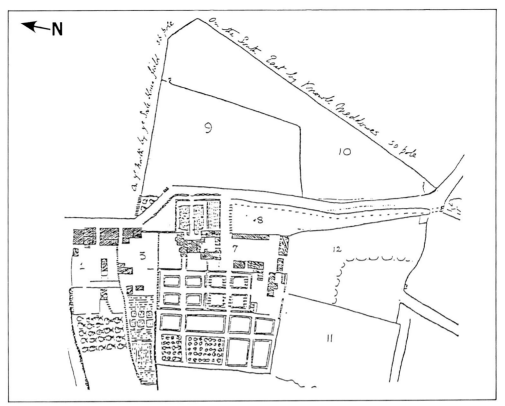

12. Brick House (surveyed and drawn by Richard Adams, 1709)

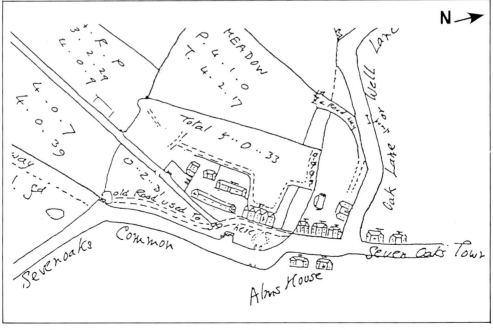

13. Brick House (estate map drawn by John Bowra of Groombridge showing the old and diverted roads and the almshouses but not School House

PARK GRANGE

Over the centuries one house after another stood on the site of Park Grange Boarding House.

The first we know of, Park Place, was owned by George Lone during the Civil War. Lone was a Royalist and his estate was sequestered. In 1654 it ,was acquired by Thomas Lambard who probably rebuilt the house, renaming it Brick House (opposite, **12**). He also re-aligned the road in front of it as it runs today. The estate map of 1780 (opposite, **13**) may well represent the same Brick House.

By 1770 Multon Lambard II, grandson of Thomas, owned the house. Improved almost beyond recognition as Park Place again (below, **14**), it remains in the family until 1841, when they moved to Beechmont.

The present Park Grange (next page, **15**) was built by Sir George Berkley, as Park Farm in the 1860s, and sold to Charles Plumtre Johnson in 1911. The School acquired the bulk of the property through the Johnson Trustees in 1948.

The substantial estate has provided playing fields, staff houses and workshops, including those for Vista. The house was first used as a boys' boarding house (next page, **15**), but is now a girls' house. An annex containing additional study bedrooms for 19 girls was completed in 1992 (next page, **16**)

14. Park Place replacing Brick House c. 1789 and replaced by the present Park Grange c. 1865

15. Park Grange photographed in 1986

16. Park Grange, the new Annex opened in 1992

village stands an old half-timbered house traditionally known as Caxton's House and traditionally reputed to have been his birthplace. There is no actual evidence to support this legend, but it may be mentioned that a gold coin of the reign of Edward III, a Rose Noble, was found embedded under a brick floor in one room. This proves at least that chronologically the legend is credible, for the reign of Edward III, 1327–1377, antedates the birth of Caxton, which occurred somewhere between 1412 and 1423. The practice of embedding a coin of the same year as the building is well known, and it is thus established beyond question that the house was already standing when Caxton was born.

Lady Nicholson then quotes Caxton's remark that he was "bounden to pray for my fader and moder's souls that in my Youth sent me to Schoole", reminds us of the foundation of Sevenoaks School and concludes: "It is thus possible, both chronologically and geographically, that the boy Caxton attended this school".

G M Trevelyan has memorably saluted William Caxton as the man who, as translator, printer and publisher, laid the foundations of literary English and of the great triumphs of our language in the following century. He pictures his press as "a battering-ram to bring abbeys and castles crashing to the ground, a tool that would ere long refashion the religion and commonwealth of England".

Latimer and others had hoped that the confiscation of the vast wealth and lands of the monasteries would lead to increased investment in the relief of poverty, in education and in true religion. In fact, most of the wealth was sucked into the King's coffers emptied by his expensive French campaigns and other extravagances. Many schools, particularly those jointly endowed with chantries, suffered a serious loss of income. As for the great tracts of land, these were rapidly sold off, so that in the end the main beneficiaries were the squires, the new class of land-owning gentry who were to dominate rural England for centuries. Many soon became very rich indeed. Having bought estates cheaply from the Crown, they profited from the land-hunger of a rising population: rents climbed steeply, and only the yeomen – freehold farmers or peasants with tenure on fixed rents – were protected from the continual devaluation of the coinage.

However, many of these new country gentlemen were conscious of their own good fortune and of the cruel plight of the poor. Some, especially if they had frequented the Court, had been touched by the New Learning and the desire to study the original classic texts. And so the last decades of the sixteenth century and the first few decades of the seventeenth saw the foundation of many new Grammar Schools and a flood of donations, bequests and endowments to existing ones. Sevenoaks School was to have ample cause for gratitude for the interest taken in its fortunes by the local gentry.

CHAPTER THREE

A Queen's Grammar School

In 1555 Ralph Bosville, Gentleman, of Lincolns Inn, purchased the great estate of Bradbourne from the Crown. In the century that followed, as the state of the roads and the efficiency of transport improved, many distinguished lawyers and merchants established their country seats in the area. A few of these were to become the Great Houses which so dominated local history (and local maps) for the next three centuries. Many of their owners figure prominently in the history of the School thanks to the interest they took in its welfare, but Bosville holds pride of place. He began researching the School's origins with a view to procuring for it, as Lennox puts it, "a foundation more suited to its increasing importance". This was not long in coming, for Bosville, Clerk to the Court of Wards, was held in high esteem at Court, and shortly after her accession the young Queen Elizabeth visited him at Bradbourne. In 1560 Letters Patent were issued under which Town and School were "incorporated" into one body. In effect this provided a new constitution for the school, which with the almshouses was in future to be administered by two Wardens and four Assistants (Governors), all six annually elected, who apparently were also given certain responsibilities for the town. Her Majesty, in granting the School the right to bear her name and the use of a common seal, was acting in the "certain and sure knowledge that our parish of Sevenoaks in the County of Kent is a place fit and proper for teaching and instructing boys and youths, both because it is very populous and full of young people and also because in past times a large number of boys and youths have assembled here from the neighbouring towns for the purpose of acquiring knowledge". Here we have clear evidence that the school was flourishing, no doubt benefiting from the renown brought to Sevenoaks by the noble and eminent owners of Knole.

Whether Bosville was motivated by a suspicion that the administration of the school was not all that it should be we do not know, though it is certain that he discovered, and was shocked by, the "feeble and weak" terms of the long lease granted to Anthony Pope. In any case, his initiative unquestionably improved the management – not least because it was decreed that Bosville, and subsequently one of his heirs resident in Kent, should always figure among the Assistants. Thus began an association between a great family and the School that was to last until 1761.

It is at this moment that the oldest surviving Minute Book of the Corporation – effectively the School's governing body – begins to record its yearly activities. We half expect to catch a distant echo, behind the prosaic entry dated 1576, of some of the stirring events of the previous twenty years: the death at the stake of Latimer, Ridley and Cranmer; the accession of Queen Elizabeth; the Act of Uniformity; the birth of Shakespeare; Drake's preparations for his journey round the world. But no, all we have is a list of rents collected from the School's properties; and though we can just about conjure a romantic picture of an increasingly populous and thirsty London at the mention of *Harte's Horn* and *Starr Inn*, Sevenoaks with its five or six hundred inhabitants calmly awaits the protection of the surrounding great estates.

Gordon Ward's map of the town as it was at this time shows the Bosvilles' Bradbourne estate just to the north. According to one of the historians of Lady Boswell's School, the mansion in which Margaret was born in 1594 was large and rambling, and the estate consisted of 1,221 acres of land, ten smallholdings, fourteen gardens, five orchards, two barns, three watermills, a stable, a dovecote and the manor of Blackhall. Immediately to the south of the School, Sevenoaks Common had been "emparked" and a substantial house (Brick House) built where today Park Grange stands; its owner, Richard Lone, had bought the land from Thomas Potkin in 1559. Both served as early Assistants to Sevenoaks School. To the East was Knole, soon to be the country residence of Lord Buckhurst, Lord High Treasurer of England; in 1603 Thomas Sackville, Baron Buckhurst, was created Earl of Dorset by James I, and began to carry out his princely plan for the development of the great house. Nearly four hundred years later, the School has good reason to thank the unhealthy airs of London that led the ancestors of our many benefactors, and of our current President, to seek a Place in the Country.

The "newe house" mentioned in the 1576 Minute may possibly have been

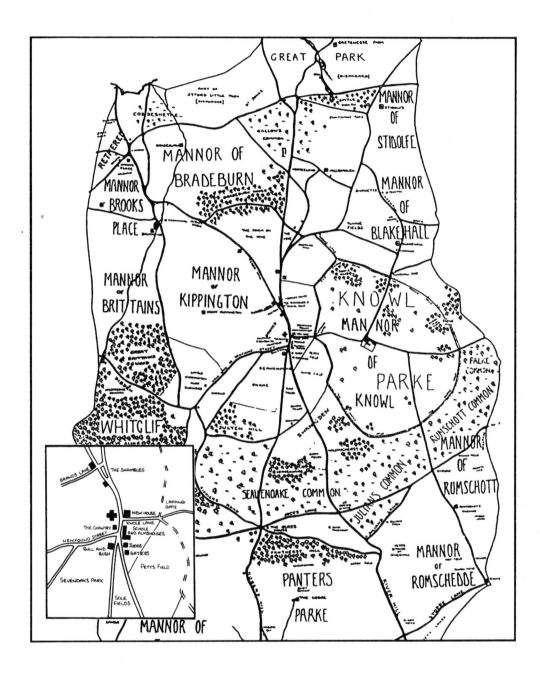

Fig (xi) In about 1950 Gordon Ward compiled this map from local records. It attempts to show the town of Sevenoaks in Elizabethan times and the large estates surrounding it – Knole, Greatness, Bradbourn, Kippington, Sevenoaks Park (Park Grange). In the inset the site area of the School and the layout of the buildings are only approximate. The New House was to become Manor House, and the Bull and Bush the Royal Oak.

the New Inn opposite St Nicholas. Acquired by Archbishop Bourchier for the Knole estate, it might have been leased to the Corporation, then re-leased to provide this income.

The 1574 Statutes and Ordinances

One of the duties laid upon the new governors was that of framing Statutes and Ordinances "to be approved of by the bishop of the diocess, for the regulating the master and usher". These were duly produced, signed by the Archbishop of Canterbury and promulgated in 1574. The previous year Queen Elizabeth had been the guest of her relative Lord Buckhurst of Knole, the son of her old servant Sir Richard Sackville. No doubt during her visit she would have listened to a Latin oration from the Master of the newly honoured Queen Elizabeth Grammar School. It is quite likely that – probably in the presence of her old friend Ralph Bosville – the subject of the forthcoming Statutes and Ordinances would have been raised, and this lends credence to the suggestion that the royal influence can be discerned in parts of the document, particularly in those concerned with punishment. At one point, when the hours of attendance at school have been stipulated – six till eleven and one till six in summer, seven till eleven and one till five in winter – we read: "The scholar offending herein to be corrected by the said master . . . *but not rigorously*". This merciful provision indicates an attitude all too rare at the time, and reminds us that the unfashionably gentle Roger Ascham, author of *The Schoolmaster*, was not only a friend of Sir Richard Sackville but had been tutor to the Queen herself. Though it was to be many years before continental humanism began seriously to influence the practice of teaching in England, is it too fanciful to suggest that, if only for a moment, a distant echo of the ideas of Erasmus and Montaigne was heard in deepest Kent? After all, Erasmus had collaborated with Dean Colet in founding St Paul's School in 1512, and the Statutes and Ordinances laid down that teaching at Sevenoaks "be ordered as the school of St Pauls in London".

The chosen Master is to be "an honest and mete man . . . *not being in holy orders..*". As in the case of the 1432 will this seems surprising for now the directions concerning religious observances are quite strict. The boys are to pray at the beginning and end of the school day, as well as "when they go to play", saying "such prayers as shall be appointed by the Lord Archbishop of Canterbury's Grace, written in a table and kept in the school . . . and every Friday morning throughout the year, go orderly to the parish church of Sevenoaks" to hear the Litany and to give thanks for the benefits bestowed upon them by their benefactors. It may be that the meaning was "*not necessarily* being in holy orders", in recognition of the scarcity of well qualified ordained teachers: this chimes with the fact that though the next Master, Edward Cotton, was not ordained, his successor Richard Buckley appointed in

THE FIRST MINUTE

The earliest Minute Book we possess runs from 1576 to 1742. The first entry in secretaryhand is reproduced opposite. A translation is offered below. The Harte Horne in Petty Wales is the London property gifted to the School by William Sevenoaks' will of 1432 (pages 22 and 33). The "land in Sevenoaks" is referred to on pages 26 and 28–30 and the "new house" on page 35 and 37.

1576	**Anno XVIII E R**	
Harlinge	The accounts of John Harlinge and Edward Lusted Church Wardens and also Wardens of the School given up before the	
Lusted	Parson Vicar and his Assistants with others of the Parish the xxviiith of September Anno Regni Regni (sic) Elizabeth XVIII as followeth:	
	Imprimis received of Mr Pope for one quarter of the Harte Horne in Pettywales due at the Feast of St Michael last before the date hereof	50 shillings
	Item arrearages of one quarter year	50 shillings
	Item for the rents of the new house then due	40 shillings
	Item for one quarter of Harts Horne due at	
	Christmas following	50 shillings
	for arrears due at this time	50 shillings
	for rent fo the new house then due	40 shillings
	Item for one quarter's rent of the Harte	
	Horne due at our Lady's Day following	50 shillings
	the rent fo the new house then due	40 shillings
	Item for one quarter's rent of the Harte Horn due	
	at Midsummer following	50 shillings
	for the rent of the new house then due	40 shillings
	Received of Thomas Godwyn for one whole year's rent	
	of the land in Sevenoaks	38 shillings
	Sum Total .... 24 pounds	18 shillings

Fig (xii)

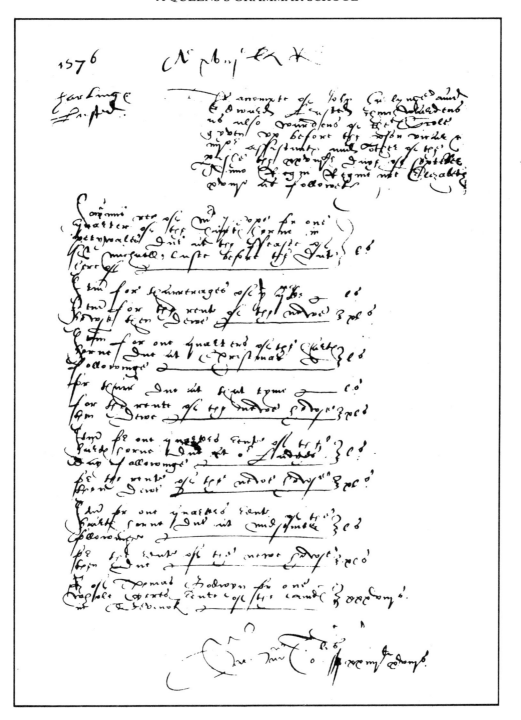

Fig (xiii)

1596, apparently was. Lennox records that he had seen an old copy of the Ordinances bearing a marginal note that evokes a flavour of the violent religious differences of the time: "No scollars to be taught but such as come to church. Recusants' children barred".

This all too fleeting glimpse of the life of a sixteenth century schoolboy makes one curious to discover just how he spent his long days. The Statutes of our "model" school, St Paul's are hardly revealing as far as the curriculum is concerned. Despite Colet's enlightened views, education was still seen as essentially a religious activity designed to encourage good conduct, right thinking and upright character. As an aim this sounds unexceptionable, but the means employed were archaic – an arid linguistic grind involving endless repetition and daunting feats of memory. The task of Grammar Schools was to teach Latin – and Greek if a teacher could be found – and this they relentlessly did by way of the 'trivium' or threefold path of learning: Grammar, Elementary Logic and Rhetoric. At St Paul's the pupils were to be instructed "all way in good litterature with laten and greke and good auctors, such as have the very Romayne eliquence joyned with wisdome, specially Crystin auctors that wrote their wysdome with clene and chast laten". This was quite enlightened for the time, for more often the texts studied were chosen more for the 'scientific' accuracy of language than for originality or interest – the bishops, already worried about the new printing presses spreading subversive ideas in the vernacular, saw to that!

It is hardly surprising that children subjected to this regime should frequently have grown restive and required stern "correction". The teacher depicted on the School Seal is holding a birch of formidable proportions, and we can only hope that Sevenoaks did not follow St Paul's in the practices current at the end of the previous century. Lawson and Silver quote from a Declamation (probably written by Bishop Alcock of Ely) made by the Boy Bishop in 1490. At seven infancy gives way to adolescence, "in the which age is the breaking of every child to goodness or to lewdness". So now the master "giveth commandments to the child in his growing age. And he break them he is sharply corrected. There is no fault that he doth but he is punished. Sometime he wringeth him by the ears. Sometime he giveth him a stripe on the hand with the ferrule. Sometime beateth him sharply with the rod".

Were subjects other than the classical languages taught at Sevenoaks at this time? The town no doubt had its "petty schools" which taught spelling and reading, sometimes writing and counting as well if the teacher – perhaps a tailor or weaver or shopkeeper making a little money in his spare time – was capable of taking them that far. The children of the very poor either had no education at all, or had to be content, or more likely malcontent, with a little sporadic teaching given in church by the parish clerk. Perhaps there were a few "dame schools" too, where three or four children clutching their hornbooks would sit at the feet of a widow or spinster in her cottage. But for the increasingly affluent yeoman classes of the area, ambitious for their children, the Grammar School was the only available 'ladder' up which a bright boy could climb towards university, the church, the professions or the higher reaches of commerce. Children of the parson or of one of the smaller local squires might well have attended. Some would stay until they were fourteen, when the very clever might enter university. Others, if they could afford it or were lucky enough to win a scholarship, might transfer to a bigger school and enter university two or three years later. Others, quite probably the majority of the Sevenoaks boys, would begin their seven years of apprenticeship in one of the crafts or trades administered by the various Guilds, just as William Sevenoaks had.

From this last group would come the successful merchants and self-made men who gave so generously to charities – particularly to those concerned with education – in the late sixteenth and early seventeenth centuries. Their motives were varied and often mixed, but one must have been their recognition of the growing need for literate and numerate apprentices in a whole new range of skilled occupations: book-keeping, surveying, cartography, ship-building and so on. Now it seems unlikely that such men would support schools entirely dedicated to the study of ancient languages, and equally unlikely that such schools in smaller towns would attract sufficient pupils to survive. Thus it seems certain that Sevenoaks pupils would have had access to the teaching of English and arithmetic or accounts – either given by part-time teachers or perhaps by the Usher in the form of paid Extras. We shall see until well into the nineteenth century that many Sevenoaks headmasters regarded the teaching of anything other than classics as beneath their scholastic dignity, but were not averse to letting their Usher supplement his meagre salary by taking in boarders, or even by teaching these lowly subjects. An Item in the Statutes of 1574 throws some light on the standing of the Usher:

> The said usher shall have of every scholar coming to the same school, at his entrance, one penny sterling; and every quarter, of every scholar one penny during his continuance in the same school – towards his entertainment. And the said usher therefore at this charges, shall cause the school to be swept and made clean once every week.

The problem of reconciling the nature of local needs with the high aspirations and statutory duties of a grammar school was to vex governors and headmasters of Sevenoaks School for three centuries to come. One way of attracting bright boys, and firing the ambitions of their parents, was to offer scholarships to the fast expanding universities of Oxford and Cambridge, and early in the seventeenth century Sevenoaks was provided with two. In 1618, accomplishing the wishes of John Spratt, late Vicar of Sevenoaks, his executor Edward Sisley endowed an annuity of fifty-two shillings towards the maintenance of an Exhibitioner at Sydney Sussex College: "one poor scholler" was to be elected every seven years by the Wardens and Assistants "with the advice of the schoolmaster". The Wardens were duly grateful to the yeoman, explaining in their letter to the College that Spratt had died before including the bequest in his will, and that Sisley had acted "being not thereunto bound by any act of the testator, but touched in conscience, and always affecting good and charitable acts." In the following year another local worthy, Robert Holmden, left his London property called "The George on Horseback" to the Leathersellers Company. Out of the income the Company was to provide, every four years, a Scholarship of £4 a year tenable by a Sevenoaks School pupil at either of the two Universities.

One indication that the School was taking local competition seriously is that in 1617 a complaint was made to the Archbishop of Canterbury that the Vicar was taking pupils, teaching them Grammar amongst other things: such poaching was not to be tolerated! It was not, and the rival establishment was ordered to cease its redundant activities forthwith.

CHAPTER FOUR

From Blome to Burlington
(1600–1730)

The leisurely pace of this narrative will shortly quicken, not so much into a trot as into a series of substantial leaps until we reach the nineteenth century. This is not because nothing of interest was happening in and to Sevenoaks School: boys, teachers, headmasters and Governors must have come and gone, learning, playing, teaching, administering. Some of them were doubtless admirable people, others little better than rogues. Many will have been men of strong convictions, passions and prejudices of which we would like to know more. Some boys will have worked hard, moved on to university and "done well"; others will have struggled, played truant, been mightily punished, left early, and often – *plus ça change* – done even better. Here and there we hear a voice, glimpse a face, sometimes only a name, but too faintly to warrant a pause that could not possibly do their owners justice.

Two names that deserve mention in the early seventeenth century are those of John Blome and Thomas Pett (a descendant of one of our early benefactors). Blome had served as Warden and was clearly worried about the state of the school building. At his death in 1624 he left a sum of money towards

43

its rebuilding, but stipulated that it should not be paid until the work had begun. As things turned out, this was very sensible of him, for the new stone building did not go up until 1631. The work was overseen by Thomas Pett, a wealthy local gentleman who served continuously as an Assistant from 1626 until 1667, the year of his death. He was probably responsible for persuading a number of parishioners to contribute what they could towards the cost: "4 bundles of lathes" and "a Fayre tree" came from two well-wishers, while others gave as much as £10.

We don't know how long the work took, nor where the school was housed while it was going on, but the Corporation Minute Book indicates that the situation was dire. The School is "so ruinated that of necessity the same must be pulled downe" and "new built in manner and forme followinge, that is to saye in length from one outside end to the other ffyfty ffoote and in breadth twenty ffoote and somewhat more, and in height eleuven ffoote from the grownd flower to the top of the second flower which is to be builded with stone". The walls are to be twenty inches thick, there are to be "nine Ffayre wyndowes of free mason worke, a dore Case and two loopes of the same worke and a water table round about the schoole of ffreestone the flower to be boarded and joysted throughout". Benches for boys are set against the walls all around the schoolroom: above are a gallery and chambers for the Master and Usher. There are four tile-covered gable windows in the roof, and in front of the building a courtyard divided from the road by a stone wall.

Pett must have had School affairs very much at heart, for in 1643, "att his owne proper Charges", he began a long and tedious lawsuit in the Chancery Court "against the cheeife Assistante . . . ffor divers wronges and injuries done . . . to the great prejudice and hinderance of the livelihoode and maintenance of the said Freeschoole and Allmespeople".

It is difficult to guess at the number of pupils who moved back into their fine new building, probably only twenty or thirty after the disruption of the move. This was a quite normal size for Grammar Schools at the time. In his *Seventeenth Century Kent* C.W. Chalkin estimates the population of Sevenoaks as eight hundred in 1660. Even by the end of the century, when there were at least twenty-one such schools in the County, he believes that "At Sevenoaks and Tonbridge, two of the most richly endowed schools, the numbers of boys were probably only fifty or sixty". Then, as for the next hundred and fifty years, school rolls tended to fluctuate frequently and violently throughout the year: many boys, apart from those intending to go on to university, would drift into school for a year or two, then leave to help their families or to enter an apprenticeship. Frequent illnesses, sometimes fatal, added to the uncertainty.

John Donne, great poet and stirring preacher, was Rector of St Nicholas' from 1616 until 1631, but is not recorded as having ever preached there during his

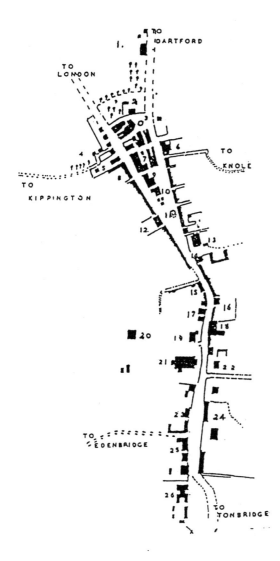

1. House, farm buildings, orchard, etc. called St. Botolph's or Bethlehem, later Bligh's Farm.
2. Blackboy Inn and Garden, on Blackboy Lane. The only existing Sevenoaks hostelry which has borne the same name in four centuries. Probably called after the Blackboy family, not the Blackamore page at Knole.
3. The Market House.
4. Old houses on Brand's Lane, which led to the footpath to Kippington.
5. The large yard and stables of The Bull Inn, now the roadway of South Park. The Inn was on the east side of London Road. It had once been The Swan, is now The Dorset Arms.
6. An Inn and yard, later The Rose and Crown. Webb's Alley nearby was the traditional route between the town and Knole.
7. The Shambles.
8. An Inn later the Crown and The Royal Crown.
9. The Market.
10. An ancient Inn on an island site. It has had many names through the years, is now The Chequers.
11. The Market Pond.
12. A large timber framed private house. Perhaps then called "Bishop's House".
13. The Red House and Grounds.
14. An Inn, recently The Carpenters' Arms.
15. An Inn, The Six Bells.
16. An Inn, at one time The Bull.
17. An Inn, recently The Coachmakers' Arms.
18. A large private House, now The Old House. Said to have been the Inn kept, around 1510, by the father of John Frith, protestant martyr. Also to have been once called "The Three Cats".
19. The Vicarage.
20. The Rectory.
21. St. Nicholas' Parish Church.
22. The New Inn, now The Manor House, Sevenoaks School.
23. An old framed building now called "The Old Post Office", said to have once been an inn.
24. The Almhouses and Sevenoaks School, before the present stone buildings.
25. The Royal Oak Inn.
26. Sevenoaks Park, also called Brick House.

Fig (xiv) This map, from Sir John Dunlop's "The Pleasant Town of Sevenoaks", was compiled from old manuscripts, documents and drawings of varying dates and accuracy. It attempts to show the town as it may have been in 1687. The layout of the school buildings (shown at 24) however, seems more consistent with Burlington's eighteenth century design with flanking almshouses, rather than Blome's seventeenth century (1631) single schoolhouse. The building shown at 26, on the other hand, seems accurately to represent Thomas Lambard's much improved Brick House of 1654 later to be developed into Park Grange Boarding House (see Illustrations **12–16**).

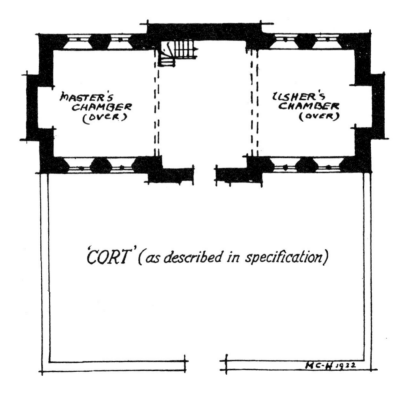

MASTER'S CHAMBER (OVER)

USHER'S CHAMBER (OVER)

'CORT' (as described in specification)

H C-H 1922

Fig (xv)   Plans for the rebuilding of Sevenoaks School in 1631

visits to Knole. Perhaps it is just as well: who knows what terror his torrential and tormented sermons might have struck into the hearts of hard-pressed Sevenoaks boys who had just "gone orderly" over the road to pray? However, in 1636 an almost equally dramatic and charismatic personage came on to the scene, this time one whose family was to influence the School's fortunes. This was Sir Thomas Farnaby, great-grandson of an Italian musician, grandson of the Mayor of Truro, son of a London carpenter. A product of Merton College, Oxford, he became one of the most famous – certainly one of the wealthiest – schoolmasters and classical scholars of his time.

An account of Farnaby's early life written in 1808 by the Reverend Mark Noble catches something of its breathtaking pace: "Gaily volatile, he quitted England and Protestantism for Spain and Popery. He found an asylum among the Jesuits. Restraint soon tired him. Joining Drake and Hawkins, he braved the ocean". (He was with Drake and Hawkins when they died in the Caribbean and he returned to England in their ship). "Sick of the sailor's life, he fought against the Spaniards in the Netherlands. Learning at length won the palm. Landing in great distress in the West of England, he assumed the surname of Baynraf, the anagram of his own. His poverty was so great that he was obliged to wander from village to village, teaching the horn-book to the cottagers' children for a precarious bread".

He finally established a school in Somerset which was enormously successful. Moving to London, such was his fame that by 1630 he was running an Academy for three hundred sons of the nobility. In 1636 the plague drove him from London to Sevenoaks, where he purchased Great Kippington for £2,200 and continued to teach many of the pupils who had followed him. We cannot imagine that he particularly encouraged contact between his young sprigs and the boys of the little local school, but the next four generations of Farnabys were to serve as Assistants at Sevenoaks School from 1667 until 1782.

In 1606 Lord North had discovered the curative value of the Wells near Tunbridge, and as they began to attract fashionable society from London so the condition of the Rye road through Sevenoaks improved, and stage-coaches became more frequent. This may well have influenced Farnaby's choice of Kippington, for many of his pupils' families were likely to have patronised the new spa.

In 1643 Sevenoaks' strategic position brought it briefly into the thick of the Civil War. Confident of the loyalty of the gentry of Kent, the King hoped with their help to reduce London and subdue the Parliamentarians. Dr Alan Everitt, not long ago a member of the School's History VIth, has in his *Civil War in Kent* shown that "small though it was, the town controlled not only the entrance into the county along the one road from Oxford, the king's headquarters, south of London, but also the strategic Darent Valley, with its road to the Thames near Dartford and its command of the three roads from the capital into Kent". In July the gentry of West Kent came armed, with their tenants and servants, to rendezvous on the Vine with the local Royalists led by Farnaby of Kippington, Lone of Sevenoaks Park and the Rector of St Nicholas'. The sight and sound of four or five thousand armed men being harangued by the likes of Farnaby must have made these few days memorable ones for the town's children briefly freed from the academic grind. However, they were soon to be back at work.

Disheartened by two days of heavy rain, and by the news that the Parliamentarian army under Colonel Browne was already at Bromley, the assembled "rude multitude" began to melt away. The five or six hundred who remained when Browne arrived were pursued down the hill as far as Tonbridge, and the Sevenoaks Royalist rising was over. Farnaby was sent to Newgate Gaol for a year, his mansion at Kippington sequestrated; he died in London in 1647. The Rector, Nicholas Gibbon, was removed from office and replaced by a "preaching minister" appointed by Parliament. The Earl of Dorset was severely punished: for a year Knole was taken over by a heavily guarded County Committee of Kent, and the contents of seventy-four rooms were sold.

Though the School's prospects were obviously indirectly badly damaged by the fines and other penalties inflicted upon local gentry, one consequence was to prove greatly to its advantage. George Lone of South Park was a Catholic: he was "sequestered for recusancy" and forced to sell his lands. In 1654 he sold Sevenoaks Park, today's Park Grange, to Thomas Lambard of Squerries in Westerham. Nine years later Lambard, grandson of the great historian of Kent, became one of the Assistants of a School with whose affairs his descendants were to be almost continuously involved for the next two hundred years.

Despite the straitened circumstances of many of its erstwhile patrons, the School was to receive one last generous endowment before the century was out. In 1675, in memory of her late husband Sir William, Lady Boswell (née Bosville) of Bradbourne established at "Jesus College in Cambridge two scholarships XII pounds per annum each: ye Scholars to be called Sr. Wm. Boswells Scholars and to be chosen out of Sevenoaks School (and for want of lads fitting here then from Tonbridge School) and upon every vacancy 3 pounds a piece to two of ye fellows of Jesus College; to come over to prove ye capacities of ye lads". Lady Boswell had served as an Assistant, as had her beloved husband after many years in the Hague as the representative of King Charles I. Mention of the possibility that there might not be enough "lads fitting" at Sevenoaks School may indicate that our numbers were low. Reasons for this would not be far to seek. There was much poverty in rural areas after the Restoration; as rents fell and prices rose, the value of many school endowments declined steeply, bringing the temptation to charge even Free Scholars just a little more. The 1662 Act of Uniformity, making statutory the licensing of Masters by the Bishops, was never effectively enforced, and in a society split as never before between church and chapel this meant that the numbers of unlicensed schools run by non-conformists multiplied. They were the more attractive in that they offered the 'vocational' subjects scorned by the Grammar Schools. Moreover, the suspicion was growing in many influential quarters that too much education of the lowly was a potential cause of social unrest, so that little philanthropic idealism survived the puritan revolution.

The Archbishop's Long Arm

When starting to consider the School's fortunes in the eighteenth century, Lennox aptly quoted G. M. Trevelyan's strong words: "The period of Walpole and the Pitts was the heyday of unchallenged abuses in all forms of corporate life. Holders of ecclesiastic, academic, charitable and scholastic endowments had no fear of enquiry or reform. Schoolmasters could draw their salaries without keeping school; Universities could sell degrees without holding examinations or giving instruction. Churches, Universities, Schools, Civil Service and Town Corporations were all of them half asleep". And Lennox, a loyal but honest man, felt constrained to add that from this heavy indictment "it would be useless to claim more than a partial exemption for the Corporation responsible for Sevenoaks School". It is perhaps as well that the evidence is too patchy and unclear to enable us to apportion blame to individuals, for many of them bear names we properly honour and list among those of our greatest past and future patrons and friends. That there was a degree of corruption is possible, that there was gross neglect at times is certain.

Already in 1696 it was clear that the Corporation was impatiently trying to shake off the supervision and interference of the Church, when William Lambard put a set of pointed questions to Counsellor Gifford. Who should elect the Master? Must he be in holy orders or not? Was it essential that the Archbishop of Canterbury confirm the appointment? Gifford replied that the Archbishop had merely the right of confirmation, not of election, and that "Whosoever is put in by the Parish as aforesaid to be Schoolmaster may act as Schoolmaster though never confirmed *if the Archbishop do not stir against him*". Gifford also believed, wrongly, that William Sevenoaks' will had decreed that the Master should *not* be in holy orders (this error may have been due to a mis-translation of the Latin original, perhaps also responsible for the oddity noted in the 1574 Statutes). The next Headmaster, Elijah Fenton, appointed in 1706, was not ordained, and for the moment the Archbishop did not "stir". Even had he wished to, it is not clear what action he could have taken against an unconfirmed Master. As Gifford pleasantly puts it: "I do not know that he can be liable to any punishment whatsoever; nor can he be easily turned out, although not well put in". There is some evidence that the Archbishop had been convinced that the habit of appointing Masters in Holy Orders was indeed contrary to the Founder's "true intention"; if so, the Corporation may simply have been irritated to have their field of selection narrowed in this way, for the Universities were in steep decline and sound Masters were hard to find; a Mr Bloome, appointed in 1695, had lasted less than a year! Whatever the motives

MARGARET BOSWELL

Margaret Boswell was a remarkable woman. The great grand-daughter of Ralph Bosville (of the 1560 Letters Patent – see page 34), she married William Boswell, accompanying him to Holland where he served as Ambassador during the English Civil War. Widowed, she inherited the Bradbourn estate (after lengthy legal battles) and set her own determined mark upon Sevenoaks. At 65 she became the School's first woman Assistant (Governor) in 1660. The minute opposite of 1663 show her dominant signature allowing the accounts for the year (they show a 2% surplus of income over expenditure); other parishioner members of the School Corporation appended their marks. The minute of 1680 below shows her signature (actual size) when she was 85. The minute records a payment to a Mr Weston for the care and pains he had taken in the management of the School, but it defines the £15 paid as a gratuity "not to be drawn into precedent for the future". Her co-governors included William Lambard II, Francis Farnaby and John Blome (son of the rebuilder of the School in 1631), all families long associated with the School.

Margaret Boswell died in 1682. Her memorial now on the wall of the north aisle of St Nicholas' Church, contains a Latin verse including the lines (translated)

> Go ask in Sevenoaks, that town so fair,
> Where grateful hearts her bounty can declare.

Her "bounty" endowed two scholarships for Sevenoaks School lads at Jesus College Cambridge, the Lady Boswell Primary School in the town, and numerous apprenticeships for young Sevenoaks teenagers.

Fig (xvi)

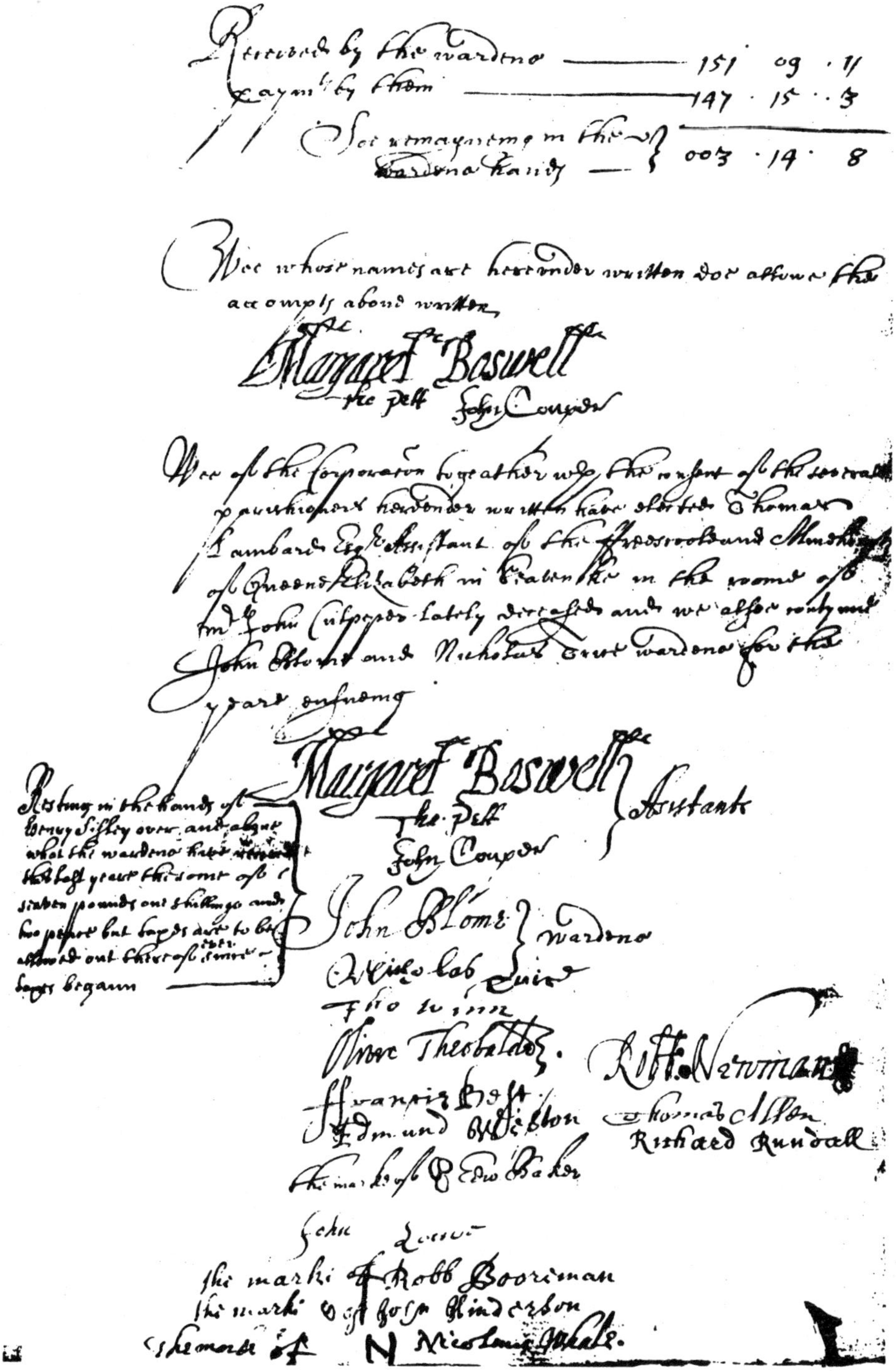

Received by the wardens ————— 151 . 09 . 11
Payments by them ————— 147 . 15 . 3
See remayneinge in the
wardens handy — } 003 . 14 . 8

Wee whose names are hereunder written doe allowe the
accompts above written

Margaret Baswell
the pett   John Couper

Wee of the corporacion togeather with the consent of the severall
parishioners hereunder written have elected Thomas
Lambard Esq Assistant of the freeschoole and Ministry
of Queene Elizabeth in Crambrooke in the roome of
Mr John Culpepper lately deceased and wee also continue
John Abbott and Nicholas Crux wardens for the
yeare ensueing

Resting in the hands of
henry Sisley over and above
what the wardens have received
the last yeare the some of
sixteen poundes one shilling and
two pence but longs are to be
allowed out thereof somme
longs begann

Margaret Baswell   Assistant
the pett
John Couper

John Blome } Wardens
Nicholas Quin
Tho winn
Oliver Theobalds .   Robt Newman
Francis Hoest
Edmund Welton   Thomas Allen
                           Richard Rundall
the marke of P Edw Baker

John Laun
the marke of Robt Boorman
the marke of hosp Kinderson
the marke of N Nicolas Wale .

Fig (xvii)

51

of those concerned, there was a great deal of mutual suspicion in the air, and clear signs of uneasiness in at least one of the School's administrators, probably William Lambard. In his private jottings it is clear that the Corporation had come in for some criticism, in one case apparently for wining and dining themselves too generously on the Charity's funds:

> As to the dinners charge, formerly more has been spent in one year than we have in ten years. Sed quomodo loqueris de hoc, for fear of being called to an account – by a commission for charitable uses, – or by Original bill in Chancery – but this was done in the troublesome times.

At times there is a certain shrillness in the protestations of innocence:

> As to the charge of the barne, the land without it is not worth halfe the money, besides it was so promised before the lease was sold – for land in ye same place may be hired almost as cheap and as good land.

Elsewhere we find that "the Archbishop has a long arm – therefore take care what we doe – for a breach of trust may cause an alteration in the settlement".

The length of the Archbishop's arm was soon to be tested. In 1721 the school buildings and the almshouses were "very ruinous and decayed", and when the Crown expressed an interest in buying the Corporation's London property the Assistants responded enthusiastically. The property, variously known as Sevenocks Key, Hartshorn Key and Wooll Key, adjoined the Custom House; it included 55 feet of river frontage and stretched back 112 feet to Petty Wales Street. The terms offered were £2,500 in cash and an annual rent of £550 in perpetuity. Twentieth century Bursars may shudder at the settlement, but at the time it was not a bad bargain – and of course it would represent great wealth to a Corporation whose annual income was less than £200. But first an Act of Parliament was needed to authorise the sale, and in the House of Lords the Bishops put their foot down. It is quite possible that they had got wind of some maladministration by the Wardens and Assistants, and were genuinely concerned as to their competence to handle such large sums in the best interests of charity. Sir Charles Farnaby, in a meeting with the Bishops of Salisbury, Lincoln and Norwich, was told the extent of the supervisory role they wanted: the Archbishop of Canterbury must be a "Perpetual Visitor", and all Ordinances must be confirmed by him or, in case of difference, referred to the Lord Chancellor. Knowing that the Bill would not pass if the Bishops opposed it, and that the matter would then come before the perhaps even more dangerously inquisitive Court of Chancery, the Corporation yielded, the Act was passed, the sale completed, and in 1724 work began on the new building to the design of Richard Boyle, third Earl of Burlington.

An auspicious combination of circumstances, one might imagine: great wealth and a great architect. Exactly what went wrong we do not know, but the Corporation seems to have been in no great hurry to spend the £2,500 (which they had swiftly invested in South Sea Stock), and the work was to drag on for the next seven or eight years, during which time the Master, John Simpson, and his no doubt dwindling band of pupils, were accommodated elsewhere outside the town. Most of the work was carried out by local builders and craftsmen, some of whose tenders indicate less than total confidence in their clients: one "will Give now Credett after ye Gob is finished;" another insists on "Reddy Mony but No Trust Pay as sonne as finished."

By 1728 the old buildings had been knocked down and the new ones were half up, when a "greate rain" and hard frost did so much damage that expert opinions were sought. One judged the situation "more frightfull than despirate" and thought it could be put right for £100; the other recommended complete demolition and rebuilding, and this was the expensive and time-consuming course of action adopted.

In Chancery

The disaster, for which the Wardens and Assistants could hardly be blamed, may nevertheless have stirred their critics into action. In May 1728 proceedings were launched in the Court of Chancery by a group of parishioners headed by Dr Fuller. The defendants were the four Assistants, Sir Charles Farnaby, Thomas Lambard, William Bosvile and Thomas Petley, together with three Wardens. The comprehensive allegations included the following:

1 That the Assistants clung to office without annual re-election;
2 That they chose as Wardens, for reasons of private patronage, men unfit to hold the post;
3 That much of their business – e.g. the election of officers, the passing of accounts – was done privately, when it should be done under the supervision of the Rector and parishioners;
4 That they had removed the accounts book from the vestry "in order to conceal their transactions";
5 That having received the £2,500 intended to pay for the rebuilding of the school, they had pulled it down but "neglected to rebuild";
6 That for years they had neglected the management of the school and allowed many irregularities and abuses, such as the failure to appoint an Usher.

The defendants' answers, as reported, were cool, even disdainfully languid. They agreed that they "continued in office", but doubted whether annual elections were "essentially necessary"; agreed that they had chosen a miller, a baker and an inn-keeper as Wardens: this was not because they happened to be tenants of theirs but because they were among "the most fit and proper inhabitants" of the town, as stipulated in William Sevenoaks' will; yes, they had removed some papers from the vestry, but only because they were rotting and illegible; no, there was no Usher, for there were not enough pupils to justify the appointment of one; far from neglecting the School they were proceeding to rebuild it "with all expedition", and had "caused to be begun" an almshouse; as for the money, their investment in South Sea Stock had already earned the Charity a profit of £1200.

The Chancery Court's first decree was not acceptable to the defendants: for instance, they did not want their old account books to be made available for inspection by Dr Fuller's party. The matter was referred to the Lord Chancellor, who gave his judgement in February 1729. Since both sides were allowed their costs out of Charity funds, he must have felt that, though Dr Fuller and his friends had been justified in bringing the action, the defendants had been guilty of nothing much worse than negligence – and of a rather cavalier attitude towards the intentions of the founder. In future, they were told, all elections must be conducted properly, and the Assistants chosen by not fewer than eight parishioners. Past accounts were to be allowed to stand, but strict rules were laid down for future auditing: accounts were to be "made up and adjusted" in the presence of the Rector or Vicar and those parishioners paying scot and lot. The defendants were urged to push vigorously ahead with the rebuilding, and both parties were asked to submit to one of the Masters of the Court their proposals for the future disposition of the Charity's now almost embarrassingly large income.

For the next six years suggestions and counter-suggestions flowed thick and fast between the Chancery Master and the Assistants, who were not always agreed among themselves as to how to spend all that money. Build a workhouse and a pesthouse for the whole parish, said Sir Charles. Not permissible under the Founder's will, ruled the Master; why not buy two fire-engines instead, and an infirmary for the use of the Charity? Dr Fuller's friends suggested that the annual surplus income of £156 should provide an extra 2s. 6d. a week to the sixteen outpensioners, leaving £40 for repairs and "putting out apprentices", and £12 for "an English Schoolmaster for teaching 15 poor boys Read Write and Arithmetick". Mention of boys reminds us that somewhere outside the town limits poor Mr Simpson – who was to prove a disaster in his own right – was waiting to move into the new building. This he did in 1732, probably with only a handful of boys to occupy "a row of forms all round with a Deske before it of Good Yellow Deal, the Floor on the outside the Deskes to be raised 9 inches above the floor in the middle for the children to sitt upon". Just how much the buildings had cost is unclear, though a letter written in 1730 by Thomas Harris, an agent acting for the defendants, mentions that £10,000 had already been spent and that £5,000 more would be needed to complete it.

The scheme finally approved by all parties – though not until a year after Dr Fuller's death in 1734 – authorised the investment of £1000 in South Sea Annuities, and ruled that out of the dividends and other surplus income four scholarships should be established at Oxford or Cambridge, available to poor boys who had been educated for three years at Sevenoaks School. Since each was worth £15 a year for seven years, it might have been hoped that such handsome prizes would bring clever boys flocking to sit at Mr Simpson's feet, but it was not to be. Instead, the other provision for disposing of surplus income – by placing out apprentices and later helping to set them up in trade – was to dominate the Corporation's "educational" activities for the next hundred years.

In 1753, in "A POEM Humbly Inscribed to His Grace the DUKE OF DORSET", a certain W. Harrod was fulsome in his praise of Queen Elizabeth, and of her Grammar School and Almshouses in their fine new building:

> Her name is stamped eternal in the hearts
> Of ev'ry worthy, ev'ry honest *Briton*;
> But how much more on Thee, distinguish'd *Sev'noke*?
> Thy stately Seminary ever stands
> A witness of her love, Her love to Thee.
> Thy FARNABY and FENTON ever live
> Enroll'd in records of eternal Fame:
> And HOLME now labours in the pleasing toil.
> *Nature* adorn'd in all the dress of *Art*,
> The pomp of Learning, and the force of Science,
> Confin'd to Virtue, and by Reason curb'd,
> Creeps from its tender buds, wide opes its folds. . .
>
> On either Hand a lovely Fabric stands
> Where Woe finds comfort, and old Age repose.

CHAPTER FIVE

A Century of Struggle
(1730–1830)

The Lord Chancellor's 1735 Order gave the Corporation clear instructions "for the Disposition of the Surplus of their Trust Estate". They were to meet twice a year, on the first Monday after Michaelmas and the first Monday after Easter week, "in order to Appoint and place out such Apprentices out of the poor Inhabitants of Sevenock as shall appear to them most proper".

Their first meeting was in October 1742, and for the next sixty years the Minute Book is dominated by the names of apprentices and their masters: often there is no mention of either School or Almshouses. It is probable that some of the boys were Foundation Scholars at the School, but the majority were not; some were no doubt pupils at Lady Boswell's School, whose Trustees were also funding apprenticeships but had less money to spare; some, depending on the nature of the trade they were joining, would have had little or no education at all.

The lists show the great variety of craftsmen and tradesmen practising in Sevenoaks in the eighteenth century: among the forty or so we find blacksmith, lath cleaver, collarmaker, cordwainer, perukemaker, hatter, vintner, glover, brazier, clocksmith, cutler, cooper, hollow turner and pattenmaker (clog-maker). The "masters" were on average paid £8 to take on a boy for seven years. Life for an apprentice was not much fun; the historian of Lady Boswell's School quotes from a typical indenture: "Matrimony he shall not contract or solemnize, Taverns, Inns or Alehouse he shall not resort to or frequent, at Cards Dice Tables or any other unlawful game he shall not play, nor from the service of his said master night nor day absent himself". Interestingly enough, among the 330 apprentices "put out" between 1735 and 1837 and for whom the Corporation spent a total of £2870.2s.6d, appear the names of four girls: in 1759 an Elizabeth Oliver was bound to a miller in Chevening, and next year her sister Mary went to a blacksmith in the same village. In 1777 one Mary Richardson, on payment of £8, was "put out" to Philip Fletcher of Halsted who described himself as a Labourer. Strapping girls, one can but hope!

Meanwhile, seemingly unable to benefit from all this largesse, the School – in so far as the Minutes afford us brief glimpses of it – was struggling. In 1748, over the signatures Dorset, T. Farnaby and H. Bosville, the Wardens are requested to report on the State of the School. How many scholars are there now, and how many have there been over the past ten years? The Wardens' report must have startled the Assistants: there are just four pupils! and Mr Simpson, when asked how many there were in previous years, "his Answer was that he could not tell". The Wardens continued (speaking of the School as if it had nothing at all to do with them) that according to "the best information we can get" there had been "a great many Scholars" when Mr Simpson arrived, "but from that time the Number gradually lessened . . . and that the School has continued declining ever since". Summoned to explain himself, Simpson resigned and was instantly replaced by Edward Holme. The fact that the two Wardens, Messrs. Novice and Nash, continued in office apparently without reprimand suggests that it was not regarded as part of their job to keep an eye on the School. It does seem surprising, though, that over ten years none of the Assistants had noticed the virtual disappearance of their School!

Two years before his downfall, on the afternoon of Saturday, October 4th, 1746, poor Mr Simpson's attention must have been caught by a great stir and commotion opposite the School, in front of a blacksmith's where now the Royal Oak Tap stands: the great preacher John Wesley was in town. Did Simpson let his sad little gaggle of boys watch and listen? Wesley's Journal does not mention them.

We took horse at 9 a.m. and soon after 1 p.m. came to Sevenoaks. After refreshing ourselves a little, we went to an open place near the Free School (Sevenoaks School) where I declared to a large wild company 'There is no difference; for all have sinned and come short of the Glory of God!' They grew calmer and calmer till I had done and then went quietly away.

For two years after Mr Simpson's dismissal, the Corporation awarded no more apprenticeship grants, for they had to meet bills for repairs to Holland's Coffee House in London and to the School House Gallery in St Nicholas'. (These heavy wooden galleries in the north and south aisles, and at the west end of the church, may have been erected during the Commonwealth, or very early in the eighteenth century. Boys from the School had pews allotted to them in the south gallery. In 1827, when there were not enough boys to fill them, a solemn Agreement was signed by the Churchwardens, four Assistants and two Wardens, giving the public the right to use two of the school pews until such time as they were needed again for boys. When the galleries were taken down in 1878, as part of the Revd Samuel Curteis's efforts to brighten up the gloomy old church and restore it to its earlier elegance, boys were seated in the old Chantry Chapel). However, even while relentlessly pursuing one of their School Lands tenants for arrears of rent, the Corporation did discover that the Holmden Exhibition administered by the Leathersellers Company had been vacant for some years, and in 1750 awarded it to one William Hicks Coppard "to receive the benefit thereof, and all Arrears that are now due". In October 1752 three former pupils recently admitted to St John's College, Cambridge applied for, and were awarded, £15 Scholarships – which is evidence that even in these difficult years some boys must have been learning something at Sevenoaks. In the same year four poor children from the Seal and Kemsing area were admitted to the School "without Fee or recompense", as John Porter had wished: perhaps the "ladder" has been set up again?

It would be tedious to relate in detail the recurring preoccupations of our Wardens and Assistants as recorded in the Minute Book, but a small selection will perhaps give some idea:

April 1755. The Wardens are to obtain estimates for repairs needed to the Almshouse sheds "and the two Boghouses belonging to the Schoolhouse".

September 1768. "Ordered that the Wardens do forthwith purchase a proper Fire Engine for the use of the Corporation and the Assistance of the Parish", and pay someone to look after it.

September 1769. The Master, the Revd George Davis, asks for and is granted two Exhibitions for his son Montague at Oxford.

January 1777. A Mr Marmaduke Lewis has applied for an Exhibition for his son, who is "shortly" to enter Oxford. Application rejected, since the boy intends to go to Westminster for two years "for further improvement in learning" before entering Oxford.

September 1831. Three widows are to be reprimanded for absenting themselves from the Almshouses. Moreover, relatives of pensioners who die there are taking away and selling the year's allowance of fuel.

September 1841. Widow Pointer to be admonished for her drunken-ness. There is a report that a widower is harbouring a woman in the Weald Almshouses. To be admonished. (The Weald Almshouses had been given to the Corporation by Multon Lambard in 1831).

The lists of apprentices, the award of the Exhibitions, the arrivals and departures of Masters, the announcement of the letting by public auction of the School Lands, the termination or renewal of other leases, the occasional misbehaviour of pensioners or tenants – such was the normal fare at Corpora-tion meetings. They did not always take place as regularly as they should have done – between October 1771 and January 1789 only nine were minuted, or about one every second year. Between 1802 and 1806, and between 1821 and 1825, there were no meetings at all. There is no indication that serious attempts were made to implement the rules the Lord Chancellor had laid down concerning the election of officers: indeed, elections are not mentioned at all before 1834 when, after a perfunctory "re-election" of the previous year's Assistants, an objection is laid against one of them, the Countess of Plymouth, on the grounds that her appointment constitutes a breach of the Act of Incorporation. This is casually brushed aside, "this meeting considering that no sufficient cause had been assigned for rejecting the appointment of the Countess of Plymouth".

In 1771 the Wardens are sternly told to "adhere themselves strictly to the business of this Trust, and also that they allow no Extra money to the Alms Rows People or otherwise without Special Order". This, together with the decision a few years later to require proof of residence at University from would-be Exhibitioners, suggests intermittent attempts to tighten things up. On the other hand, in 1814 the Assistants admit that the whereabouts of the premises in Bread Street, London, from which they have received £9 annually since 1543, are "not exactly known". Shortly afterwards, a letter of Byzantine impenetrability shed no light at all on this, nor on anything else:

The undersigned is able to inform you of something to your advantage on receipt of your promise to reward him one quarter of the value of some property you may receive in consequence of his discovery for his troubles when so received.
Respectfully,
Joseph Ady,
Hatter
No.16, Houndsditch London.

The Assistants, intrigued, asked the Wardens to investigate "the advan-tage that would result from a disclosure of the Information alluded to", and to

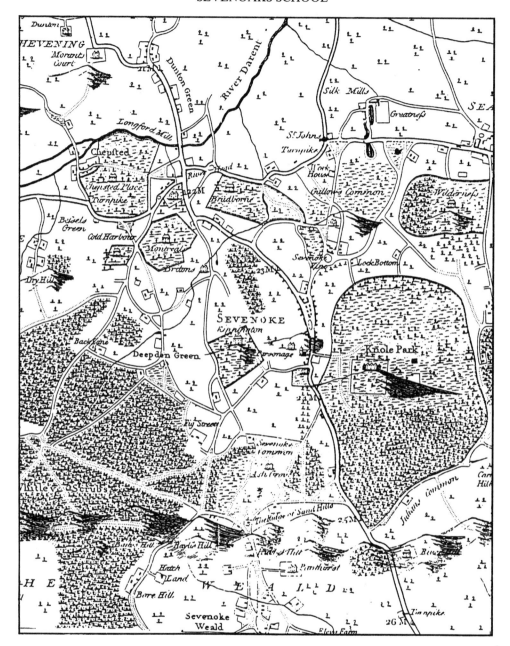

SEVENOAKS IN 1780

Fig (xviii) Hasted's map of 1780 shows the town very little changed since Elizabethan times (see map on page 45). The surrounding estates now include Wilderness and Montreal, the latter given by a grateful nation to Earl Amherst to commemorate the conquest of Canada in 1759. The Amherst family served on the Governing Body from 1789 to 1924. The School site is now accurately marked; the Burlington buildings could have been shown, but are not. Park Grange is shown where it lies at present.

report back to them; prudently, they then asked the Clerk to sign this particular minute. Alas, that is the last that is heard of the mysterious hatter!

In the early years of the nineteenth century there are signs that some parishioners were impatient to make the Corporation more accountable. In 1798 it had been ordered that printed copies of "all the wills, letters patent, decrees and other documents relating to this Charity . . . be deposited and kept in the Chest belonging to the Parish Church, for the benefit and perusal of the Parishioners paying Scott and Lot". In 1825, "upon the application of Several of the parishioners," fifty more copies were printed and distributed "among such of the parishioners not provided therewith" together with copies of the Balance Sheet of the Accounts. The Assistants were not entirely happy about this, and at the next public meeting decreed "that all future applicants for such Books and accounts shall produce to the Clerk of this Corporation a written order from one of the Assistants . . . and without which order no books or accounts shall be given".

The always precarious financial situation was not helped by the non-payment or late payment of rent by some of their tenants, who in 1827 included the Marquess of Camden from the Wilderness and Mr Geoffrey Pett: the latter owed £47.10s.9d, but this was reduced by £18 when the Wardens "possessed themselves of One Stack of Hay on the Premises" and had it valued by Colonel Austen's bailiff. They did have one windfall at this time, when they began to enjoy the benefits of the Will made in 1814 by Widow Susanna Nash. She had left £1200 in 4% bank annuities, the interest and dividends to become available to the Corporation on the death of her daughter: strictly the money was meant to be divided amongst the Almshouse residents, but it seems that the dividing line between the two accounts was not always impeccably observed. Whether or not it was in this case, the Minutes repeatedly mention the need for frugality. In 1837 two outspoken parishioners, Messrs. Mount and Luckhurst, forced the acceptance of a decision to cease the payment of £5 to the pensioners on Christmas Day.

What had become of William Sevenoaks' "free schoole to sweet learning, to renowne", intended to benefit the poor boys of the neighbourhood? There were never more than a handful of local Foundation Scholars in the School at any one time, though there might be as many as forty boarders. Incoming Masters would often bring their boarders with them, and take them away when appointed elsewhere, so that numbers fluctuated alarmingly. From the Master's point of view, free place boys were both a nuisance and a financial burden. They were not really "free" any longer, since they were charged £3 or £4 for "extra" subjects such as writing and arithmetic, as well as for slates and paper. Often so poorly grounded as to be almost unteachable when they weren't truanting they were also taking up a place that could have gone to a fee-paying boarder. From the Assistants' point of view, anything that reduced the Master's income was to be avoided. A Master successfully conducting a thriving boarding school could happily be left to his own devices. Grateful to be free of interference from the Corporation, he would often dismiss, engage and pay for his own assistant teachers, buy his own furniture, arrange for school cleaning and repairs and even, to protect his profitable privacy, forego the miserly £50 a year the Corporation were supposed to pay him. On the other hand, an unsuccessful Master with a lot of free place boys would be constantly at the Corporation's door with complaints and requests for help.

There was little consistency in administrative matters. Sometimes an Usher was allowed, sometimes not; sometimes his salary was paid by the Corporation, sometimes by the Master. Dr Whitfield (Master 1771–1788) built up numbers and was allowed an Usher from 1775; the Revd Gervase Whitehead (1789–1812) clearly needed one while the School flourished, with nearly sixty pupils; but it is difficult to understand the need for one in 1831, when under the Revd John Wilgress (1812–1831) numbers had fallen to one boarder and six day boys! Needless to say, by the time his successor, the Revd Edward Heawood (1831–1838) moved in with twenty boarders from Goudhurst, the Usher had moved out.

The term of office of the Revd James Wallace, who arrived in 1839 with twenty boarders, was unfortunately cut short by his death four years later, (his widow was given less than two months to auction off the furniture and vacate the premises), but not before he had put to the Corporation a strong case for being allowed a paid Usher. More importantly, his well-researched "memorial" urged a fundamental reconsideration of the way the Charity's funds were allocated. Pointing out that the Founder had wished the Master to receive two thirds as much as the total allocated to the Almspeople, he demonstrated by a simple sum that since the latter were receiving £353.12s, he should be getting not £50 but £235! The reaction of the Assistants is not recorded, nor is it noted that any of them attended the late Master's funeral.

Wallace was simply re-stating what had been reported in 1819 by the Commissioners on Education of the Poor, though they had not been arguing the Master's case. They regretted that there were seldom more than seven boys "on the foundation" i.e. educated free, while the Master in his spacious rent-free house "maintains there a considerable boarding school". They felt that "this, as a free grammar school, appears now to fall very short of effecting the intentions of the founder". Why then did they sadly conclude that, "according to the circumstances and exigencies of the present time, we do not know that a better apportionment could be made"?

The fact is that Sevenoaks School, along with many other endowed Grammar Schools at this time, was struggling in a trap from which the Commissioners could see no escape. When they asked Gervase Whitehead why so few poor children came forward he was in no doubt: "The reason I conceive to be, that the mode of education, namely, classical learning, is not generally adapted to the condition of the persons who would be entitled to apply for it. There are other schools in the place better adapted to the circumstances of the neighbourhood". In other words, the *really* poor children either didn't want to, or couldn't afford to come. But wouldn't they be educated free? Yes, in Latin and Greek, and with a little bit of English thrown in; but if they wanted teaching – as they all did – in reading, writing and arithmetic, then they must be charged, for otherwise the School would be mis-applying the Founder's endowment, which had been specifically intended for a "classical" school.

"What class of persons generally send their children?", the Commissioners asked the Revd Wilgress. "The children are generally sons of tradesmen and farmers". "Have you ever had application for poor children?" "I have never had any application but from those of the description I have mentioned". One may well wonder why, since the Assistants had apparently already condoned such substantial departures from the founder's wishes, they didn't feel able to challenge this constraint; but it has to be remembered that the English obsession with rigid class divisions – something William Sevenoaks couldn't possibly have foreseen – was already well advanced. Though all-powerful Commerce had now displaced the old Aristocracy and the Church, all three still shared a strong suspicion that to over-educate the *really* poor was at best inappropriate, at worst positively dangerous. Even as ardent a supporter of educational reform as John Locke thought that mental culture was not for men of low condition, while Hannah More, whose simple, uplifting moral tales sold two million copies in 1795, thought writing was an unnecessary accomplishment for the poor.

We begin to see things more clearly. The Assistants didn't really know what was going on in school, for the two Wardens appointed to look after practical problems apparently did little more than claim their riding expenses for rent-collecting; effectively the Master was left to sink or swim, attracting wealthy boarders as best he could, putting up with as many "poor scollers" as he had to but not going out of his way to ease them up the ladder of opportunity so dear to the hearts of William Sevenoaks and our other early benefactors. Thus it would probably be wrong to condemn too quickly all those concerned with the affairs of Sevenoaks School in those corrupt times. There is ample evidence that most of our Assistants were upright men with a strong sense of the responsibilities of rank, active in many philanthropic and charitable enterprises. It may well be that in the case of the School they despaired, like the Commissioners, of finding a way out of the trap, and so turned their benevolent attentions elsewhere – for instance, to the rebuilding of St Nicholas', or to Lady Boswell's little English School, which since 1675 had offered primary education to fifteen poor boys in the town. The names of many of our Assistants –

Bosville, Betenson, Austen, Lambard, Farnaby, Petley, Curteis – are from the beginning found listed as Trustees, and it was largely due to their efforts, above all to those of Lord Amherst, that in 1818 two new National Schools, one for boys and one for girls, were able under Lady Boswell's name to move into fine new buildings in London Road.

Nevertheless, though our administrators' sins may have been merely those of omission and neglect, they did result in abuses, and in a serious failure to fulfil the wishes of the benefactors. Between 1721 and 1842 only thirty-one Exhibitions to Oxford or Cambridge were awarded, and it is certain that many of them went to fee-paying boarders who were not entitled to them. When we discover that several Exhibitioners went on receiving their grants years after they had left university, our only consolation is the proof this offers that incompetence, not greed, was responsible. And what of the four £15 scholarships established on the instructions of the Lord Chancellor in 1735? Well, quite a lot were awarded up to 1803, but then they petered out. Between 1814 and 1829, when the Revd Wilgress was Master, only one was given, and that one to his nephew.

CHAPTER SIX

Some Masters, Some Boys and a Housekeeper

We know little about the Masters who taught the boys of Sevenoaks School before the nineteenth century. This is a pity, for some of them were no doubt worthy men and good scholars who did their best to sugar with humanity and affection the bitter gruel of "gerund-grinding" and catechism, often obliged to teach single-handed a class of widely varying ages and abilities. On the other hand, some were probably minimalists doing just enough to earn their salary but not enough to risk increasing the size of the School and their own workload.

After Thomas Hales, the only other name we have in the fifteenth century is that of William Younge, and all we know about him is that when he was Master in 1498 he was the defendant in some obscure lawsuit.

In 1560 William Painter, aged about forty, succeeded his father as Master of Sevenoaks School, but remained only a matter of months. Probably his mind was on other things, for in that same year he published an English translation of a Latin tract, *Antiprognosticon*, written by his friend William Fulke to disprove the claims of astrologers. Painter had left St John's College, Cambridge, without a degree, and so was strictly ineligible for the Mastership; however, he was not without influential friends, and when his father fell ill he somehow managed to get himself ordained by the Bishop of London and moved into the schoolhouse. It was possibly just as well for the School that almost immediately he was offered, and accepted, a permanent post as Clerk of the Ordnance in the Tower of London. On paper this was worth eighteen pence a day, but in fact, by borrowing freely from the funds under his control, he became very rich, married and bought lands. In 1586 he was ordered to pay the Treasury £7075, and confessed that he also owed the Queen £1709. 17s. 3d. The following year he was accused of false book-keeping in collusion with Ambrose Dudley, Earl of Warwick, but still managed to retain his profitable post until his death in 1594.

Painter's only claim to fame, or perhaps even to respectability, is as the author of the *Palace of Pleasure*, a collection of translations from French and Italian, "beautified, adorned and well-furnished with Pleasant Histories, Tragical matters, and Excellent Novells selected out of divers good and commendable authors". The latter included Boccaccio and other "shameless" humanists, and the book largely inspired Ascham's condemnation of the evil effects of the dissemination in English of Italian literature; but it was hugely popular – and important in that it provided Shakespeare, Webster, Jonson and others with a rich storehouse of plots.

In 1610 a certain Humfrie Frank, "an insufficient and disordered school-master", was expelled as a result of legal proceedings brought by Sir Ralph Bosville. A few years later he was appointed Headmaster of St Olave's Grammar School, but the appointment was disallowed by the Bishop of Winchester. All the interesting details are lost to us, as is any significant information about his successors at Sevenoaks until the eighteenth century. In the *Autobiographies and Letters of Thomas Comber, sometime Precentor of York, Dean of Durham (Surtees Society 1946)* there is a glancing reference. In 1653, when the School was in the hands of John Hooper, formerly usher to Thomas Farnaby, the future Dean was eight: "and was then removed to the great free school at Sevenoaks to Mr Hooper, but falling into the measles I was taken away . . .".

Elijah Fenton was Master from 1706 to 1711. Surprisingly, Dr Johnson judged him "an excellent versifier and a good poet", though Southey dismissed him as "a Poet Minorite, whose productions are more characterised by indecency than wit". Perhaps he had been shocked by "Olivia":

> Olivia's lewd, but looks devout,
> And scripture-proofs she throws about,
> When first you try to win her;
> Pull guineas out

And never doubt
To find the saint a sinner.

However, Fenton was capable of more serious – if rarely more entertaining – work, and Pope thought highly enough of him to employ him as collaborator in his translation of the *Odyssey*. He had been intended for the Church, but when he graduated from Jesus College, Cambridge in 1704, his principles prevented him from taking the necessary oaths. "By this perverseness of integrity", wrote Johnson in his *Lives of the Poets*, he was driven out a commoner of nature, excluded from the regular modes of profit, and reduced to pick up a livelihood uncertain and fortuitous" as a teacher. Though we have no confirmation of Johnson's assertion that the School was "brought into reputation" during Fenton's brief tenancy of the schoolhouse, we do know that when he was lured away "with promises of a more honourable employment" he had considerable success as a private tutor. The Earl of Orrery, his former pupil, declared that "he was never named but with praise and fondness, as a man in the highest degree amiable and excellent". Kind and considerate, he was however far from energetic: Pope said that he died of "Indolency and Inactivity", while Johnson's description hardly suggests that he would have made a particularly dynamic Headmaster:

Fenton was tall and bulky, inclined to corpulence, which he did not lessen by much exercise; for he was very sluggish and sedentary, rose late, and when he had risen, sat down to his book or papers. A woman that once waited on him told him, as she said, that he would "lie abed and be fed with a spoon".

One interesting fact that has recently come to light, thanks to help from the Revd F. W. Austen and Mr Charles Lees, is that while Fenton was Master his Housekeeper for two or three years was none other than Jane Austen's great-grandmother Elizabeth Austen. According to *Jane Austen her life and letters, a family record*, by William and Richard Austen-Leigh (Smith, Elder, London 1913), Elizabeth's rather feckless husband died in 1704, leaving her with six sons and a daughter in poor circumstances. Obviously a determined and resourceful woman, anxious to give her children a decent education, she moved to Sevenoaks, and in return for looking after the Master and a number of boarders was granted free education at the Grammar School for at least four, possibly five of her sons. The boys seem to have made the most of the opportunity. Thomas Austen became an apothecary in Tonbridge, where his brother William practised as a surgeon. Francis Austen became a lawyer in Sevenoaks, amassed a considerable fortune in 1743 and bought The Red House; he died there in 1791 at the great age of ninety-two, having served as an Assistant at the School for nearly twenty years, as did his son Francis Motley Austen, who sold The Red House in 1796 and bought Kippington from the

Farnaby estate. Francis Motley's son, Colonel Thomas Austen, who was an active Assistant for forty years, further sealed his close connection with the School's history when in 1837 he bought Sevenoaks Park, today's Park Grange, from Multon Lambard.

Jane Austen's grandfather William, the Tonbridge surgeon, died young, and his orphaned son George was supported by uncle Francis of Sevenoaks. Francis sent him to Tonbridge School where, after winning a scholarship to Oxford, he eventually returned as Second Master. Later granted a living near Basingstoke, he married a Miss Leigh, and Jane Austen was born in 1775. Thirteen years later she was to visit her great-uncle Francis in The Red House, four years before his death.

The only other eighteenth century Master of whom we can form some sort of picture is the Revd Gervase Whitehead, who conducted School affairs between the resounding dates of 1789 and 1812. We cannot here write as fully or as entertainingly about him as did Lennox, who clearly revelled in the access he was given to the privately printed papers of the Woodgate family of Summerhill. In these Whitehead emerges as an amiable, mildly absent-minded scholar – he was a Fellow of Jesus College, Cambridge, and second Chancellor's medallist – who engaged in a gently persistent, if unimpassioned and ultimately unsuccessful, courtship of several daughters of the Vicar of Seal, William Humphry, the Woodgate's son-in-law. Whitehead resigned his Mastership to become Domestic Chaplain to the Duchess of Dorset, who then appointed him Vicar of Seal on Humphry's death. Though something of a social lion, he was politically a shade unworldly; in 1820, when George IV was trying to divorce Queen Caroline, "Mr Whitehead's praying for her spotless Majesty two Sundays has excited a great oration . . . Lord Camden spoke to him on Sunday and certainly he has laid himself open to a severe reprimand from his Bishop". In financial matters he was apparently less out of touch, for when he died in 1838 he was said to have accumulated a fortune of sixty thousand pounds.

The Revd John Wilgress (Headmaster 1812–1831) was a keen cricketer, as recalled in *Memories of My Early Life* by Charles Wordsworth, later Bishop of St Andrews. Charles captained the Oxford Cricket XI in 1827 and 1829 and rowed in the first Boat Race; his brother Christopher became Bishop of Lincoln.

When my father left Bocking for the double preferment of Lambeth and Sundridge, given him by the Archbishop in 1815, [my education] was carried on under Dr. Wilgress at Sevenoaks; my brother Christopher being at school with me for a short time. . . . Kent was the foremost cricketers' county, and Sevenoaks a cricketing centre, and when matches were played on the well-known "Vine" ground, we schoolboys, marshalled by the usher, were taken to see them, Dr.

Wilgress himself sometimes making one of an eleven. . . . Once when we were playing a game on our school ground, I made a good catch, and the Doctor happening to see it, as he was standing just then at his study window, threw me out a sixpence as a reward for my dexterity . . .

The Revd Edward Heawood, who was Headmaster from 1831 to 1837, is remembered only for the verve with which he solicited the post. Though assured by the Corporation's clerk, Mr Cole, that the attendance of candidates was not required, he insisted on putting up at the Royal Oak "opposite to the object of our ambition: that should any interrogatories be found necessary or desired, I am on the spot ready to obey any summons". Duly rewarded for his enterprise, the new Master-elect expressed his appreciation to Mr Cole:

"I am told the Goudhurst coach is apt to be in a desperate hurry passing through Sevenoaks without stopping. Will you desire your servant to look out for it on Monday as by it I shall beg your acceptance of the first and last joint of Pork fed by me at Goudhurst and offered for your acceptance. Hope it will prove good!". A little later, announcing his imminent arrival from Goudhurst with twenty boarders, he sent his man-servant on before him: "He will amuse himself Brewing a Batch of Beer, getting stock of wood and coals, cropping the garden and the like, all which will most materially benefit my convenience."

Two years later the School does not seem to have prospered under his breezy rule as much as the Assistants may have hoped, for when Lady Ashburnham made enquiries about it she found "that it is considered as only a preparatory school, that all the elder scholars have left, and that those who remain are only little boys, in number about twenty".

The Revd William Presgrave's appointment in 1843 caused some excitement in town when it was discovered, the day before term was due to start, that he was an undischarged bankrupt. The Assistants were naturally alarmed, but somehow or other he managed to ward off his creditors and retain the Mastership, though he seems to have remained in financial difficulty right up to his death in office, aged only forty-three, eleven years later. A further strain must have been imposed by a certain Mr Kelson, father of a day pupil whom Presgrave esteemed "the most dangerous and troublesome of all youths I have had to manage during an experience of fifteen years". Kelson senior thought his sickly, lazy, congenitally untruthful offspring could do no wrong and was being shamefully treated. He was being unfairly put into detention, kept from a meal despite a doctor's letter, punished in private instead of before the whole school, publicly called a "sneak" by the Master; he was "retrograded both in Latin and Writing", and is "deficient in ready reference to the rules of Syntax"; he was unhappy about the new writing and the introduction of the *metal pen*. Accused of neglecting the little paragon, the Revd Presgrave explodes:

> Neglect of duty! No! I deny the charge. Mrs Presgrave's frequent remonstrance is that I shall injure my health by my too long and close attention to my scholastic duties. Did Mr Kelson ever see me or hear of my leaving the duties of my situation even to enjoy any of the rational recreations of life? No! I am neither Florist! Fisher! or Fiddler!! (Qui fugit molam fugit farinam).

Another of his pupils, William Franks, writing to his parents in 1846 (see opposite), seems all that the Revd Presgrave would have wished for.

There is quite a lot of evidence that the School's reputation under Whitehead stood high. In 1800, when at the age of sixteen George Humphry entered Jesus College direct from Sevenoaks School, his letter of recommendation stated that he was an excellent scholar in Greek and Latin, and had been educated "partly by his Father and partly by Mr Whitehead of your College who keeps a very admirable School at Sevenoaks". The letter goes on to admit, however, that the boy is not strong in Mathematical science, "for which in general boys at Sevenoaks are not sufficiently put upon train". Poor George, a sweet-natured and courageous youth who was to die of lung trouble before taking his degree, laboured long hours to repair the deficiency and "to keep up with the young men who come out of the North in Mathematicks; they come up having all Euclid and the greater part of Algebra at their fingers' ends, so that it is with great difficulty that I can keep with them". Presumably the young men from the north came either from grammar schools less strictly bound by their statutes to an exclusively classical curriculum, or from proprietary Modern Schools which were able to tailor-make their courses to the changing needs of the universities and of society.

In the same year that George Humphry went up to Cambridge, the five year old future historian George Grote entered the School. Exactly what arrangements were made for boys of such tender age we do not know, nor how common their presence was. His admission may have been at the personal request of the Lambards, who were friends of the Grote family and would be "available for the boy's protection and care, should sickness or accident overtake him". In fact, as was quite common at the time in the case of small grammar schools, Sevenoaks was being used as a Preparatory School, in this case for Charterhouse, to which the boy transferred in 1804. In Mrs Grote's *Personal Life of George Grote* she tells us that she had already taught him to

70

My dear Parents,

It is with great pleasure I have to inform you that our Midsummer Vacation commences on the 24th of June and will terminate on the 30th of July.

I hope you will find me much improved in my studies.

I am now learning the Latin Accidence, Butters Etymological Spelling, History, Geography, Writing, Arithmetic, and Sunday Lessons.

We have had during the half year several interesting Lectures on the nature and properties of the gases.

I am, my dear Parents,

Your dutiful Son,

William Franks.

Sevenoaks.

May 28th 1846.

Fig (xix)

read and write, and had even grounded him in the rudiments of Latin before sending him to Sevenoaks. "At this school the future historian . . . evinced a decided aptitude for study, being rarely found behindhand with his tasks, and ranking habitually above boys of his age in the class to which he belonged. In the holidays his mother caused him to devote a portion of his time to his lessons, to which habit, however, he never showed, or indeed felt, any reluctance".

To prolong for a while the relief of dealing, not with statistics and generalised comments but with real named men and boys, we can here take advantage of the Woodgate Family History to record a life-long friendship forged at Sevenoaks between two boys whose destinies were very different from those of Grote or young George Humphry: Henry Hardinge and John Woodgate.

"John was sent to school at Sevenoaks, a big boy for his age; and his first day there some of the other boys had got hold of little Hardinge, and were roasting him before the fire, according to the genial custom of the times. Though only a 'new boy', John made such a fuss that Hardinge was released: and to attest his gratitude, carved him a small wooden boat, for many years preserved in the family".

Both went into the army on leaving school. Woodgate, whose parents then owned Riverhill, joined Sir John Moore's forces in 1805, when he was just seventeen, served with heroism in many engagements in the Peninsular War, and was several times severely wounded. On one occasion his friend, now Sir Henry Hardinge and a Divisional Commander in the Peninsular, wrote to John's father: "I have very great pleasure in affording to the Father of my old schoolfellow and to his Kentish friends the very proudest consolation you can all feel, that whilst stepping beyond the line of his Duty your son received his wound in evincing a courage and determination that the bravest cannot surpass and which his Regt. and Friends cannot too much admire". Happily, John Woodgate survived and lived until he was eighty.

Henry Hardinge's brilliant career is part of our national history. Having lost a hand at Waterloo, he became Secretary of State at War in 1828 and Governor-General of India in 1848. Returning to England as Viscount Hardinge of Lahore he became, on Wellington's death in 1852, Commander-in-Chief of the British Army and subsequently Field Marshal. As a boy, his aunts had made him hang with his arms from a door in order to stimulate his growth; at his burial, on his coffin was laid the sword of Napoleon given him by Wellington. A General Order issued to the Army declared that "The Queen has a high and grateful sense of Lord Hardinge's valuable and unremitting services, and in his death deplores the loss of a true and devoted friend. No sovereign ever possessed a more honest and faithful councillor, or a more loyal, fearless and devoted servant."

CHAPTER SEVEN

The Victorian Era: I

June 13th, 1832. A General illumination on account of the passing of the Reform Bills for England, Ireland and Scotland. Every house in Sevenoaks was illuminated. Transparencies in many of the windows . . . a portrait of Grey and another of Lord John Russell. The union band marched several times through the town in procession. Had about 20 rockets some Bengal Lights and 3 Fire Balloons being sent off from the centre of the town: the largest was in sight nearly half an hour.   (From C.J. Knights's Diary)

. . . . (before you come to Seven-Oaks) saw a most beautiful and rich valley, extending from East to West, with rich corn-fields and fine trees; then comes sandstone again; and the hop-gardens near Seven-Oaks, which is a pretty little town, with beautiful environs, part of which consists of the park of Knowle, the seat of the Duchess of Dorset.
   It's a very fine place. . . . The gardens and houses all look neat and nice.
                    (From William Cobett's *Rural Rides*, 1833–53)

The Educational Background

It is tempting, and easy, to deride the astonishing muddle into which English education got itself in the course of the nineteenth century, to castigate the hypocrisy and callousness of those who thwarted the reformers' zeal and left the great majority of children condemned to no education at all, or to a

73

pathetically inadequate one based upon a self-serving belief in divinely ordained class divisions. In fact, that would be far too simple, and not entirely just, for the muddle resulted as much from the virtues as from the vices of our society. While France and Prussia, with a single-minded awareness of their national interests, were rapidly evolving centralised State systems of education, England's advance was hampered by the very vigour of its opposing voices, the passion of opposing ideals, fears and hopes. Though our School's struggles were mainly with smaller, more pragmatic problems like leaking roofs and blocked lavatories, it nevertheless suffered sufficiently from the larger conflict to justify a few words here.

The most glaring need for educational reform was amongst the very poor, many of them suffering vile urban squalor and the exploitation of child labour brought by the Industrial Revolution. Elementary education thus became the focus of attention during the first half of the century: the Grammar Schools and others in the secondary sector had to wait. The multiplicity of views on the nature of the required reforms reflected widely different ideas about what education was *for*. The Church of England and the nonconformist churches were mutually suspicious, but were united in their resistance to State intervention, and to any attempt by the Liberals to topple religion from its central place in the school curriculum.

On the whole, where the poor were concerned, education was seen less as a birthright than as a containing exercise. Some doubted the wisdom of doing anything at all. In his *History of English Education*, H. C. Barnard quotes from an 1807 Commons debate on the Parochial Schools Bill, which would have offered two years of free education in monitorial schools for those who could not pay fees. A Mr Davies Giddy felt that to educate the labouring classes of the poor "would be preudicial to their morals and happiness; it would teach them to despise their lot in life, instead of making them good servants in agriculture and other laborious employments. Instead of teaching them subordination, it would render them fractious and refractory, as was evident in the manufacturing counties; it would enable them to read seditious pamphlets, vicious books, and the publications against Christianity; it would render them insolent to their superiors". This view was not confined to a few blinkered extremists: throughout the century the belief was to persist, even among the most compassionate and idealistic reformers, that some are born to lead and govern, other to toil, and that it would be absurd to offer them the same kind of education. If anyone foresaw the evils of Disraeli's Two Nations, he would be reminded that 'character will out', and that the great principles of Free Trade and *laissez-faire* would enable men of real worth to leap the divide by means of self-help and sturdy independence. The poor must not be molly-coddled: "Let there be no lamentation of their condition", said Burke, "Patience, labour, sobriety, frugality and religion should be recommended to them".

If this sounds insufferably smug, we have to remember that certain duties and responsibilities were laid upon those fortunate enough to have been born to lead. Though not all made any great attempt to discharge them, some remarkable men and women did, and perhaps without this nineteenth century English middle-class version of *noblesse oblige* there might have been no William Wilberforce, no Robert Owen – and no Butler of Shrewsbury, Arnold of Rugby or Thring of Uppingham. And probably, without those three great Headmasters and their followers, the Grammar School would have died before the end of the century; for though the Established and the Nonconformist Churches, the Evangelicals and the Utilitarians and the new Industrialists found it difficult to agree about how – or whether – to educate the poor or train their teachers, all could find plenty to criticise in the endowed schools, including the great ones: there were, for instance, five rebellions at Winchester between 1770 and 1818. Riotous behaviour, debauchery, bullying, overcrowding, an absurdly irrelevant curriculum (and of course the brutal floggings necessary to teach it) – these were the charges commonly levelled against them. Obviously, the little one-room country schools – the pattern of the majority in the first half of the nineteenth century – were less subject to these abuses than were the bigger schools, but in none of them could life have been very pleasant for the pupils, however enlightened their Master.

Ironically, the abuses and excesses common in the big Public Schools at that time played a significant part in determining the nature and ethos of the best schools in the country, both grammar and public, for the next hundred years and more. We are inclined to forget, when noting the complacency and hypocrisy of the Victorians, just how many powerful voices were clamouring for moral regeneration, for higher standards in both public and private life, and condemning the uncritical glorification of science, material gain, popular democracy and mechanical religion.

Arnold of Rugby had no wish to rival the gloomy prophetic thunderings of Carlisle, and certainly not to abet Newman's efforts to revive a supine church by means of "objects so pitiful" as ritual, robes and symbols. What he wanted to do was to "introduce the principles of Christianity into men's social and civil relations". Many shared this aspiration, but Arnold's originality, and his genius, emerged in the practical method he chose. An inspired and inspiring teacher, he saw the communication of knowledge as a moral act, or rather as just one part of an education of the whole man. "His favourite idea", wrote Basil Willey in *Nineteenth Century Studies*, "was to introduce 'the highest principles of action into regions comparatively uncongenial to their reception'". One of these "uncongenial regions", Arnold readily admitted , was boyhood itself, because "from the natural imperfect state of boyhood, they are not susceptible of Christian principles in their full development upon their practice, and I suspect that a low standard of morality in many respects must be tolerated amongst them, as it was on a larger scale in what I consider the boyhood of the human race". Such realism implied no watering-down of his expectations of his pupils: on the contrary, his School became a microcosm of his ideal world, and his Prefects were given great powers and responsibilities; with them and with his other Sixth formers he spent a great deal of time both in and out of School, treating them as "gentlemen". The pursuit of excellence in all spheres of activity – social, intellectual, spiritual, physical – was encouraged not as a means of defeating one's competitors but as the only road to a truly Christian life of self-fulfilment and self-respect. More imaginative teaching methods were introduced – historical, philosophical and political lessons were drawn from the classical texts – and the curriculum was broadened to meet the needs of individual children.

The above digression, if such it be, cannot be justified by any startling immediate changes in the life of a boy at Sevenoaks or at any other small grammar school then struggling to preserve its dignity with very limited resources, bound by its statutes to fulfil a dual role that made the 'family' cohesion of Arnold's school quite impossible: a handful of poor "Free Place" boys had to be given rudimentary instruction in the 3 Rs – for each of which they had to be charged as Extras – while at the same time the brightest children had be groomed for entry to Oxford or Cambridge to preserve the School's fragile claim to academic respectability. Nevertheless, the ideals of those first great Headmasters were widely admired, and it was not to be long before our Assistants were openly admitting that "a really first-rate Headmaster" would be essential to attract more pupils and lift the School out of obscurity.

At Sevenoaks, both public esteem and physical comforts were scarce for Masters and boys until well into the second half of the nineteenth century – the more so since, as we have seen, little attempt was made to distribute the Charity's income according to the wishes of William Sevenoaks: the almshouses continued to receive by far the greater part. Not that the income could always be counted on. Tenants of School properties in both London and Sevenoaks had frequently to be pursued for arrears of rent, and in 1814 Anthony Pope's former property in Thames Street – variously known over the centuries as "The Anchor and Hope", "The George", The Tobacco Rolls" and "Holland's Coffee House" – was destroyed by fire and had to be rebuilt, only £500 of the £1300 cost being covered by insurance. Usually, when a new Master was appointed, the Assistants would make a token effort to meet the early requests of the keen new man for a lick of paint here, a few repairs there, perhaps a few pounds more for advertising and School Prizes; all too soon, however, his demands would elicit the familiar courteous regrets that the state of the Charity's finances simply could not justify further extravagance.

The Reverend Crofts

Soon after the Revd. Christopher Crofts had been elected Master in 1854, he asked for some repairs to be done to the School House. It is perhaps a measure of the increased involvement of our Assistants in School affairs that Lord Holmesdale and William Lambarde personally accompanied the surveyor to inspect the state of the building. It was agreed to re-paper all three floors, but a watchful eye was kept on the quality of paper: "for the drawing room floor 2d, for the next floor 1.1/2d and for the Attic 1d per yard. The new Master to select the papers, and if beyond the sums allowed and stated then the new Master to pay the difference in price". More importantly, there were to be new desks in a completely new lay-out in the Schoolroom, and new lavatories, at a total cost of £257 (see Figs (xx), (xxi), (xxii) on page 78). Croft's unctuous letter of thanks is worth quoting in full:

> My Lords and Gentlemen,
> It is with sentiments of sincere pleasure that I beg to express to you my thankful acknowledgment for the very handsome and liberal spirit in which you have been pleased to listen to my requests relative to the improvements at your Grammar School. I feel that so valuable a proof of your confidence and of your kind desire to contribute to the domestic comfort of my Boys, my Wife and myself ought to act upon me as a fresh stimulus to the zealous discharge of my duties. It will be my earnest and constant endeavour to show by my conduct that I duly appreciate the call thus made upon me, and while it will be my study so to conduct the Working of the School as to render admission within its walls an object of desire to the Parish and Neighbourhood from the benefits of the education and training there given, it will be my pride to make and to keep up the Fabric and its grounds an ornament to the Town.
> > I have the Honor to be
> > My Lords and Gentlemen
> > Your very faithful and
> > Obedient Servant
> > Chr. Crofts   Clk
> > Master.

Crofts' arrival coincided with the first serious attempt by the Charity Commissioners to deal with some of the anomalies that had crept into the administration of Sevenoaks School: the absurd imbalance in the distribution of income between School and Almshouses; the inadequate number of Foundation Scholars amid the fee-paying boarders; the woefully inappropriate curriculum. Above all, they clearly felt that the Trustees (the Assistants) had been both casual and high-handed in modifying the scale of payments and the qualifications required of applicants for admission to the School: the implica-

Fig (xx)

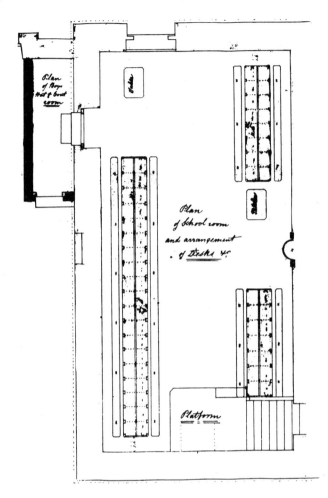

Figs (xx), (xxi) and (xxii) The new desks that Crofts asked for and received are illustrated below and their arrangement in the old School room to the left. Sixty-eight desks were provided in 1855. As there were no boarders in that year and only 26 day boys, most of the desks remained unoccupied. When Crofts left in 1879 there were still no boarders and only 11 day boys. Nevertheless School House was extended (upwards) to provide dormitories for 32 boys, a re-arranged School room for 80 and two classrooms for 25 boys each. If this implied a capacity for 150 pupils, it was not until the 1920s that it was filled.

Figs (xxi)   **Figs (xxii)**

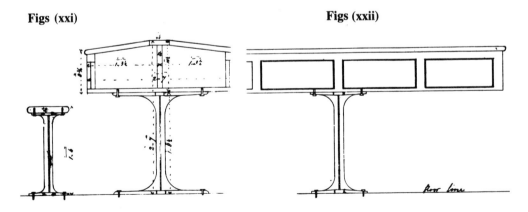

tion is that they thought *anybody* was being admitted if he could pay the capitation fee which had been raised to £5. These matters "should not remain matters of discretion, especially where the Trustees are subject possibly to frequent change".

The 1855 Scheme

The Trustees were summoned to attend at the Master of the Rolls' Chambers in Chancery Lane on March 7th, 1855, to be told about the new Scheme for the Management and Regulation of the Charity. Earl Amherst and Colonel Austen pleaded ill-health, Lord Holmesdale was busy at the County Assizes, so only William Lambard and one of the Wardens, Isaac Corke, attended. It would be tedious to rehearse here all the details of a Scheme which was never fully implemented – partly due to a lack of enthusiasm among the Assistants, partly because the funds simply were not available – and which in any case was to be replaced twenty years later. In summary: eight "Assessors", resident parishioners selected by the Court of Chancery, would vote with the Wardens and Assistants at the annual elections; a Clerk and a Receiver were to be appointed to help the management; the Master was to be in Holy Orders, with a salary of £150 and a capitation fee of £3.3s.0d. (but bright boys aged twelve from local elementary schools and from the parishes of Seal and Kemsing would have these fees paid by the Corporation) and the privilege of taking up to thirty boarders; there was to be an Usher at a salary of £100; no more than £30 a year was to be spent on placing out apprentices; the school age was to be from eight to eighteen; £10 a year would be available for Prizes; one Exhibition of £30 was to be substituted for the two of £15. As for the curriculum, all fears of betraying our Founder's stipulation of a largely "classical" diet seem to have disappeared. "The instruction to be afforded in the School shall be in the principles of the Christian Religion, the Greek, Latin, German Languages and Literature, Writing, Arithmetic, Land Surveying, Book-keeping, Geography, Mathematics, Drawing and Designing, General English Literature and Composition, Sacred and Profane History, the Principles of Chemistry and Physical Science generally, and such and so many other Branches of Education as shall . . . be necessary to render the Foundation of the most general use and benefit, and as the state of the Revenues of the School will admit, and so as to give to the Boys a sound, religious, moral and liberal Education".

Passing from these confident prescriptions to the familiar realities of the Minute Book, we can no more convict the Corporation of bad faith than we can credit them with an excess of zeal for the reforms. They were obliged immediately to borrow £425 to pay Law Charges due to the Chancery. The Master's salary was raised to £100, not £150, and out of this he paid £40 to his new Usher, Samuel Howlett of Caius College, to supplement his Corporation salary of £60, which was all they could afford. However, it seems likely that the Revd Crofts' wife was a lady of means, and for sixteen years they took no boarders and managed on the capitation fees – £82 from twenty-six day boys in 1855 – together with their share of the Extras earned from teaching French, German or Drawing.

If the Revd Crofts was under any misapprehensions as to the readiness of the Assistants to contribute to his domestic comforts, he was quickly disillusioned.

> Ordered – that the Clerk do write the Head Master and acquaint him, that the sum of 9s. 6d for removing the snow 3 times from the roof of the School House and the sum of £1:12:0 paid to Mr Fawkes for repairing the slating are disallowed.

> Ordered – that the Clerk do see the Charity Commissioners and obtain their opinion whether the Head Master having discontinued his Boarders the Corporation should be liable to the Rates and Taxes for his House in future or whether the Capitation fees would carry the Taxes.

> The Receiver laid before the Meeting a long letter from the Head Master of the Grammar School respecting the impure state of the water in the well from which his house and premises were supplied. It was decided that an official reply should be made to the Headmaster that for the present this Meeting would adjourn the subject.

In 1863 the Assistants and the Charity Commissioners agreed that the Usher should be allowed to take a limited number of boarders into his house. The Commissioners pointed out that the Scheme imposed an "absolute prohibition" upon such a move, but in view of the Headmaster's refusal to accept boarders they deemed it "advantageous to the School and to the public" to allow it while Crofts remained in office.

In 1870 Mrs Crofts died, and the widower began making alterations to the house to accommodate his married son and family. The Corporation reprimanded him for not first asking their permission, and warned him that on his departure he would be responsible for the cost of restoring it to its proper state "so as to fit it for the reception of boarders again". Crofts obviously thought this a bit mean, but rose above it: "I beg to present to the School the value of all the improvements that have been made . . .". The following year, with school numbers beginning to fall – they were to be down to eleven by the time he resigned – he was obviously finding life hard and thinking of taking boarders for the first time. As a consequence he requested, and was granted, permission to abandon the division of the School Year into four Quarters, and to adopt instead a three-term year "because at almost every School of any reputation the Vacation begins just about the time of its termination at this school". Two years

BUILDINGS 1890–1900

17.   The Assembly Hall/Gym (left), built in 1890 and Cottage Block (1900), the first permanent buildings since School House and the Almshouses were erected c. 1730. Photographed 1909

18.   The Assembly Hall interior, photographed 1932

19. A general view photographed during First World War showing School House on right, the assembly hall/gym in middle and the laboratory and workshops (added in 1900) on left

20. The swimming bath built in 1900, photographed in the 1930s

SWANZY BUILDING 1925

21. View of east front of Swanzy Building seen from Knole Park. Photograph of 1932

22. A similar view in 1993

23. View of east front of Swanzy Building from Jockey's Platch, photographed in 1932

24. The same building in 1987

25. The west front of Swanzy Building on right facing the 1890 Assembly Hall/Gym on left, enclosing Sennocke Close. Photographed in 1932

26. The Swanzy Chemistry Laboratory in 1932

SCIENCE BUILDINGS

27. The Science Block built in 1957 seen across Jockey's Platch

28. The Science, Electronic and Computer Building erected in 1988 masking the 1957 science buildings

JOHNSON BUILDINGS 1925–32

29. Johnson's Boarding House given by the family in 1927

30. The Johnson Hall opened in 1934 as photographed in that year from School House garden

31. The Johnson brothers' first gift to the School was a flagpole (1925). Photographed in 1956 (with the Headmaster's Austin Somerset car on left and the author's Singer Gazelle on right!)

32. The Johnson Hall, interior 1932

33. The Johnson Library, conversion 1976

34. The Pavilion on the playing fields in Solefields Road (1949)

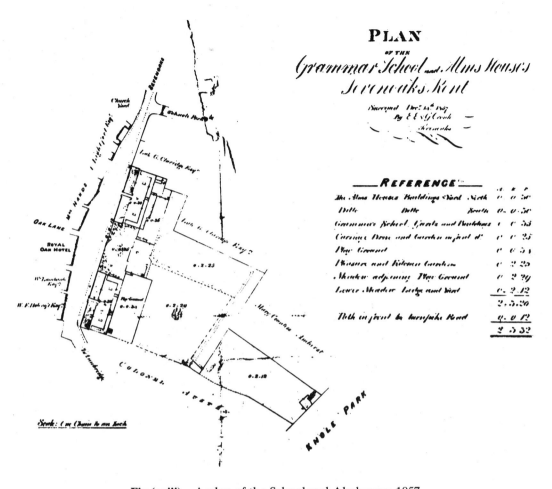

Fig (xxiii) A plan of the School and Almhouses 1857

later he asked to be allowed to let the Schoolhouse during the summer vacation: the Corporation somewhat frostily consented.

Things were not going well for the Revd Crofts, and it is difficult to decide how much sympathy he deserves. In 1874, his son having embarrassingly resigned the Second Mastership after only a few months – the Bishop of London had appointed him British Chaplain in Bonn – he was pleading unsuccessfully for a salary of £120 to attract a Maths graduate to fill the position, since the cost of living had risen dramatically since 1855: "At that time, to quote one instance only, I used to pay for butcher's meat 7d per pound. I now pay 11d and 12d". Later that year, once again reprimanded for letting the House without prior permission, he apologises for having incurred the Corporation's displeasure but "I desire to state in reference thereto that in June last my health began to give way, that my sleep became broken and unrefreshing, and that I used to wake with a violent headache and a painful tension across my forehead which gradually grew more intense and sometimes lasted throughout the day".

The Taunton Commission and the 1877 Scheme

When we joined the School the Head Master's second Wife had recently abolished the Boarders, and his third wife did not re-establish them. I have always considered that this was most detrimental to the School. [Crofts] found that on one occasion he could let the School for the months of June and July: with the result that our summer holidays suddenly began about the 7th June and ended about the 24th July. (S. Hyde Turner, 1870–76)

In 1864, The Schools Enquiry Commission was appointed under the presidency of Lord Taunton. One of its aims was to examine the widespread abuse by grammar schools of ancient endowments, many of which were being applied to instruction of a very elementary kind, showing as little regard for the "classical" aspirations of Founders as for the actual needs of the time. An extremely comprehensive questionnaire was compiled, to which Trustees (Governors) and Headmasters were required to respond. The answers supplied by Crofts illustrated not only his desire for a quiet life – "State of school buildings?: Good;" "Difficulties?: None" – but also help us to understand why, while Tonbridge was rapidly and energetically approaching the status of a "proper" Public School (with 104 boarders, 66 day boys, prefects and monitors, fagging, flogging and caning – but also with a Headmaster anxious to lift the restriction of Entrance and University Scholarships to local boys, in order to bring in more bright boarders), Sevenoaks (with no boarders, no prefects or monitors, nor corporal punishment) seemed blissfully content to forego any such ambition.

The "luminous and exhaustive" Taunton Report, as it was described by the 1894 Bryce Commission, also throws useful light on the sometimes loosely employed designation of schools as First Grade or Second Grade:

The term First Grade implies that the School has at least 10% of its whole number of scholars above the age of 16 years, the number given by that percentage not being less than 4.
  The term Second Grade implies that the School, not being qualified for the First, has at least 10% of its whole number of scholars above the age of 14 years, the number given by that percentage not being less than 4.

Thus, Tonbridge was listed as a "Classical First Grade School", Sevenoaks as a "Classical Second Grade School" – even though Crofts declared that he and his parents valued the school mainly for its "Comprehensive commercial education with Latin and French". At Tonbridge, no boys were taught Book-keeping or Mensuration, Physics or Natural History, though a few took Chemistry; at Sevenoaks, there were substantial numbers in all these classes, though of course Science was taught only from books in the absence of laboratories. Not surprisingly, Tonbridge had many more "Class A" parents (Independent, Professional or Mercantile) than Sevenoaks, particularly parents of boarders. The Tonbridge Headmaster declared that 23.8% of his pupils were "destined for university", while Crofts claimed 13.1%, which may well have been a trifle optimistic: the Commission discovered that there were only three boys at Oxford and Cambridge who had entered university within one year of leaving Sevenoaks, while there were nineteen from Tonbridge.

One hundred years later, a Sevenoaks School Headmaster was to bless the Revd Crofts for having "missed the Arnoldian boat" which might have carried us towards the lofty exclusiveness of some great public boarding schools. He thus played his part in prolonging into the next century the School's "medieval-modern oddity", and its eventually fruitful openness to new ideas. At the time, however, he had his critics. The Assistants were inclined to lay all the blame for a further intervention of the Charity Commissioners, and for the 1877 Scheme, at the door of the Revd Crofts and his agitation for a pension. In fact, as early as 1872 the Commissioners had been unhappy about Sevenoaks, and had seriously contemplated affiliating the other Grammar Schools of West Kent to that of Tonbridge; moreover, there was an influential body of opinion in Sevenoaks urging that when Crofts resigned the School should become a County School, in which case an even more drastic amendment of the Scheme would have been required.

In summary, the new scheme replaced the Wardens and Assistants by fifteen Governors: one *ex officio*, the Lord of the Manor of Knole; six Representative Governors (one the nominee of the Archbishop of Canterbury, one of Jesus College, Cambridge, three chosen by the Sevenoaks Local Board and one by the School Board for Sevenoaks); eight co-optative Governors, in future to be approved by the commissioners as "competent persons duly qualified to discharge the duties of the office". The Headmaster was not necessarily to be in Holy Orders, and the Archbishop's ancient privilege of "licensing" new ones was abolished. The school age was to be from nine to nineteen; the concession available to "natives" of Sevenoaks, Kemsing and Seal was reduced from full to half fees.

Dr Gordon Ward lamented that thus "a scheme came into being which repealed all that was left of the constitution of Queen Elizabeth" (for instance, the new curriculum was decidedly "modern" and Greek had become an Extra at £3 a year!), and that the new Governors had lost control of the funds now vested in the Charity Commissioners. "Thus Sevenoaks School was brought into line with other educational establishments, and thus also it must have lost much of that interest which attaches to actual responsibility". Whether this gloomy retrospective analysis might have been justified had it not been for the devotion and generosity of certain Governors, the valiant efforts of Headmasters, and eventually the admirably open-minded and sympathetic approach of the County authorities, is open to conjecture. At the time, clearly, much depended upon the choice of Crofts' successor.

Now in his seventieth year, Crofts announced that he was "disposed to resign", and asked the Corporation to grant him a pension. He declared that he had spent £1200 of his own money on School House and the premises, and that for the first seven years of his Mastership he had received only £100 of his £150 salary whilst also supplementing the Usher's salary by £40 a year. The Corporation regretted that they had no funds to provide a pension, and would he please tell them *when* he was leaving? Crofts thanked them for their regrets and said that he was staying.

In 1875 pressure was mounting on the Corporation to do something about the School. The town was changing rapidly. The Forster Act of 1870 had paved the way to compulsory attendance at elementary schools. The arrival of the railway had begun to reduce the dominance of a few old families, for many of the wealthy new "upper middle class" residents – mainly bankers, merchants, brokers – were, in Sir John Dunlop's words, "men who had a strong belief in the merits of private enterprise and, therewith, a notable sense of the civic duties which were incumbent upon wealth and influence". Soon men like F. Swanzy and W. J. Thompson (who in 1854 had bought Kippington from the Austens) were forcefully articulating local dissatisfaction "as to the condition of the Grammar School and Charity generally". Mr Swanzy was invited (at his request) to meet the Assistants, upon whom he urged "the great desirability of superseding the present Headmaster in his office with a view to the appointment of a younger Man who would take Boarders in the School and so tend to the great advantage of the Town".

Meanwhile the Revd Crofts had submitted his case for a pension to the Charity Commissioners and refused to budge, despite considerable moral and financial pressure, until their new Scheme was in force. To the great consternation and indignation of the Assistants, the Commissioners decreed that Crofts' pension was to be £75 per annum! In September 1877 he left the School, unlikely to have been convinced by the Clerk's assurance of "the regret of the Corporation at the termination of a connection of such long standing".

What did the boys make of the Revd Christopher Crofts and his School? We have one set of memories, those of the late S. Hyde Turner, who was a pupil in the 1870s. His mother took him and his brother to School House in 1869 for a preliminary interview with the Headmaster. He remembered thinking him somewhat "oily" on that occasion.

> He was an elderly man of dignified presence and of courtly manners. To our relief he told our mother that never during his career as a master had there been any occasion for him to resort to that last extreme – a flogging; but, as we discovered later on, there were equally efficient punishments of other kinds, including detention and the writing out of innumerable pages of class books, interspersed with terrific clouts over the head.
>
> The Head Master taught Latin, Greek, French and English – on reflection, I think the old man did not do so badly considering the material. Grammar was especially well taught, and he loved the classical authors. Mathematics were taught throughout the School by a clever but extremely impatient Irishman. There was also another assistant, not clever, more patient, and hopeless as a teacher and disciplinarian.
>
> As the numbers of the School declined, it was difficult to avoid winning a prize of some kind at the annual Christmas distribution. The distribution was usually done by the dear old Nobleman, who was known as 'Farmer Amherst'. The Head Master was generally impressed to the point of tears.

For the Revd Crofts had always believed in Speech Days. They were an occasion for high sentiments and fine words, for moving displays of self-deprecation, unity and mutual admiration by management and staff. As reported in the South Eastern Gazette of December 24th, 1861, he thought that they were

> productive of great and general good. They created in the minds of the boys a healthy tone; they provoked an honourable emulation; and as the year drew near to its close he could see that the spirits of those who thought they were likely to be the successful candidates for distinction received the gladdening influence by laying to heart that they were shortly to receive the reward due to their industry, perseverance, and good conduct, and that they should receive that guerdon at the hands of his lordship, in the presence of the clergy and gentry of the town and neighbourhood.

"Earl Amherst said that he could not permit the able, energetic and affecting address of their esteemed head master to pass without a few words." Fortunately less lavish with them than the previous speaker, "he declared that he felt highly honoured to be called upon to distribute the prizes, and to support so excellent a master as their school then possessed".

CHAPTER EIGHT

The Victorian Era: II

The last quarter of the nineteenth century was a particularly taxing time for grammar schools. They were facing increasing competition from the more lavishly financed – and often more efficiently administered – proprietary schools, which were not only able to offer the whole range of 'modern' subjects to attract the commercial middle-class, but were also building and equipping science laboratories. As if this were not enough, many rate-supported Board Schools were improperly developing 'Tops' and thus trespassing into the field of secondary education. The Taunton Commission, and the resulting Endowed Schools Act of 1869, loosened many of the shackles restricting curricular development in grammar schools, but did not supply the funds to pay for new teachers and equipment.

Another factor was the 'Darwinian' belief, rapidly gaining ground throughout the Victorian era, that public examinations were the only way to select those best fitted for advancement. The iniquitous system of "payment-by-results" as applied to the Board Schools had resulted in an even greater reliance on mechanical rote-learning of the 3 Rs: Lawson and Silver quote a turn-of-the-century judgment that "the examination system controls education, and in so doing arrests the self-development of the child, and therefore strangles his inward growth". Though the best grammar schools were now dedicated to the

Arnoldian belief in self-development and a "rounded education", they could not remain aloof: parents now expected their children to be prepared for the Royal Society of Arts exams, or for entry to Sandhurst or Woolwich or the Civil Service. Foreshadowing the debate about League Tables in the 1990's, this new emphasis upon practical achievement meant that grammar schools, however 'hampered' by their humanitarian ideals, were forced into the market place. Some did not survive; others survived, diminished, slipping meekly into the State system.

When Crofts departed, the new Governors, now including the redoubtable W.J. Thompson as a representative of the Sevenoaks Local Board, appointed the usher, David Chapman, as Acting Headmaster and set up a Committee to report urgently on the state of the School's finances, and on "the best mode of carrying out Clause 28" of the new Scheme. This had briskly announced that the Governors, "as soon as conveniently may be .. shall provide proper school buildings suitable for not less than seventy day scholars and thirty boarders, and planned with a view to convenient extension. Such school buildings shall include a library, a laboratory and a gymnasium, with proper fittings and appliances".

The Committee recommended: selling The Anchor and Hope as soon as the lease was out; putting the School Lands up for sale (the Vine Court Estate had recently been sold off at £1000 an acre) or on building leases; repairing and repainting School House, putting in new drainage and a new staircase, and extending the building northwards into the small kitchen garden and yard. The new dormitories were to be provided by taking off the roof of the south wing and putting on another floor (so much for Palladian symmetry!). Tenders had been obtained from four local builders, that from Wiltshire of Sevenoaks (£2,383) just undercutting that from Durtnell of Brasted. These alterations, overseen by the architect, Mr Hooker, would provide dormitories for thirty-two boys, a School Room ('by rearrangement of desks') for eighty boys and two Class Rooms for twenty-five boys each.

Finally, they recommended that in order to secure a really first rate Headmaster he would have be guaranteed a salary of £400 for the first two years, clear of the profits he might make on the boarders; he would not receive capitation fees during that time; boarders were to be charged £60 a year, "natives" £8 and all others £15; there were to be no Extras. Since funds were low, each Governor was asked to pledge £20 a year for two years in order to pay the Headmaster's salary: this "proof of their personal interest would be a strong encouragement to any Headmaster to undertake the making of the School".

Birkett (1878 – 1898)

There were sixty-seven candidates. Six were short-listed, their ages ranging from twenty-seven to thirty-four. Daniel Birkett, twenty-nine, was appointed in January 1878, but the School remained closed until the dormitories were ready in June: the Inspector of Nuisances had reduced the number of beds available from thirty-two to twenty-one in consideration of "the amount of air to be allowed to each boy". The other building work dragged on for several months more, hindered by bad weather and strikes among Mr Hooker's workforce. In fact, some of the contracted work had still not been completed two years later.

Birkett wasted no time when he finally moved in. It was resolved "that the course of instruction be that of a Modern School of the First Grade with classical instruction for those Boys who were intended for the Universities". He spent £25 on advertising for pupils, appointed a French Master, M. Doret, at £50 a year, a mathematician and scientist, Mr Vinter, as Second Master at a salary of £200 (Chapman had resigned and was soon part of the competition, running Turret Lodge School in the town: "Instruction, thorough; Situation, healthy; Dietary, first-class; Discipline, parental; Comforts, equal to home'). Birkett bought a bell "for the summoning together of the School", a clock and several "Wall Maps to illustrate Geographical and Historical Lessons". He asked to be allowed to appoint teachers of Drawing, Singing, Drill and German (though the German teacher was to be paid by the Headmaster). He had the playground gravelled and employed a gardener at £1 a week, of which the Governors agreed to pay seven shillings.

The Governors, eager to support Birkett but not wishing further to reduce their income by selling more stock, began taking a tougher line with non-payers, and refusing to grant remission of fees to boys who were absent for less than a whole term. However, by the end of 1879 they were beginning to pull on his reins. The Headmaster's request for an additional resident master to help supervise the boarders was at first turned down for lack of funds, though they did allow him £12 for gymnastic equipment.

For a few years all went fairly well. By May, 1880, there were eleven boarders and thirty five day boys in the School: two years earlier there had been no boarders and only eleven day boys. Birkett had had the School Field levelled for cricket, and was himself paying the lease of a small field for football. Mains water had been laid on at the generously low charge of £5 per annum, probably due to the fact the W. J. Thompson was a director and one of the founders of the Sevenoaks Water Works Company. The Visiting Examiner "formed the opinion that the School is in a state of admirable discipline".

Yet the boy standing second in order of merit on the School List, one W. H Swaffield, was only thirteen years old, and no Exhibitions could be awarded since no pupil was old enough to enter University. Birkett pleaded for the provision of more Scholarships to enable boys to stay on longer, and to attract into the School "boys far better grounded and prepared than, I regret to say, are many of those whom I have been obliged under present circumstances to admit .. It would be well if it were more generally understood by the public that this School has been organised by the Charity Commissioners as a 'First Grade Modern' and not as an Elementary School". Thompson, now Vice-Chairman, conferred sympathetically with Birkett, but told him that the Commissioners would not allow further funds to be taken out of capital. In the end Birkett agreed that his salary should be reduced to £200, but that he would receive a capitation fee of £4 for each boy in the School up to one hundred boys. At the next Governors' Meeting Thompson produced a list of Gentlemen prepared to contribute to a Scholarship Fund and proposed that four small Exhibitions should be offered over the next three years, but the Motion was lost on the Chairman's casting vote.

There is no doubt that Birkett was an able, energetic Headmaster, proud of the School and determined to raise it into the "first rank". He and his wife were spoken of affectionately by pupils, staff and Governors. It is sad to watch, through his twenty-year struggle to raise standards, increase numbers and improve facilities, the gradual waning of hope and enthusiasm. In 1880 he had listed some of the "attractions – I would almost say essentials" – in which Sevenoaks was deficient. The growing importance of games and athleticism is striking:

   1 Covered Play Ground
   2 Detached Infirmary
   3 Library
   4 Fives Courts
   5 Studies for the Senior Boarders
   6 Separate Cubicles in the Dormitories
   7 Cricket Ground
   8 Gymnasium
   9 Carpenters Shop
10 Laboratory for Science Teaching
11 Swimming Bath

Without at least some of these, he predicted, the School would inevitably remain small. And so it proved. In 1881 the Charity Commissioners refused the Governors permission to sell the School Lands, or to develop them for building purposes. They argued that too much building was going on, that even new houses as close to the station as St Botolph's Road were still for sale, and that as the town developed and mains services and roads were extended, so the school property would dramatically increase in value. This momentous – and probably wrong – decision effectively dashed all Birkett's hopes and condemned him to years of penny-pinching, during which he frequently had to dig into his own pocket: he paid to convert and equip two rooms as a workshop; rented part of the School Lands for cricket and football pitches; and contributed generously to the establishment of a Library (a collection of books, not a building).

Nor were the Governors loath to help, frequently contributing £10 or £5 each to reduce the annual deficits or to fund an occasional Exhibition; William Thompson endowed the Kippington Prize for English Literature, John Clabon the Clabon Prize for Good Conduct.

But the books had to be balanced, economies had to be made: the admirable Mr Winter was asked to accept a lower salary and sadly resigned, becoming Vice-Principal of the Church of England Training College in Culham; his successor lasted only two terms. The Drawing Master's and Drill Master's salaries were reduced, and cuts made in the amounts available for School apparatus, Examiners' Fees, Advertising and Printing. As for the Headmaster's "essential" improvements, the only one the Governors felt able to contemplate was a corrugated iron roof over part of the playground, "for the accommodation of day boys bringing their dinner in wet weather. These boys now use the School room, and thus prevent the ventilation of it between School hours".

Meanwhile the "Anchor and Hope" was proving more of a liability than a source of income. Having fallen into dilapidation between a succession of defaulting tenants it had now been burgled: "found unfast by the Police . . the pewter had been stripped from the counters and the brass taps wrenched off". Put up for sale, it attracted no viewers at all; the Agent supposed that "the uncertainty as to Public Improvements and Fish Markets, and Custom House, probably deters any one from entering upon such premises at present". Consequently, Birkett's attempt to force the Governors' hand by announcing that he had brought a lathe and a good supply of tools for the proposed Workshop fell sadly flat: the Workshop was "deferred".

Only occasionally downcast, Birkett struggled on. A fire in School House set his wardrobe alight and destroyed some of his clothes. In 1883 he agreed to a further cut in his and his assistant teachers' salaries "until the pension to Mr Crofts falls in". With numbers fluctuating between forty-five and fifty-five, he still managed to offer the full range of subjects proper to a First Grade School, and was congratulated by the Examiner on finding a place for Drawing and Vocal Music: "It is pleasing to notice that, amid the multiplicity of other studies, a certain amount of time can still be accorded to these humanising and delightfull occupations".

It seems that some of the inhabitants of the town were less complimentary. In the 1880s the *Sevenoaks Chronicle and Kentish Advertiser* ran a rather fatuous column called "Sevenoaks Sayings", amongst which we find: "I think of all the idle and pedantic portion of the community which exists, schoolmasters are the very essence". An advertisement for Cassell's Popular Educator asserts that a reader "will understand the greatest part of what is going on around him, which is a great deal more than can be said of the best Greek or Latin scholar".

Birkett had heard "disparaging remarks on the Status of the School". He analyses the problem for the Governors: Local Elementary School standards are low, and though Sevenoaks is now offering both Modern and Classical studies the new Entrance Examination required by the Scheme is excluding "the class of tradesmen," who feel disgruntled and accuse the School of not fulfilling its responsibilities to the Town, "in the sense of 'the tradesmen of the town'. The School seems to me not intended for any particular class, but for all who reach a certain educational standard at a certain age. This is the standard required by First Grade Schools, and is naturally higher than that of the so-called 'Commercial' or (technically) 'Middle Class' and Second Grade Schools".

"The Boarders now in this School, and nearly all the Day Boys, are the sons of gentlemen, so that there is very little of that 'mixture of classes' of which parents often complain".

"I believe that the School will succeed by strictly keeping to the Scheme and maintaining the position laid down for it there – provided the people of Sevenoaks will recognise that position. If however the School is to be constantly regarded, by many of the middle and upper middle-class residents, as containing chiefly boys of a lower social grade than their own (which is not the case), the Scheme as it stands cannot be worked, and should perhaps be altered to one of a lower Grade".

Poor old School: lower class children are not 'suitable', tradesmen class children are not up to it educationally, and upper-class children look down on it socially! It is clear that Birkett was less preoccupied with increasing the opportunities available to the underprivileged than with maintaining and raising the "tone" of the School: "At present the School is maintained chiefly by the Boarders, who are all of a high class, and who naturally give its tone to the School". But more are needed, and so we are back to the "essential attractions" – for which there are no funds . . .

In my day the School was known as Queen Elizabeth's Grammar School. There was only one building with a very small piece of ground attached not large enough for any games. Our recreation was taken in a field at the other end of the town beyond the Cricket ground. I forget what the numbers were, but I should say well under 100 in all, and a very small proportion of boarders. I was there from September 1884 to, I think, the end of 1888 when I went to a crammers at Folkestone for a year before getting into R.M.C. Sandhurst.

Mrs. Oxtoby was the Matron, a stout and very efficient lady, who was always very kind to me.

(Major-General Sir Jocelyn Percy, K.B.E., C.B., C.M.G., D.S.O.)

A New Beginning?

In 1884 Birkett and the Governors agreed to take a gamble. The task of balancing the School's income and expenditure was handed over to the Headmaster: he was to be responsible for meeting any deficit, and all profits would go to him. No doubt he was tired of having to get permission for every small item of expenditure, for every move that he felt might benefit the School; for their part the Governors, many of them successful businessmen and believers in free enterprise, probably thought that nothing could be lost by giving the young man his head. It was suggested that they all contribute towards paying off the present deficit in order to give him a clear start.

Only one of them had serious doubts: "Major German stated his conviction that the School would not improve – it was too far from the general public; there were higher class Schools on the one hand and also lower class, working a lower fee attracting day boys. He had withdrawn his sons on account of the social element and as he was not willing to personally assume any pecuniary liability he begged to withdraw from the Board and then left the room".

By 1888 it looked as though the gamble of giving Birkett "sole conduct of the School" had succeeded: there were three resident and one non-resident graduate masters, three non-resident teachers of specialist subjects, thirty-three boarders (some of them rooming in the Usher's house nearby) and twenty-seven day boys; a small Chemistry Laboratory had been set up; there had been successes at cricket and football; the annual Sports Day, Concert and Dramatic Entertainments were well established; places had been won at Oxford, Cambridge and Woolwich; the bold step was about to be taken of having the Upper School examined by the Oxford and Cambridge Examination Board. At that year's Distribution of Prizes William Thompson, now High Sheriff of Kent, was fulsome in his praise of Mr and Mrs Birkett ('for every true wife present knew the power of a sympathetic heart and watchful eye to cheer her husband in any difficulty'). Sevenoaks and Maidstone newspapers reported his speech in full.

There were some, he knew, who differed as to the constitution of the school He thought the Commissioners had exercised a wise discretion when they followed what they believed to be the original intention of the founder, and made it a first grade school. A school like that, he believed, conferred upon the town of Sevenoaks directly and indirectly, greater benefits than would a school of lower grade, merely intended for the trade of the town. The school was open to the tradesmen of the town, and they had boys of intellect and character fit to avail themselves of its advantages, and every boy born in Sevenoaks and Seal could attend at half fees. No one, therefore, need be shut out of the benefits of the school of his native place, and if the boys would remember that among the peers of the realm at the present moment they had one whose grandfather was a butler, and among the foremost statesmen of the day one whose father was a newsmonger, they would see that in England everything was open to him who tried.

Thompson was a member of a wealthy Mincing Lane family of tea brokers. A devout, evangelically-inclined Christian, he was a churchwarden of St Nicholas', and in 1880 he and his sister had built St Mary's in Kippington. A true Late Victorian, he passionately urged the assembled boys to pursue beauty, wisdom and right conduct: "With Ruskin they might enter into kings' treasuries and walk in queens' gardens. Let them study eagerly every good book, everything that would lead them to a higher tone of life . . Let them not be afraid of enthusiasm: the boy without it was nothing worth".

Mr Thompson then quoted Young's lines on Death, and concluded as follows: Oh, my boys, my young men rejoicing in the strength of your youth, consecrate your powers to the power of the good and of the beautiful. Scorn a lie. You must to yourself be true; and believe me that as every sin committed dogs a man to his last hour, so every good thought, every act of self-denial, every influence for good will attend you as guardian angels, and make you realise to the full the picture in the first Psalm, and while you are doing your duty to God on earth you are denizens of heaven itself, for Heaven is with Him. Farewell! (Loud applause).

Within years of this stirring occasion numbers began steadily to decline, particularly among boarders. It is difficult to account for this other than by the superior facilities available at other schools, which Birkett had always feared. Despite the opening in 1890 of the handsome Assembly Hall/Gymnasium (the ragstone building on the west side of Swanzy Close, linked by an arch to School House), pupils and funds became scarcer and scarcer.

The Technical Instruction Act of 1889 was to prove important to Sevenoaks. The growing awareness that Britain was fast being overhauled in terms of industrial and technological efficiency by other nations forced the authorities to recognise that the country was not fishing deep enough in its pool of talent. Though it would be many years yet before the death of the old conviction that different social classes must be educated quite differently, some enlightened voices were calling for the notional 'Ladder of Opportunity' to be properly and securely set up, so that able poor children in Elementary Schools could gain scholarships to the Grammar Schools and thus on to University. The Act empowered county and county borough councils to make grants and provide scholarships to secondary schools, including the endowed Grammar Schools in those localities where there was no other 'rung' available.

In 1893 the Technical Education Committee of the Kent County Council offered us help, and the following year the Governors, rather reluctantly, agreed to accept £50 a year to encourage Technical Instruction, together with two £10 scholarships available to Elementary School children. Their reluctance sprang partly from their fear that Sevenoaks School might lose what social status it had, partly from a suspicion of state interference, for the price of this aid was the appointment of two K.C.C. representative Governors to their board.

Birkett was in a quandary. He believed in the 'Ladder', but he wanted the children to be selected on academic merit and not simply on "nomination" by the parent school: "The requirements of the higher School also must be borne in Mind". He was afraid that too many inadequately-grounded children from elementary Schools, arriving too late and staying only a year or two, would lower the "tone" of the School, deter boarders – and not benefit much themselves. He pleaded the case of local parents of modest means who had not sent their children to Forster's overcrowded Elementary Schools, "and who may justly claim a share of the benefits" of scholarships to Sevenoaks. Could not funds somehow be found to revive the Foundation Scholarships, which were not tied to Elementary Schools, and not one of which had been awarded for seven years? Was it essential to go on giving the half-fees concession to "natives" whose parents could easily afford the full fee, in preference to perhaps brighter boys outside the "native" area whose parents could not? In 1895, three out of fourteen boarders and eighteen out of thirty-one day boys were paying the reduced fee, which meant a serious loss of income to the School and a considerable strain on Birkett's own finances, for his capitation fee for "natives" had been reduced from £4 to £2. Not only had he contributed generously towards the cost of the School House extension, the new School Room, the little Chemical Laboratory: "I have long been providing a better Staff than the Endowment warrants, by supplying board and lodging for two, and sometimes three, assistant masters entirely at my own cost".

The Governors agreed that two Foundation Scholarships should be available to "non-natives" under the age of thirteen, and these were advertised. Pressed by the Technical Education Committee for details of proposed improvements in accommodation and science facilities, Thompson, Lord Hillingdon, Sir Mark Collett and one or two other Governors personally pledged a total of £100 and asked whether the committee would match this. Not ambitious enough, replied the Committee: the School needed a decent workshop, Laboratory and Science Lecture Room, and their Committee would give £250 if the School could raise the same amount. The Governors consulted the Charity Commissioners, who suggested that the Lower Thames Street property might be sold. Instead, the Governors launched a General Appeal to

94

the residents of Sevenoaks and the neighbourhood. This fell only £60 short of its target, but by 1897 the cost of the new buildings had soared to £900!.

Meanwhile the urban District Council had offered £2,500 for five acres of the School Lands east of Hollybush Lane, next to the cricket field which Birkett was renting. The Governors replied that since the U.D.C. wanted the land for a cemetery, this would eventually reduce the value of the remaining land for housing development, but they would consider an offer of £1,000 per acre. The U.D.C. backed away.

☆ ☆ ☆

In October 1897 Birkett wrote to the Governors: "I much regret to inform you that I find the conditions of the Headmastership, always difficult, are now almost impossible; and I am compelled to tender my resignation of the post". After twenty years he had come to the conclusion that his struggle to maintain Sevenoaks as a First Grade Classical and Modern School was doomed to failure. An important factor must have been adverse local comments occasioned by the poor performance of his boys when for the first time the whole school was examined by the Oxford and Cambridge Schools Examination Board in 1896. At both Higher and Lower Certificate Level they had been sitting exams designed for children as much as two years older than themselves. Sevenoaks had no Sixth Form: there were three boys in the Fifth, aged 16, 17 and 18; seven in the Fourth, aged from 15 to 18; twelve in the Third Form, mostly 14 or 15, but two of 13 and one of 17; ten in the Upper Second, from 11 to 15; fifteen in the Lower Second, from 10 to 13. The wide age-range in each form gives some idea of the difficulties encountered by Birkett and his staff in teaching children coming into the School from widely differing educational backgrounds; once in, the appalling attendance records of some of them prevented any academic progress, and they would "stay down" year after year. On the face of it, Birkett's decision to expose all of them to the Oxford and Cambridge examination was suicidal, though it is just possible that it was a calculated shock-tactic to convince the Governors of the need for increased resources and a more realistic admissions policy. In the event, none of the three Fifth Form boys gained a Higher Certificate (the national pass-rate was 58%), only three Fourth Form boys gained Lower Certificates, and the Examiners' Report on the lower forms made depressing reading.

> **Chemistry**: "The answers to the questions on bromine and sulphur were meagre and scrappy. Some experimental work would be beneficial to them".
> **Mechanics**: "All the work sent up was of poor quality . . "
> **Arithmetic**: "These boys were clearly unequal to the paper".
> **Latin**: "No boy gained half marks and six fell below one-fifth of the maximum".

French: "One boy in the Upper Second sent up a fair paper, but all the rest were exceedingly poor .. ".

By the end of 1897 the number of boarders had dwindled to ten, and at the Christmas Prizegiving Birkett delivered his valedictory speech. He recalled that he had arrived twenty years earlier "full of hope and enthusiasm. The fine situation of the School, together with the new conditions established by the scheme of the Charity Commission, seemed to augur well for the future of the School". But he had been surprised to find "no school plant or apparatus of any kind .. no library, only a few desks and forms of venerable antiquity, two volumes containing lists of entries during the past quarter of a century, and an empty cricket box". Though numbers had remained small he believed, with Arnold, that size was not important in "a school of christian gentlemen". He saw virtue in being able to recall the face of every boy who had passed through his hands. He was proud of his part in the inauguration of The Old Sennocki-ans' Club, in the nourishing of a true esprit de corps and a lasting affection for the School. Mentioning without bitterness the great personal sacrifices he had gladly made towards providing a library, a chemistry laboratory, a workshop and the new Schoolroom, together with facilities for cricket, football and tennis, he warmly thanked the Governors for all the support they had been able to give him, his staff for their loyalty and hard work, and concluded: "I sincerely trust that the School may, before long, be placed, once for all, on a firm basis, that it will then receive a widely-extended support, that its progress will be continuous, and its prosperity without a check". (Loud applause).

The Chairman, W. J. Thompson, was typically fulsome in his praise of the Birketts, and obviously genuinely sorry to see them go: "They owed more to the influence of Mrs Birkett than any tongue could tell. They had felt the influence of a true woman permeating through the school, and if they may not have had her virtues emblazoned on their walls .. " Another Governor, John Clabon, "was convinced that from the very first day on which Mr Birkett accepted the position of headmaster he had done all that a man could do".

CHAPTER NINE

Interlude
Primroses in Knole

It is heartening to know that while Governors, Headmaster and his staff were wrestling with harsh financial realities, all was not gloom among the pupils. Dr. Cyril Bailey, C.B.E., F.B.A., M.A., D.Litt., LL.D., Fellow of Balliol and Public Orator of the University, was one of Birkett's boarders. "The Head Master was always attired in a black, full frock coat. He had a massive, leonine head, with sandy side whiskers. I suppose that in those days he was only in this thirties, but I always felt he was at least ninety! His was a very awful and terrific presence". Some of this distinguished Old Boy's memories were printed in *At Honour's Game*.

"I was at the School from 1882 to 1884. It was, by the way, in those days known as Queen Elizabeth's Grammar School, and in the light of the development of the Grammar Schools under the Education Acts and in view of the personality of Queen Elizabeth II, I rather regret the change. The 'Public School' element which has been introduced and strengthened in it is just what was wanted to give it, together with the continuous local association, the character of the ideal Grammar School of the twentieth century, in which many streams should meet.

"The School building was not then very different from what it was when I last saw it in 1938 – a substantial stone building of a basement and three stories. The western end was the Headmaster's private house. The other end was the School House and showed traces of its original Grammar School character. In our time the main hall was the teaching room of the Headmaster, who occupied a dais at the top, while his class sat at desks on the floor below on both sides. Next to him came the Second Master, who taught from the floor with his class ranged on either side, and beyond him at the bottom of the Hall the Usher. This School block was entered from the gravel playground by a flight of steps downwards into the basement and then another flight upwards. Above the Hall were two dormitories capable of accommodating some 30 boarders. At the side of the playground the ground fell rather steeply in a rough field on which there was as yet no Johnson's Hall.

"There was a considerable cleavage, not in any way acrimonious, between the boarders and the day boys, . . the sons of residents and shopkeepers in the town or of farmers in the vicinity . . A few came in by train from stations on one of the two lines – remember that there were no bicycles in those days. I don't think that there was much cohesion among the day boys or any definitely dayboy society.

"The boarders, on the other hand, were a pretty close corporation, not local in character, but drawn from the professional classes, largely in London. There were about 30 of them, who slept in the two dormitories over the Hall, seniors below, the juniors above, in the spacious long room with plentiful windows on three sides, looking on Knole Park and over towards the Weald. As the School House was at the time the last building at that corner of the town, its position was commanding.

"When we were assembled for meals in the lower room the upper dormitory boy had to take his chance, I remember, particularly at tea time. It was the custom to butter one's bread first and then toast it over the top of a half-moon shaped fireguard, where it dripped onto the metal floor. The big chaps had their go first and the state of the guard and its floor by the time that the boys of the upper dormitory got to it was amazing. I have often thought since of the maids cleaning it up next morning, but they always did.

"Besides the three permanent members of the staff . . there were visiting masters, of whom I remember two particularly, both rather distinguished in their respective ways. One was W. G McNaught, singing master, at that time leader of the Tonic Solfa movement. It has always been rather despised by orthodox musicians, but I am glad to have been instructed in a system which gives one an idea of the relation of one key to another and the development of one out of the other. It is pretty ludicrous to have a party of grown persons chanting tafatefe-ta-tay but it does make the sense of rhythm a reality. The other master was Henri Buet, the author of several books of instruction in French. He used the little classroom at the foot of the stairs, and his lessons were very far from being the farce with which the lessons of Frenchmen are usually associated . . Was there any other Master? If there was, I have forgotten. But I must add the School Matron, who had the name of Oxtoby, which I have never met before or since. She tended little hurts and ailments, and cast a friendly eye upon us in our small troubles.

"We boarders went on Sundays to the services at the Parish Church – a few yards on the other side of the road towards the town. We had pews reserved for us in the south aisle and the simple services and straightforward sermons of the Vicar, the Rev. T. S Curteis, were just the thing for us boys. The Vicar and his family too were good friends to all the boarders, and used to have some of us to meals and to the Vicarage and its garden.

"The other friend was 'Mother' Eames, who kept the baker's shop about a quarter of a mile down the road to the town. She was a kindly, cheery body who took an interest in us and we liked her, but we liked still better her buns, which had a peculiar flavour of their own.

"I used to sweat and sweat at being a good goalkeeper at the head of the stairs into the House but it was no joke stopping a gravelly ball; as a reward I once kept goal for the School against Sutton Valence but have no recollection of what happened. The school Soccer Ground was about half a mile from the School; it was a most extraordinary field, shaped like the letter U with sides rising up from a more or less level bottom. Gerald persuaded our cousin, N. C. Bailey, then captain of England, to bring a side against the School. He collected E. C Bambridge and his international brother; they were quite unable to contain their laughter when they saw the ground . . the ball centred from the wings, came down with the fury of a jet-bomb into the middle of the forwards and had to be steadied onto the ground.

"Cricket was played on the great historic Kent ground of the Vine and I am always glad and proud to have practised and played on so famous a ground. There was a famous local county cricketer – one Tonks or, as I think, Tong, whom we used to worship at the boundary rails.

"But my memory of outdoor life at Sevenoaks was not primarily of games or friends . . It was just the Cockney boy's adoration of the country, which he had never really known before. From the School House there were three possible roads into the country. The road straight on, if one was coming from the town, was perhaps the least attractive, though it had fine open fields one of which we systematically trod at the beginning of the summer term, because it was reputed to have larks' nests – but we never found one. Just opposite the School gates ran the road, first down then up, to Kippington, where one of the School Governors lived, Mr Thompson I think, with whom I established connection by winning the Junior Kippington Essay Prize.

"But it was really at the back of the School where nature kept her chief joy and surprise, for that was Knole Park . . Opposite the Church you plunged down a steep road, which took you at once into the Park. On the hill in front of you rose the House, a lovely and vast Elizabethan structure which Lord Sackville told me had seven miles of roof – a terrifying prospect for repairs. We used to regard the house with remote veneration, and to be in it and traverse the great galleries and find the family living in one end of one of them was an amazing experience. But we boys of the eighties, who were given the freedom of the Park, would wander past the house and among the herds of, I think fallow deer, out towards the outer boundaries. In a wood overlooking the Weald I remember what seemed to me then the most wonderful primrose corner, full-to-bursting with great blossoms. I wonder who knows that spot nowadays and whether they enjoy it as much as we did then. It was indeed a fairyland and its discovery the culmination of the joy in the Sevenoaks country. How much I should like to know whether these things are still there and whether they make the like approach to a mid-twentieth century schoolboy".

CHAPTER TEN

The Old Man
(1898–1919)

The *Sennockian* had appeared for the first time in the Easter Term of 1895, and had recorded the inaugural meeting of The Old Sennockians' Club at the Holborn Restaurant, with Birkett in the chair and twenty Old Boys present. The menu (overleaf), priced 3/6d, promised well. In April 1898, in the same restaurant, fifty members came to say farewell to their President: "The toast was drunk with musical honours, and three times three for Mr and Mrs Birkett".

The Sennockian of Summer Term, 1898, whilst welcoming Mr and Mrs Heslop, was in rather sombre mood: "Probably nothing feels a change so deeply as a School the change of Head Masters. The status of the School may be altered for better, or worse. Success may follow, or failure. The staff recognises the stranger hand, joyfully or regretfully, the boys wonderingly. Old boys feel a little alienated. All is thrown again into the melting pot".

In fact, within a few months of Heslop's arrival, everything was going swimmingly. The local School Board had heard a rumour that the Governors had been infected by Birkett's pessimism and were proposing that the School should abandon its aspiration to First Grade status. There is no evidence that

Fig (xxiv)   An Old Boys' dinner menu of 1896. The meal cost 3/6d.

this is true, but the Board's letter is interesting in showing increasing local support for the School and a realisation of its potential value to the town:

This Board having charge of Public Elementary Education in the Town and District and being especially interested in the Education of the Inhabitants, desires respectfully to express to the Governors its strong conviction of the great desirability of maintaining the present Educational Standard of the Grammar School. They hold this opinion because (among other reasons) (1) the interests of the Town require such a School, the number of residents who would use it being rapidly on the increase; (2) in view of the fact on which all Educationalists are agreed that a National System of Secondary Education cannot be much longer postponed it would be a great boon to all classes of the Inhabitants to possess Graded Schools through which Boys could pass from the lowest to the highest; and because (3) if the Standard of the School is reduced it will be impossible at any future time to raise it to its former Grade.

This was just the sort of endorsement that Birkett had long hoped for, and it is an additional irony that – within two years of the Governors refusing him a pension on the grounds that "they had engaged Mr Heslop on the condition that the whole income of the Foundation would be available for the conduct of the School" – the School was to have many of these "essential attractions" for which he had almost wearied of pleading. Governors, parents and some local residents responded to the Chairman's appeal and contributed to a fund to match the County's grant for a new Laboratory, Workshop and Lecture Room (at the south end of the new Assembly Hall and what was to become the Swanzy Block).

George Heslop was thirty-nine when appointed, and he came with an impressive reputation. *The Sennockian* reported with awe that "Mr Heslop found six boys at Sandbach School, and he turned it, in an incredibly short space of time, into the centre of education in that part of Cheshire, a flourishing School of 107. That a similar success awaits his work here is, we are sure, the wish of everybody".

It is not clear from the records how many boarders Heslop brought with him from Sandbach, or how many joined him later, but E. J. King-Farlow, writing in *At Honour's Game*, recalled that there were several boys from the North in the School in 1903, and thought that the Headmaster had probably lured down some of the best games players – including all seven Rigby brothers! – because of his own great love of sport. However he managed it, we know that by September 1899 there were sixty-four boys in the School and Boarding Accommodation was *full*!

Heslop had been appalled at the state of the School House when he moved in: "The old range was quite worn out and there were no means of cooking a dinner for the increased numbers . . . Every tap in the house was found to be leaking. The water supply to two closets was out of order. A urinal in the house was in a filthy and disgusting condition . . . The drains were blocked and sewage was discharging into the lower passage . . . The boys' lavatories and baths were unfit for parents' inspection and consequently unfit for a boy's use. All sinks had to be repaired and cleansed. A sink on the second floor required instant removal. The rotten and horrible condition of its surroundings obliged the workman to leave the job for a time".

To their credit, the Governors decided not to approach the Charity Commissioners for permission to raise the money: Lord Hillingdon and Thompson each gave £100 immediately, and Thompson and one other Governor promised a further £220 to pay for the drainage work.

Heslop kept up the pressure, enthusiastically and generously supported by his Chairman. Both were keen to capitalise on the improving relations between Town and School. Thompson not only paid £100 for the rebuilding of the lavatories in the playground,but gave one hundred guineas to provide full gymnastic apparatus in the new Volunteer Drill Hall – his own gift to the Town – on condition that the School might use it "at stated periods upon reasonable terms" – and perhaps use it for Prizegiving too. The Headmaster, obviously supremely confident of the School's bright prospects, suggested that the capitation fee payable to him should be raised to £5 per boy up to a school roll of sixty, but that beyond that number the fees should be invested for the general good of the School. This generous gesture was accompanied by his insistence upon the urgent need for a Sanatorium and a Swimming Bath. He thought that the latter would cost £800 and was confident that the money could be raised 'independently of the School Funds'. The cost of the Sanatorium was estimated at £500, and "the Chairman very kindly offered £250 towards the amount, and the Head Master was given permission to put the matter forward provided the remaining £250 could be found".

In September 1899 Thompson, now eighty-three years old, made the radical suggestion that reporters should be allowed into the Governors' Quarterly Meetings: "It strikes me – that were we more frequently before the town – with the present satisfactory position of the School – we should create an interest among new residents . . . and gather round us those ready to give material aid . . . We are a rich neighbourhood but the School's position is unknown – that it has no funds to fall back upon and that all improvements . . . must be met by outside liberality".

This was too much for some Governors (we do not know which, but the Minutes record that several leading Governors were absent) and Thompson was obliged to withdraw the suggestion in the face of strong dissent, unrepentantly clinging to his opinion "that the more all things connected with the School were before the public the better it would be for the School in the future". The Minutes cagily conclude: "Some further conversation took place and experiences were referred to and the subject dropped".

By March 1900, the indefatigable Thompson had raised £430 from "several Gentlemen in the District" and wanted a further appeal made to the public. He was supported by General Luard, but clearly some Governors felt that too much begging was demeaning: it was decided instead to approach the Commissioners for leave to borrow the rest.

By the summer of 1900 the new Laboratory Buildings were up, and the Governors asked the K.E.C. Technical Education Committee for their cheque.

The Committee refused to pay up until the buildings were properly equipped with adequate scientific apparatus, half the cost of which they would be happy to meet. The Governors replied indignantly that the labs *were* properly equipped. Only after a year of cool exchanges was it discovered that the Committee thought that Sevenoaks had applied to be recognised as a fully-fledged 'Science School'. At last the Governors agreed to spend £43 on new equipment for the Workshop and the Laboratory, the K.E.C. cheque arrived and the impatient builders, Messrs. Wiltshire & Son, were paid. Meanwhile the new Swimming Bath and Annexe (which was to serve as a Sanatorium, a new dormitory, and as a classroom for the Preparatory Class of younger boys proposed by Heslop) were nearing completion. Numbers were steadily increasing, and the Second Master Mr Stephenson was given permission to accommodate in his house some of the overflow of boarders.

Despite, or perhaps because of this flurry of confident activity, the financial health of the School remained fragile, and between 1901 and 1904 Heslop saw the capitation fees due to him reduced from £5 to £4, then £3. By this time he had completed his "annexation" of The Beacon Preparatory School in St John's Road and raised the School roll to one hundred, sixty of them boarders. The School was now bursting at the seams, and obliged by the Charity Commissioners to make substantial yearly repayments of money raised by selling Consols. A more timid or less ambitious man might have thought that this was the time for retrenchment, but Heslop's confidence was unshaken: with the permission of the Governors he threw himself into the organisation of a Bazaar to raise funds for a new Pavilion on the Cricket Ground.

There is no doubt that Heslop did much to raise the standard of games at Sevenoaks during his early years. Sporting prowess and Manliness were ideals fiercely pursued by the big Public Schools during the late nineteenth and early twentieth centuries, and many little Grammar Schools adopted them with enthusiasm. Sometimes this enabled them to turn disdainfully aside from direct competition with exam-orientated "commercial" schools, and to flaunt an intellectually spurious élitism based on class-pride and a contempt for trade; in other schools such as Sevenoaks, where of course snobbery was not unknown, it did something to unify the diverse community under successive scholarly Headmasters who happened also to be fond of games. It must be admitted, if contemporary witnesses are to be believed, that under Heslop greater emphasis seems to have been placed upon physical than upon mental agility: swimming, football and cricket flourished, and very full fixture lists were established. In the Summer Term of 1900 fifteen cricket matches were played on Wednesday and Saturday afternoons (against Skinner's, Mercer's, Cranbrook, Penshurst Park, Battersea Grammar School, Brasted C.C., Southborough School and the Sevenoaks Town "A" Team amongst others), and in the following term there were no fewer than twenty-one football fixtures between September 29th and December 15th: apart from schools, opponents included a Stock Exchange XI, Guy's Hospital "A", London Hospital "A", Holmesdale F.C. and Richmond Association F.C.

In 1904 that great benefactor and friend of both town and School, W. J. Thompson, died. Soon, however, we were to be equally indebted to Francis Swanzy, Governor of the School and Chairman of the Urban District Council. In 1910 he contributed half of the £4,750 paid by the Council for the School Lands, which enabled the School to buy part of our present Solefields Road playing fields from the Sevenoaks Park Estate Company.

Between 1904 and 1919 the affairs of the School can be but dimly followed, at least so far as "official" records are concerned. The Governors' Minutes have been lost; only one issue of *The Sennockian* has survived, and the Minutes of the Kent Education Committee are unrewarding. This is a great pity, for these were stirring times for the town and critical years for the School, and it would have been interesting to eavesdrop gubernatorial discussions as the School strove to keep pace with the rapid expansion and changing needs of the community. Edwardian Sevenoaks was still a place of rigid social classification. The "carriage folk" in the old great houses and the newer spacious mansions would hold their annual "Servants' Ball" for their large domestic staffs, and to these the local tradesmen would be graciously invited. Another self-contained group consisted of the professional men – lawyers, doctors, clergymen and schoolmasters. Sir John Dunlop has underlined the importance of "the growing army of junior workers in London. They were the clerks in law offices, the book-keepers in merchant firms, the more senior salesmen in retail shops", who walked from their homes on the lower slopes of the hill to travel third or second class from Tubs Hill Station.

Exactly why the School with its new amenities did not flourish as Heslop and Thompson had hoped we do not know, but its ambiguous social status – Birkett's constant worry – must have had much to do with the decline in the number of boarders from sixty in 1904 to nineteen in 1919. In January 1918, when it was "recognised" under the Regulations for Secondary Schools, it became eligible for the first Grant approved by the Board of Education (£238 for the first six months). At the same time it agreed to admit, each year, 25% of new boys on County Scholarships; but even before these significant developments, few boys had been coming from private schools.

If we do not have the Governors' Minutes, we do have a few glimpses of Heslop's school through the eyes of some of his pupils, and they suggest that, whatever its academic failings it was, for some of them at least, not an unhappy place. Heslop himself, the "Old Man" or "Judd", is invariably remembered with respect, often with genuine affection.

a very great character . . . beloved by all who knew him. He was quite a stern disciplinarian but he had a very keen sense of humour and was absolutely just. Despite the many handicaps and frustrations he had to contend with, he undoubtedly left his mark on the School . . . (E.J. King-Farlow, 1903-08).

Judd was a gentlemen, a scholar and a sportsman and held the most democratic views on discipline through the prefect system and rarely had to make use of the hickory shaft which was kept behind the study door.

It seemed that if the Old Man wanted to do anything at all, he must do it himself, and do it to the utmost of his time and ability and he would turn up for any (cricket) practice or for the three half-days practice games . . . with snappy instructions on all points.

I am always grateful to him for his patience in holding me in the bath suspended in a sling around my chest which was attached to a long pole which he held for I do not know how many hours. (N.C. Stenning, 1898-1903).

There is also Heslop's historic ride on his cross-framed Raleigh from Sevenoaks to Canterbury which he did in 2 hours and 45 minutes, and I remember his saying to me afterwards: 'Not bad for an old man'. He was then, I believe in his early forties. (G.Harrison, 1900-02).

After school hours were over, there was a certain amount of ragging between the boarders, playing games on the playground, singing and reading in the common room, and indeed we really had quite a good time.

(Heslop) would in no circumstances stand for favouritism (as between day boys and boarders) and every encouragement was given by the boarders to the day boys to enter more actively into the sporting side of the school. I am afraid it was not with great success, as the day boys were anxious to get home after school hours . . . (but) there were certainly many friendships formed between the Sevenoaks boys and the boarders; in particular I recall such families as the Knights, Ingolls, Dons, Sykes and others . . . (A.Welch, 1898-1902).

Welch was one of three brothers who had come down from Sandbach with their Head Master. They found "the villagers" quite friendly, but decided later that the reason they were invited out so often was the amusement caused by their northern accent. They devised one harmless form of revenge: they would attach a length of twine to a penny and leave it in the road where it bends south of the almshouses, then clamber up the steep wall and watch for the approach of greedy villagers, or better still of gypsies or hop-pickers in the season; holding their breath and still as stone they would wait for one of them to bend to pick it up – "then a quick yank on the twine . . . what asses they looked! and we were safe out of reach behind the wall!" On the night before the official celebrations of the relief of Mafeking, a group of boys went down town; a drunken soldier somehow attached himself to them, and under his leadership they warred with the villagers. The next night Welch watched from the dormitory window as a coach swept through towards Tonbridge "with wild hallooings and pistols fired from the roof".

Relations between boarders and day boys, when both are present in substantial numbers, are always likely to present – even in these less class-ridden days, even when the abolition of free places has sadly narrowed the social composition of the School – a problem and a challenge to Headmasters anxious to promote a sense of corporate identity. It is good to hear that in Heslop's time, long before numbers allowed the creation of Day Houses and inter-House competitions, some abiding friendships bridged the gap. The Knight family mentioned by Welch included Charles Knight, the closest friend of G. (later Sir Guy) Harrison quoted above, who remembers that "even at the age of nine he showed his devotion to Natural History. The walls of his bedroom were decorated with such delectable objects as snake skins, rabbits' skulls, owls' pellets and other interesting finds. We had many an enjoyable birds' nesting expedition together, and he was always rather more daring than I was and would climb a little further up a tree, or a little lower down a cliff than I was prepared to go". N. C. Stenning recalls that "the diagrams in his Chemistry and Euclid books at school were all converted into animals . . . He usually came to school with some kind of animal life in his pocket, and was particularly fond of bringing out in class a pair of white mice. On one occasion . . . he produced a pair of tiny tawny owls he was rearing". As a captain in The Queen's Own Royal West Regiment Knight was awarded the M.C., and after the war achieved world-wide fame as a brilliant and pioneering photographer of wild life; his books and films won both specialist and public acclaim and he lectured in many countries, often accompanied by his friend, "Mr Ramshaw", a magnificent golden eagle.

E. J King-Farlow, in *At Honour's Game*, gives us a generous selection of snapshots and memories of life at Sevenoaks School in the early years of this century. (Heslop, like Higgs-Walker later, was anxious to drop the Queen Elizabeth Grammar School designation, insisting that the Queen has "usurped" an honour due to our founder). Here are a few of them:

> When I look back, I am ashamed to recall what horrible little snobs we boarders were. Day boys were looked down upon as the 'lowest form of life'.. with perhaps the exception of a few who either excelled at sport or who were not the sons of tradesmen . . . We boarders at

Sevenoaks were also regarded as 'the scum of the earth' by the sons of gentlemen at Tonbridge School who, of course, never deigned to meet us in the realms of sport.

The standard of education at the time was extremely poor . . . Very few boys went up to the Varsity and those who did were usually the more brainy and hardworking but despised 'Daybugs', who were scornfully looked down on as 'Swots'.

Corporal punishment was extremely rife . . . for quite minor offences. I myself received 'six of the best' at the hands of the 'Old Man' after being at the School for only six weeks . . . My offence was slipping across the road in 'break' to Ma Woods to buy sweets . . . The other masters seldom gave whackings but the lordly prefects had the power of 'life and death' over all delinquents and some of them had extremely sadistic tendencies.

Detention was the most curious kind of punishment . . . If, for instance, one was late for a class or for meals, one received five minutes' detention . . . When the number of 'five minutes' amounted to a total of thirty-five minutes in the case of a delinquent, it was known as 'being over'. Occasionally a master or prefect would award thirty-five minutes all in one go. On Monday afternoons, which were half-holidays (in addition to Wednesdays and Saturdays) for those having no detention, the Detention Class was held in a classroom by a very bored master with his watch laid on the desk. There would usually be about twenty to thirty defaulters present and, at a given signal, the first five minutes commenced. Every boy had to sit absolutely still without moving a muscle. If anyone moved after say four and a half minutes, the master would rap on his desk and that period of five minutes was entirely recommenced. Woe to the boy who moved! He would receive retribution from his fellow sufferers afterwards. When a five-minute period was completed without movement, the class relaxed and the names of boys whose period of detention was up were called out and they sped out of the room and went down to the cricket or football ground . . . Boys with a total of thirty minutes could expect to be kept in the whole afternoon.

It will hardly be credited, but on Sundays we all wore top hats, from the smallest boy upwards, on our solemn perambulations to and from Church . . . Up to the age of twelve, boys wore 'Etons', or as they were more vulgarly known, 'bum freezers'. From the age of twelve, short black jackets and striped trousers. Prefects and sixth formers were allowed to wear white ties, and were also privileged to have the bottom button of the waistcoat undone. On week days, you wore what you liked – or rather what your parents liked. In early days the Norfolk jacket, with weird sorts of pleats, was the popular garb.

The swimming bath was my chief joy in the Summer Term . . .

109

Dead mice etc. had to be skimmed off the surface before one could bathe, but we didn't mind this.

Occasionally, some of the Senior boys played some very 'pat -ball' tennis on the bottom lawn with the Old Man's daughters, Evelyn and Faith. Faith, the younger daughter, also used to play 'tennis ball' football for the Boarders against Dayboys occasionally.

With regard to pastimes and hobbies, nothing seemed to be organised. There were no Societies – Debating or otherwise – and we were left to our own devices in our spare time . . . Nowadays, it seems to me that every minute of the day is planned out and scheduled.

Photography was my forte – on a commercial basis too . . . The dark room was in the stoke hole. My friend, H. W. Hamlett, was the business manager, taking the orders for prints of groups and portraits and collecting the money. And we did very nicely too. 3d. was the price for a quarter-plate print on Eastman's Solio P.O.P. – and nicely glazed too. Mounting was 2d. extra!

On the whole, the food was excellent and plentiful and was augmented by the contents of tuck boxes brought from home at the beginning of each term by every boarder and by food parcels received during the term. The menu, however, never varied, and we knew exactly what we were going to eat at every meal throughout the week. Supper, after prep. at 9 p.m., was the poorest meal – thick slices of bread and butter and glasses of water.

The classrooms, dormitories and other rooms used by the boys were lit by gas – and ordinary fish-tail burners at that . . . there must have been a considerable strain on the eyes doing prep. in a classroom lighted by four flaming gas jets on brackets suspended from the ceiling.

There was no water laid on in the dormitories, and all down the centre there were wash stands with basins and jugs filled with cold water. I can often remember breaking the ice in the jugs before performing scanty ablutions on a cold winter's morning. Two bathrooms were provided in the basement and we were allowed one bath a week, although, in summer, we were permitted to have cold baths after cricket. On my bath night, I used to boil sausages and brew cocoa in a saucepan over the gas jet in the bathroom and share them with my friend H. W. Hamlett.

Some of the smaller boys used the only other bathroom in the building, in the Headmaster's quarters. After the bath, one went in one's dressing gown into the Matron's sitting-room and made toast at the fireplace. A very kind and well loved character was the Matron, Miss Woods by name.

Soon after he left School at the end of the Christmas Term, 1908,

110

King-Farlow became Treasurer of a revived Old Sennockian Club: the Secretary was Martyn Rogers who was to die in the coming war. Though with only a couple of dozen members, they managed to run a Soccer XI and played matches on most Saturdays against other Old Boy teams: "After a match, we frequently dined together at 'Ye Olde Cheshire Cheese' in Fleet Street, where we invariably partook of the world-famous steak, kidney, lark, mushroom and oyster pudding, washed down with copious draughts of ale and sometimes finishing up with rum punch. Cost of meal, with drinks, 3s. approximately!"

Into War

My parents wanted me away from the Zeppelin raids on London. I believe that I was 9½ years old at the time. We had a charming Headmaster, Mr Heslop, a clergyman, and his lovely wife and two daughters. All able masters had been called up and we had one master who had brain storms and hit everyone in sight. The food was very good. . . .

We used to roam about in the railway tunnel at the risk of our young lives, and also to raid strawberry fields in the neighbourhood . . . There was not much heat in the buildings and we were always cold.   (N. Prince 1916–18)

In 1918, at the age of fifteen, I went to sea as a Cadet in the merchant marine. . . . I was third man in the sixth or top form of a British public school. I had had five years of Greek, Latin and French: in other words, I felt my education was complete! Since we were in the midst of the First World War, everyone as soon as he reached the height of five feet five inches, put his age up and obtained a Second Lieutenant's commission in the Army. The Headmaster published an edict that no-one's name would appear on the honour roll as serving in the armed forces unless he had entered in the proper legal manner. His son was killed in action and he later rescinded this ruling.
(Rear Admiral Gordon McLintock of the U.S. Navy)

At the outbreak of war the Club ceased to exist, but in December 1920 thirteen Old Boys met for dinner at the Florence Restaurant in Soho and resolved to reconstitute it. King-Farlow was unanimously elected Honorary Secretary and Treasurer, a post he held until 1928. The School which he loved so dearly (despite a lifelong hatred of cricket engendered by compulsory daily practices) owes much to him. "The years I spent there were extremely happy ones and, after I left, I was fortunate in retaining many friends. Alas, some of these lost their lives in 1914-1918."

Another Old Sennockian to die in the Great War was Heslop's beloved son, and this was a devastating blow to him. N. C. Stenning thought that "what he did for the School has been almost completely forgotten because . . . the general frustration which his efforts seemed to meet, added to his unconsolable sorrow at the loss in that war of his only son, of whom he had such ambitious hopes, resulted in his losing so much of that enthusiastic effort which he had so long devoted to making for the School a place in the world of education to which he was so sure it was entitled". On September 13th, 1916, Heslop was writing to a parent about his child's progress:

Leslie is doing wonderfully well in all ways and is a most plucky youngster. He gave a wonderful proof of this in the Sports but I do not imagine he has said much about it. I have noted the little matter of pocket money. Have you any more boys of Leslie's stamp in your neighbourhood? Brainy youngsters are so nice to handle. My boy was killed on the 1st of July in the first ten minutes of the great push. There is nothing to say. He had a duty to do and it was done.

In September 1917 he wrote:

My eldest girl is in France and being kept very hard at work. I have just had a letter from the Front giving me a full account of the finding and burial of my boy.. That ends long weary months of waiting and suspense. The war is very cruel. By our post yesterday I heard of the deaths of two more old boys. We schoolmasters have suffered, for though our boys are not of our blood they become very dear to us and something more than friends.

Ten years later he wrote to a historian:

You address your envelope to 'Hyslop'. There is some strange fatality about the name. My son was granted a commission as Hyslop. Representation secured some sort of attention and they kindly altered the name to Hyslope. However he was wounded as Heslop. He was killed as Heslop but they could not resist another effort and the name on the cross at the grave was Heslopp. It took some effort to secure a correction. The name seems simple enough.
      Yours faithfully,
      George Heslop

Out of the 350 Sennockians who served in the Great War, 36 lost their lives, 53 won the Military Cross, 11 the Distinguished Service Order, 4 the Distinguished Service Cross, 8 the Distinguished Conduct Medal, 6 the Military Medal, 6 various foreign decorations, while a large number were mentioned in dispatches. For a little School whose numbers between 1900 and 1914 averaged less than 75 this is a proud enough record.

Dear Mother and Millie (some war-time letters)

In January 1917 twelve year old Leslie White came to Sevenoaks School, and throughout his first year wrote home every week, sometimes twice a week. It seems presumptuous, even indelicate, to dismember his charming and carefully composed letters to his loved ones, but they do give the authentic "feel" of schoolboy life and preoccupations, which admirably complements the age-mellowed memories of older Old Boys.

I arrived here quite safely at half-past six. The boy I met in the train happened to be a monitor and has been here four and a half years. We took a taxi and paid half each. So far I don't know much about the boys or the school or anything. It is very cold and for a quarter of an hour every day we have to go into the playground and freeze . . . The matron has taken charge of my trunk and has told me to wear my blue suit and old boots . . . I am going into the third form which consists of boys from eleven to fourteen. There is one freak who looks about eighteen . . .

For the present I am more or less a 'fag' and am likely to be a new boy until I have been here a year . . . The language of one master is not all that can be expected as he called one boy a swine this morning.

We finish school at 4.15 and have tea at 5 o/c . . . We have from after tea till 7.30 to ourselves when prep starts and goes on till nine. On Wednesdays and Saturdays we are free from 12 till 7.30 except for dinner and tea . . . but we must go out in the afternoons. In the evenings we play billiards, chess and draughts or write letters . . . I have just been watching a game of billiards between two of the boys with the Old Man as prompter. It was quite exciting . . .

For breakfast we had rissoles. I have taken quite a liking to things which I did not like before, such as mince, watery rice, greens, marmalade, beetroot and stewed fruit . . . For dinner we had a most gorgeous steak and kidney pudding and leeks. We too notice the shortage of potatoes . . . I like boarding school very well but at the same time I won't be sorry when I leave. . .

As some of our old boys have won the Military Cross there is an extra half-holiday this afternoon . . . The news on the Western Front seems jolly exciting, doesn't it? Miss Heslop usually shows us the news and explains where all the captured towns are . . . Wednesday we had General French down here reviewing some troops in Knole Park. I did not get a chance of photographing him. On Friday we had a little excitement from the air. It was only a few miles away and we could hear the engines quite distinctly. I suppose I ought not to say anything about this but I thought you would like to know that I am all right . . .

There are several more cases of measles . . . the matron has caught it and had to go to bed . . . There was singing tonight and at prep afterwards there were only fourteen boys out of thirty-six present . . .

I am doing my best to train for the coming Chase by going for a sharp walk of about five miles every day . . . We have had two runs this term and I have been backer up which consists of kicking anybody who slacks . . . Please excuse my writing but . . . I have just been boxing and my hand is rather shaky. One gets excited at this for one has to be ready for the unexpected . . .

There was some fun in the dorm last night. While the maids are getting the meals ready the boys have to keep out of the dining room. Only the boys with colds are allowed to remain as that is the only room that has a fire in it . . . One of the boys had a parcel and left it in the dining room. Two boys who were in there with colds found it and thinking that the cakes looked very nice, purloined several. The prefects heard of it and decided that one of them must run the gauntlet of the dorm. The prefects and monitors being honoured personages had two whacks to every one of ours . . . He must have felt slightly sore at the end of it. I found my clothes brush came in very handy as it has a nice long handle on which you can get a firm grip.

We have despatch riders rushing past all day long between London and Tonbridge . . . We had some excitement here last night. The raid started at six and ended at eleven. Three times we were told to go from our dorms to the Old Man's dining-room and were served with biscuits . . .

The other day as we were going into tea I happened to punch the boy in front so that he nearly sat down. The Old Man was just inside the door and he caught hold of my tie and pulled me up to him so I thought I was in for a row. Instead of which the Old Man told me he was making me Scavenger prefect which is the lowest of the officials but still it is a beginning . . .

We have a good deal more time to ourselves of an evening now so the Old Man has instituted a Debating Society . . . I shall probably have to address the assembled throng. If you happen to be in need of apple cores or egg shells you had better let me know in advance . . .

Your affectionate son, Leslie

The War left its mark not only on Heslop, but also on the School itself. As the first post-war number of *The Sennockian* reminded its readers in December 1921, it had passed through troublous times. "Its staff was depleted, its work and games were disorganised, and its numbers fell until at the beginning of 1919 there were only 48 boys in the School". Heslop saw his early hopes and ideals crushed by the cruel restrictions of a bitter war and by the death of his son and so many of the boys he had nurtured. But we should recognise his very distinctive contribution to the School's story – honourable, patrician, old-fashioned eccentric that he was.

CHAPTER ELEVEN

The Aftermath of War

With no Governors' Minutes to tell us about either Heslop's resignation or about the appointment in 1919 of his successor, Geoffrey Garrod, we are fortunate in having the Report of the visit to the School of His Majesty's Inspectors in March, 1920.

This provides some interesting statistics: there were 88 boys in the School, including 19 boarders; 40 were ex-Public Elementary School pupils; 32 were under 12, 53 between 12 and 16, 3 over 16. (In the year 1918–19, there were 13 leavers under the age of 14, 5 under 15 and 13 under 16. In the same year, 11 boys under 10 were admitted compared with 1 in 1917–18). The average age of Form IV was 14.9, while the average age of boys in the top form, Form V, was 14.8 (suggesting that the three older boys were hardly academic high-flyers!).

Of the 88 pupils at present in the School 20 pay no fees: 16 of these are Free Place Scholars, 4 hold Boswell Scholarships from the Boswell Elementary School. There is one Leaving Scholarship of £4 to Jesus College, Cambridge, which may be given to a boy from Tonbridge School in the event of no boy from Sevenoaks Grammar School claiming it.

Class in life from which Boys are drawn (percentages):

Professional	20
Farmers	3
Wholesale Traders	8
Retail Traders and Contractors	11
Clerks and Commercial Agents	6
Public Service	4
Domestic Service	4
Artisans	3
Occupation, none or unknown	41

The Inspectors noted that there was also a Kindergarten class of 21 children, with an age-range of 5 to 9, being run by a separate staff as a private venture on the ground floor of the Sanatorium: "If it is proposed to continue and develop this feature of the School, the matter should be regularised by the Governors assuming responsibility for this department . . . " It seems that this little "school within a school" must have been closed, or moved elsewhere, shortly thereafter as School numbers rose, for no reference to it appears after 1920.

There was some quite severe criticism of "many defects in the present accommodation": the laboratory and lecture room are too small, and one of the classrooms beneath them cannot be used in winter as it has no heating; the Sanatorium is unsuitable, having no kitchen, no hot water and inadequate sanitary arrangements; there are no fire-escapes from the dormitories; there are not enough baths. As to the Curriculum and Organisation: the school week is rather too short at 26 hours; the teaching of English Language and Literature, History and Art is adequate, but poor in the case of French and Geography; the Maths and Science teacher is good, but there is a desperate shortage of apparatus and books; games flourish "as much as present circumstances will permit", there are no School Societies, no School Magazine and no Old Boys' Association. All in all:

The School is in an undeveloped condition. It has small numbers and inadequate accommodation. Being without a top and having no pupils who reach the standard of a First Examination, it scarcely at present comes even within the definition of a Secondary School . . . Heretofore it appears to have been conducted mainly as a boarding school; while the boarding element may with advantage be continued and developed, it seems clear that the principal function the School will be called on to perform in the future will be that of a day-school for the Sevenoaks area. By setting itself adequately to fulfil this aim, it may eventually win for itself an honourable place among the many excellent Secondary Schools of the County.

116

Garrod 1919–1925

Among the scarce reasons for this modest optimism was the School's new Headmaster – "a young man of good academic attainments and vigorous personality". Garrod, a former Scholar of Winchester and New College, Oxford, was a qualified barrister who had been Sixth Form Master at the City of London School. When he left Sevenoaks in 1925 after only six years, to become Principal of the large and prosperous Royal Academical Institution of Belfast (and later Professor of Classics at University College, Exeter), the School had been not quite transformed – there was still no Sixth Form – but clearly revitalised, and most of the foundations had been laid for its long-postponed renascence. Three Day Houses had been created: Grote, Fenton and Wordsworth; games had been made compulsory; soccer had given way to rugger; twelve Challenge Cups had taken the place of two; the School (debating) Society had been started and both *The Sennockian* and the Old Sennockians' Club had been revived. Most significantly, numbers had been trebled, and the splendid New Buildings, erected at a cost of £15,000, were nearing completion.

Much of the credit must go to Garrod and his staff, including two legendary assistant masters, H. J. "Scaly" Wright and H. L. "Jockey" White, teaching Latin and Science respectively, but he was strongly supported by a sympathetic and idealistic Board of Governors, particularly by Lord Sackville, Earl Amherst, Walter Hay (of Manor House), William Lambarde, Charles Plumtre Johnson and Sir Mark Collett. The last named, as Chairman of the Kent Education Committee, was to play a vitally important role in the evolving relationship between School and County. In 1919 a very generous County scheme to extend the School at a cost of £21,500 had been accepted by the Governors, but cancelled on financial grounds by the Board of Education.

It was at this point, with the General Strike looming and frugality the government watchword, that Francis Swanzy came dramatically to our aid. In his will he left £5,000 to the School, and the K.E.C., eager to encourage other private benefactors, agreed in 1922 to give an additional £10,000 towards the New Buildings, which would raise the School capacity to 250 pupils, including 100 boarders. It would also, Lord Sackville announced, enable the School to purchase 4½ acres of land at Solefields, to give us a good cricket field and two new soccer pitches (in fact, with the imminent arrival of the great "E. G." Groves, they would be used for rugger from 1924).

Sevenoaks was now committed to admitting an increased number of boys from Elementary Schools, their fees to be paid by the Kent Education Authority. This was what Birkett had feared, assuming as he did that this would further lower academic standards and the "tone" of the School, and drive the fee-payers away. What he could not have foreseen was the extent to which, after the Balfour Act of 1902, both national and county authorities would be prepared, even eager, to help grammar schools in areas lacking any other adequate institution of secondary education. Already in 1920 the K.E.C. had made Sevenoaks a grant-in-aid of £2,000 to help carry out essential repairs and generally smarten up the premises. The other unforeseen change, announced by Garrod at the 1922 Prizegiving, was that the Board of Education and the K.E.C. had agreed "that unsatisfactory boys . . . should give place to those who would do better" – in other words, that a new element of selection could be introduced in order to narrow the previously enormous ability-range. Hitherto, all that candidates for admission had been required to provide was a certificate of good conduct from their previous school, and they were admitted "strictly in order of application". By the end of the school year 1922-23 there were 32 free place children on the roll of 129 – just about the required 25% – but all 30 boarding places were full and demand was increasing.

Certainly, Geoffrey Garrod had no intention of presiding over a School in academic, moral or social decline. Bursting with energy and confidence, whether as proud President addressing the burgeoning Old Sennockians' Club, or as possessor of a fine voice singing sea shanties – "Billy Boy" and "Haul Away Joe" – in the Summer Concert, he was very much a "hands on" Headmaster. A former pupil, F. C. Pearce, remembered that when Jockey White would banish a miscreant from the upstairs Laboratory to stand on the platform of the outside iron staircase, "within seconds . . . the Headmaster would appear, ascend the stairs at speed, firmly grasp the wretched youth's ear between finger and thumb . . . and drag him back into the Lab. for explanations". At his last Prizegiving, in 1924, noting that the Cricket First XI had won all their matches against other schools, that a School Four was now rowing on the Medway at Tonbridge, that the Head Boy H. B. Foy had just set a new school record by swimming 100 yards in 67 seconds, that the first ever 1st XV had won a match against the Old Boys of King's School, Rochester, that music was flourishing, that the School Play had been revived with a performance of Beaumont and Fletcher's "The Knight of the Burning Pestle", and that in spite of all this one boy had gained a Higher Certificate and seven out of ten boys Lower Certificates, he concluded ringingly: "Our aim here has been to give the boys a training in discipline and self-control and especially that spirit of corporate enthusiasm which is sometimes known as *esprit de corps* and sometimes as the Public School spirit".

The Visiting Speaker, Major Ronald Williams, M.P., said that "It is a great thing, I think, this school business". But more specifically: "You are very fortunate, it seems to me, in Sevenoaks, in having two such splendid schools as Walthamstow School and this". The following February, when Miss Lilian Swanzy laid the foundation stone of the New Buildings, the Bishop of Rochester declared that: "It was to schools like this, which stood midway between the great and expensive boarding schools and the county secondary schools, that many people were now looking, and, he thought, rightly looking, for the solution of many of the educational difficulties of the time''. Things had indeed changed since the H.M.I.'s Report of 1920. And what was Birkett thinking, now an honoured guest at the sort of occasion he had dreamt of half a century before?

CHAPTER TWELVE

"Jimmy" and the Great C.P.J.

On February 23rd, 1926, Lord Eustace Percy declared the long-awaited New Buildings open. They contained five new classrooms, two new science laboratories, a new woodwork shop, new offices, new changing rooms and cloak-rooms, and a new staff room. The quadrangle they formed with the "old" Gym/Assembly Hall/Theatre/classroom was to be named Sennocke's Close in memory of the School's Founder. As at the laying of the foundation stone, Birkett was in the audience, and telegrams of good wishes were read from Heslop and Garrod. The new Headmaster, since Spring 1925, was J. A. "Jimmy" Higgs-Walker, who was to remain in office nearly thirty years before handing over to Kim Taylor.

Appointed from among 189 applicants for the post, Higgs-Walker was to prove an inspired choice. Educated at Repton and St John's College, Oxford, he had served throughout the war in the Worcestershire Regiment, in Egypt, Salonika, Mesopotamia and Italy. Teaching History and running a House at Oundle under the great Sanderson, he had been exposed to some of the most enlightened Arnoldian thinking about education available at the time. A good scholar, who respected and encouraged academic achievement, he nevertheless believed that a good school should seek out and nurture in every child the seeds of excellence. "Education", he said, "does not consist of forcing boys into a mould, but in providing the machine that would suit the boy . . .". Whether helping to run a Club or a Society or a Magazine, or performing in a musical concert or a school play or a debate, in becoming a House Official or even a Prefect, every boy was capable of being civilised by responsibility and group loyalty. Games were important to Higgs-Walker: he had done great things for Oundle cricket. A fine cricketer and fearsome fast bowler, an Oxford "Authentic" who had played for Worcestershire, he seldom missed a match at Sevenoaks. In an increasingly exam-orientated age, he was not afraid to declare that "character building is the main object of education. . . Clever men are plentiful enough; they provide many of the derelicts floating aimlessly on the sea of life; but men of character and strength of purpose are rare".

In 1956 Taylor told visiting H.M.I.s that: "What the School is, is largely Mr Higgs-Walker's doing. He is clearly the key figure in its recent history". Perhaps it would have been more accurate to call him one of the two key figures: the other was Charles Plumtre Johnson, our "Second Founder", a Governor of the School from 1913, and Chairman of the Board from 1926 until his death in 1938. Johnson liked and trusted Higgs-Walker and loved the School, which his great wealth was able to transform.

From the pages of *The Sennockian* now radiates a growing sense of a School brimming with confidence, proudly aware that it is advancing on sporting and academic fronts – and in terms of social status. In the mid-Thirties we get the impression of an organism approaching a state of near-perfect equilibrium and health.

Of course, there had been severe growing pains, and a desperate need for new clothes. The deficiencies noted in the H.M.I.'s Report of 1920 could not be remedied all at once. No doubt, without the sympathetic support of the K.E.C. and the munificence of Charles Johnson and his brother Edward, the School could not possibly have maintained the élan given it by Francis Swanzy's New Buildings in 1926. But new buildings and improved facilities do not necessarily make for a better school, any more than increased numbers necessarily make for a stronger 1st XV. Without venturing to define a Good School, one would suppose that a widely shared ethos – shared amongst past and present pupils, Staff, Headmaster, Governors and parents – is at least a very important factor, perhaps the most important of all. A narrowly prescriptive or proscriptive ethos – for instance, the all-importance or the unimportance of games or discipline or academic success – is unlikely to be widely shared: it will create stresses and conflict, arrogance and disaffection, public lip-service and private doubt.

It would be foolish to suggest that in these stirring years of renaissance no boy was unhappy, no parent dissatisfied, no Governor uneasy; but it is impossible to resist the impression of a remarkably united community, full of ideals and enthusiasm, fiercely protective of the individual, but unashamedly sentimental about the honour of the School and the achievements of its members. Speech Days, as reported in *The Sennockian*, really do feel like family occasions in the affectionate tributes given to leavers, Staff, Governors and benefactors.

What was this ethos which in those years so successfully bound the School together? It was nothing very new, certainly not revolutionary. Even to attempt to put it into words is probably to falsify it, for it stemmed from the characters of the people concerned, rather than from their ideas, from their loyal collaboration and mutual support rather than from any formal set of principles. Perhaps this is why Taylor insisted upon Higgs-Walker's key role, for in a small school the Headmaster's personal influence is powerful, all-pervasive among both staff and pupils.

Basically, it was the conviction that the ideals of the 'great' Public Schools could be applied to smaller schools, which would be much less expensive, less rigidly authoritarian and much less socially exclusive. Lord Sackville declared proudly that Sevenoaks School was "providing a course of education marvellously cheaper than elsewhere". Schools like Sevenoaks, he thought, "were now taking the place of the larger Public Schools in England". That was in 1930, when economic pressures upon parents were great, but even in less worrying times Governors and Headmaster were genuinely concerned to bring the advantages of a Public School education within the reach of as many people as possible. Two years later, at the Quincentenary Speech Day, in the presence of the Archbishop of York, Dr Temple, later to be Archbishop of Canterbury, Higgs-Walker reflected upon what the School stood for: "We are called, in a School like ours, to a definite duty in the national life. We have our chance of doing our educational duty to our Founder's district; we have the duty of meeting a national need for a full, varied, healthy, public boarding school education for the sons of those who want that education, but could not pay the fees of larger Schools; and lastly, we have the duty of performing an experiment of national value in our combination of day and boarding education into one corporate whole of incalculable value to boarders and day boys alike".

The missionary note was no mere Speech Day rhetoric. Higgs-Walker was no egalitarian – one or two of his Staff, while respecting him, thought him a little remote as he cruised past them and their bicycles in his venerable Rolls-Royce, the "Ark Royal" – but neither was he an élitist. Certainly, he believed that one of the principal functions of a Public School was to educate our future leaders, but he did not believe that all Public Schoolboys ought to be leaders, or that all our leaders would come from Public Schools.

Before looking more closely at the manifestations of this new self-confidence – the successes in games, the proliferation of stimulating Clubs and Societies, the improved academic record, praise and support from distinguished friends, rising standards in music and drama, the rapid growth of the Old Sennockian Club, the development of the inter-House rivalry – perhaps it would be salutary to remind ourselves that the very special situation of the School, midway between independence and an imperfect national system, did bring some considerable stresses and difficulties. Not all of the latter, judging by the H.M.I.'s Report of March 1939, were to be easily resolved.

As ever, the main problem was that of meeting the needs of children of widely varying academic ability and expectations, entering and leaving the School at different ages. Even as late as 1938, when in the previous three years 28 boys had won university places, six of them with Open Awards, the ages of boys admitted to the School were: 1 under 10, 9 under 11, 15 under 12, 4 under 13, 11 under 14, 10 under 15, 1 under 16 and 1 under 17. There were 31 boys in the Sixth out of a total roll of 253. Considering that when Higgs-Walker arrived there had been only eight boys in the School over the age of fifteen, things were clearly improving, but were as yet far from right. The Inspectors noted that the wide age and ability ranges had obliged the School to provide more options and smaller classes than the staff could really cope with: "It is noticeable that the Masters have very full time-tables . . . yet their loyalty and enthusiasm are such that they do not hesitate to take on other teaching groups (e.g. of Sixth Form boys) in their few free periods, in addition to . . . innumerable out-of-school activities". This bore admirable witness to the devotion of the team Higgs-Walker had assembled around him, but there was a price: "On the whole it may be said that the Masters are best at dealing with the ablest boys . . . they are not so strong at devising and developing a technique for dealing with the rank and file".

Commenting on the great strides which had been made since the previous Inspection, thanks largely to the generosity of C. P. Johnson, "whose faith in the School was and will remain one of its strongest assets", the 1939 Inspectors nevertheless felt constrained to add – and with hindsight the words contain a chill premonition of the great decision that was to be faced in 1946 – that "the extent to which the School does and can serve the ordinary Secondary School needs for boys in this particular locality seems to deserve some consideration . . . The intake and the demand for places from local Elementary Schools seem to be disappointingly low".

It may seem churlish to cast this shadow in advance over the many splendid achievements of the years between 1925 and 1939, of which Higgs-Walker, his Staff and pupils, Governors, Old Sennockians and the Kent Education Committee were so justly proud. Yet we owe it to the memory of William Sevenoaks and his fervent desire that the School should "teach and instruct poor Children whatsoever coming thither to be taught", to wonder why, amid such public acclaim, relatively few local children applied to benefit from the School's success. The population of our "catchment area" was about 40,000 in 1938. The number of boys in the School who lived in that area was 164: this gave a figure of 4.1 per thousand, against the national figure of 5.1 per thousand. There is absolutely no evidence that Higgs-Walker discriminated against boys from Elementary Schools. Could it be that the School was becoming too grand in its ambitions and pride, so that the "class factor" which had frightened away the middle classes in the nineteenth century had now begun to deter parents of humbler backgrounds? Or might there have been a general impression that the School's greatest efforts were concentrated on their brightest boys, towards the Sixth Formers whose names adorned the new Honours Board, and that it had yet to devise, in the Inspectors' words, "a suitable organisation and technique for the younger entrants and the less able boys"?

Whatever truth there may have been in these reservations, nothing can detract from Higgs-Walker's achievement in transforming the School and laying the foundations of its future growth. There is no doubting his total absorption in the School, and his ability to generate a matching enthusiasm in those around him. Charles Plumtre Johnson certainly recognised and honoured it: the genuine friendship that grew between these two men was to be of immense importance to the School's fortunes. Johnson had been a Governor for fourteen years when, in 1927, he made his first gift to the School: significantly, this was a 30 foot flag-pole to stand in front of School House and to celebrate, when required, notable feats performed by boys.

Later in that same year came the first of Johnson's "landmark" gifts. Convinced by Higgs-Walker of the need for more boarding accommodation, he presented "Thornhill" to the School. This large Victorian house, to be called Johnson's after its founder, was to double the number of boarders from fifty to one hundred. Perhaps even more importantly, under its energetic young Housemaster, Ernest Groves – "E. G.", one of Garrod's shrewdest appointments, destined to become Second Master and something of a legend – Johnson's was to spearhead the development of House Spirit, inter-House rivalry and the training of responsible House Officials, and thus successfully extend the character-forming benefits of the Prefect system in which Higgs-Walker so passionately believed.

Bathrooms and an outside lavatory block were added; the old billiard-room and cloakroom were converted into changing rooms, with baths for use after games; part of the big entrance hall was screened off as a reading room. In the east wing, the Matron's room and sick-room formed a self-contained isolation unit. From the Common Rooms, French windows led out to the stone terrace and garden. Later, Johnson added a Lodge for the houseman, just inside the entrance from Oak Lane.

One special night, for a dare, one boy climbed out onto the fire escape and was stopped dead in his tracks by a glimpse of schoolboy paradise: a bedroom, containing an unmade bed, on which lay a bare and unmade housemaid, wearing nothing but a cheap novel and an expensive-looking

124

cigarette holder. As she smoked, and read the novel, she moved her body from one erotic pose to another, presumably acting out the lurid episode. Within a minute of the discovery of this early blue video there were nearly twenty pop-eyed pupils balanced two storeys up on the narrow fire escape.
(R. Dunn, 1934–38, later Clive Dunn, Corporate Jones in Dad's Army).

The enviable arrangements at Johnson's inevitably highlighted the inadequacies of those in School House, particularly for looking after the sick. Mrs Higgs-Walker recalled that in the Summer Term following their arrival in 1925, half a dozen boys went down with measles.

For them we took a cottage which was sometimes used as an annexe to the "Pest House" (officially the Isolation Hospital) in Oak Lane. Nurses were installed, and twice daily visits to the victims inspired the purchase of our Austin 7, which was forever loved by me and hated by J. A. H-W.

Johnson's next comes into the picture; and with its usual match-winning technique produced, in 1930, a few cases of scarlet fever. The first was sent to the Isolation Hospital; the others were nursed rather grandly and magnificently at Johnson's, with day and night nurses, and a special outside staircase built for the use of the sick-rooms. As might be expected by all who know Mrs Groves, she took this upheaval in her stride and never flinched from the heavy domestic burden it entailed; but it was a red light, showing the need for a sanatorium, and the building of this was made possible by Mr Charles Johnson and J. A. H-W. The picturesque stables behind the swimming bath (once compared by an aesthetic visitor to an old street in Bruges!) were pulled down; and the architect, Mr Cable, cleverly fitted in the Sanatorium, in which infectious cases from the boarding houses were nursed up till 1939. It was staffed, when in use, by trained nurses, in those days so easily and so quickly obtained from London.

In our one serious outbreak of illness I had six nurses on day duty and five at night. The wife of the Johnson's houseman arrived at 7.30 a.m. to do the breakfasts, cleaning, etc. "Light diets" were done in the sanatorium, "full diets" and nurses' meals were sent over from the School House kitchen. In the afternoons Miss Taylor, who, for nearly thirty-five years has mended School suits not counted by hundreds but by thousands, came to do"teas". Admission to the San was something of a ceremony. There was a special clothes list, and patients were despatched with their suitcases which were duly checked and signed for. Transport from School House was by a carrying chair. Johnsonians arrived more ostentatiously by car.

☆ ☆ ☆

Another defect noted in the H.M.I.'s 1920 Report had been the unhealthy proximity of the servants' quarters to the boys' dormitories, and in 1929 C. P. Johnson provided a Servants' Hall in School House. Thanking him for this on Speech Day, Higgs-Walker stressed how grateful the School was for the many kindnesses it was receiving from friends, parents and Governors. It seems that Johnson's generosity was infectious, for over these years many gifts – some small, some substantial – flowed in, in a concerted effort to improve facilities or, in the case of School Prizes, to stimulate ever greater activity by boys both in and out of school. In 1926, Walter Hay of Manor House left £250 in his will to endow a Travelling Scholarship, and three years later his widow added a further £300: the first Scholarship was awarded to C. Clarke and G. W. A. Thomas, to enable them to spend August at the University of Strasbourg. Then came a microscope from Miss Smithett; a double bass 'cello from Mrs Runge; a cobra skin and a tiger's skull from Mr Saxton; a bat from Mr Outram for the highest score in an inter-School match; a cricket fielding machine from Colonel Laurie (a Governor and future Lord Mayor of London); a shark's jaw from Mrs Fraser; an engraving of Bowdler from Mr Clive Knocker (who was convinced that Bowdler had attended the School); an astronomical telescope from Mr Tattersall; another 'cello for the School Orchestra, this time from the Headmaster; trophies galore for House Relay Races, House Fives Competitions and so on – those are merely a selection from just three years, in the last of which, 1930, C. P. Johnson's brother, Edward, gave the School a Fives Court, the use of which was inaugurated by a demonstration match between Mr C.H. Knott and the Headmaster of Tonbridge.

This splendid and highly popular gift was the more welcome in that the old court had just had to be demolished to make way for C. P. J's latest gesture by way of the Cory Trust – the extension southwards of the Gym/Assembly Hall, with a fine new maple-wood floor, a new stage for School Plays, with a door at the southern end opening into a new Staff Room which would double as a Green Room when necessary. The new Hall was due to be baptised at Speech Day in July, 1930, but an outbreak of scarlet fever meant a postponement until October. Typically, on that occasion C. P. J. called the epidemic "fortunate" in that it had "resulted in a decision to build a sanatorium" – without mentioning that he was providing the funds. Equally typically, Higgs-Walker made great efforts to ensure that boys who had left in summer would be there to receive their prizes and congratulations, for several had been Prefects and Captains or members of School Teams in the year 1929–1930, "the most successful in the annals of the School. . . All thinking parents of boys undoubtedly appreciate the fact that without leaders of character and personality, as well as of mental and athletic skill, a record such as the past year's would have been unattainable".

Higgs-Walker was fond of pointing out that athletic and intellectual distinction were by no means incompatible. That year he was delighted to

126

congratulate J. H. Sutherland, School Captain, Captain of the undefeated First XV, on winning no fewer than three Exhibitions to Brasenose College, Oxford, one of them a County Award. The previous year had indeed amply justified the faith and generosity of the Johnson brothers and our other benefactors. J. R. Wilson had been placed second in the Public Schools Direct Entry Examination for the Royal Navy. Six Higher Certificates had been granted (two from Classical Sixth "A", two – in History and French with Latin – from Classical Sixth "B", two from the Science Sixth) in addition to five out of five Matriculations by First Year Sixth Formers, and seven Lower Certificates for Fifth Formers. The First XV had defeated the Third XVs of both Dulwich College and Tonbridge (next year Tonbridge were to honour us by putting up a "B" XV, which the School duly beat, 9–5). The 1st XI had lost only one match; Busby had made fifty playing for the Gentlemen of Suffolk C.C.; R. J. Martin, as well as playing Rugby for the Kentish Public Schools, had made a fifty and twenty, both not out, playing at the Oval for the Young Amateurs of Kent against the Young Amateurs of Surrey.

The School Society had debated several lively issues: "Capital Punishment is a Disgrace to our Civilisation" (Lost, 14–17); "The Power of Women has increased, is increasing, and ought to be diminished" (Carried, 15–12 – despite an intervention by the President, Higgs-Walker, to the effect that, even if it were desirable, it would be *impossible* to diminish their power); "The Public School system is fundamentally unsound and pernicious to the well-being of the nation" (Lost, 14–10). In this debate, Mr Littlewood (Captain of Boxing and Swimming) suggested that the public school "stifled originality and enforced mediocrity. The only reason why parents sent their sons there was the conventional idea of a "gentlemanly" training which led to that spirit of snobbery which was one of their most unpleasant features". Mr Forsey emphasised the public school's important role in educating the ruling classes. Mr Williams said that public schools "supplied something of everything and everything of something (sic) . . . without imposing any unnecessary burdens upon the individual". Answering the charge that public school-educated men had grossly mismanaged the Great War, the Headmaster pointed out that the foreign High Command had been no better, and then gave what *The Sennock-ian* describes as "a satisfactory definition of a public school". What this was is not reported, but the Secretary (J. H. Sutherland) supported him on the grounds that the public school system was at least "practical, as opposed to the more idealistic schemes advocated by Dalton and others".

The Founders of Summerhill (1921), Dartington Hall (1925) and Bryanston (1928) would no doubt smilingly have dismissed the Secretary's remarks as the product of an out-of-date system of education whose aim was to turn children into miniature adults, prematurely burdened with concepts of Honour, Self-Control and Manliness, instead of allowing them to grow freely and creatively as children. This is not the place to discuss the claims of rival philosophies of education, "Traditional" or "Progressive". Probably, as many sins against children have been committed by extremists under one of those vague terms as under the other. But Higgs-Walker was no extremist, and the objective of "wholeness" in education was close to his heart. He energetically supported all kinds of out-of-school clubs, societies and activities, and both music and drama flourished in his time.

The School Orchestra was founded by A. P. Rollett in 1927. He persuaded some boys that "playing in even a small orchestra is often as good fun" as rugger or cricket. The first practice was held in the Gym in the Easter holidays, with Rollett at the piano, Coomber playing the violin and Francis the fife. "Our hopes were dashed somewhat by the impossibility of tuning the fife to the piano"; but soon other boys and other instruments – some given or lent by parents – appeared, and when four items were played at the Summer Concert next year the orchestra boasted a piano, three violins, three 2nd violins, a 'cello, a double-base, a drum and a triangle. Apart from Rollett, the driving forces in their first year were Hounsell, who led the violins, and Pearce, a good pianist who undertook to learn the double-bass and did so in an astonishingly short time. In 1930, when the Orchestra, now enriched by a clarinet, a viola, a flute and a trumpet, played during the intervals of the School Play, Shaw's *Arms and the Man*, their performance of a Brahms Hungarian Dance and of a selection from the Chocolate Soldier was warmly applauded. When it was decided that orchestra members would be excused from the whole School choral practices conducted by John Longmire on Friday afternoons, recruitment became easier.

As for Higgs-Walker's love and encouragement of drama, only his wife Mollie could match him: both of them devoted countless hours to the production of the School Play. This event was for many boys and quite a few Staff the high point of the school year, a focus of diverse energies and talents, and over the years the Sevenoaks School Play acquired a reputation for consistent excellence which drew the attention and praise even of the national press. Dewey and Montessori, with their advocacy of "education as activity", would have been impressed by the numbers of enthusiastic volunteers involved, the corporate passion engendered, and the high degree of delegated responsibility enjoyed by stage managers, carpenters, electricians and scene painters. For *Arms and the Man* Richard Beck, who in 1956 was to be responsible for the decorations at the Melbourne Olympic Games, designed and painted the Balkan settings; much work was done by boys in the Workshop under the skilful guidance of Charles Page, who this year produced "a Serbian stove four feet square", and at other times delighted in making duck-boards, hurdles, cricket sight-screens and even boats, at prices the School could afford. Mrs Higgs-Walker, who worked with one or other master on all pre-war and post-war productions, lent her considerable expertise on make-up, costumes, and "feminine deportment for boys". Critical reviews in *The Sennockian*

MANOR HOUSE

35. Manor House from front. The site, originally thought to have been an inn (the 'newe house' of the 1576 Minute?), was acquired from Knole by Archbishop Bourchier in 1456. The present house, built in the late 18th century, was bought by the School in 1947.

36. Back of Manor House from the garden

37. Manor House entrance hall, restored after war-time dilapidations

38. Panoramic view from south-east (photographed 1993)

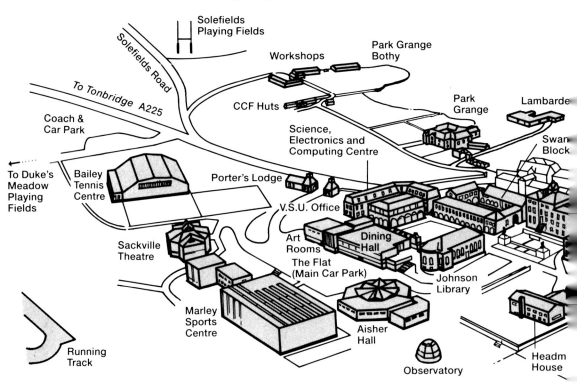

Solefields Playing Fields

Solefields Road

Workshops

Park Grange Bothy

To Tonbridge A225

CCF Huts

Park Grange

Lambarde

Coach & Car Park

Science, Electronics and Computing Centre

Swan Block

To Duke's Meadow Playing Fields

Bailey Tennis Centre

Porter's Lodge

V.S.U. Office

Sackville Theatre

Art Rooms

Dining Hall

The Flat (Main Car Park)

Johnson Library

Marley Sports Centre

Aisher Hall

Headm House

Running Track

Observatory

To Knole Park

39. Axonometric plan from north-east (drawn 1993)

40. Panoramic view from south-east (photographed 1993) (overleaf)

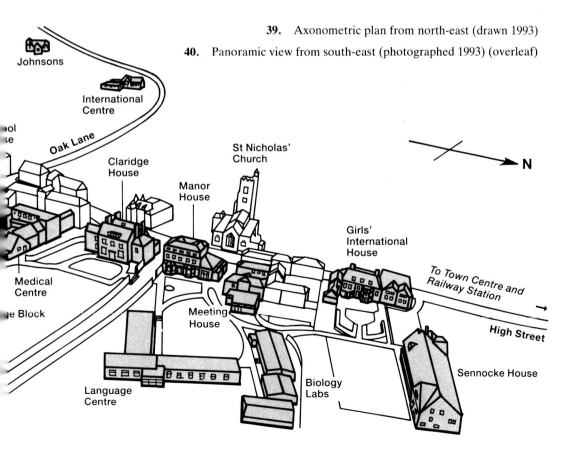

46. Sackville Theatre, built 1981

47. Bailey Tennis Centre, built 1989

sometimes ran to as much as five pages and were highly professional.

It would be impossible to do full justice to all the activities of boys and staff, all the supportive actions of parents, all the deliberations of Governors and of the Kent Education Committee, in 1930 or in any other year – and of course the problem will be greater when this modest history comes to deal with a much larger School and an infinitely wider range of activities. If we have paused on this year of relatively distinguished achievement, it is in an attempt to explain, and perhaps in part communicate, that prevailing mood of optimism and pride that swept the School onwards and upwards through the Depression and towards the war. Many more examples of social awareness, of athletic, intellectual and spiritual vitality might have been cited: the Sunday Concerts of chamber music given by John Longmire and his friends from London (a brilliant teacher, Longmire was described by his friend John Ireland as "one of the most able all-round musicians in this country"); the Form Collections to support one boy through seven years of his education in a Dr Barnado Home, and then to fund a bed in the Children's Ward at the Sevenoaks and Holmesdale Hospital; the flood of books donated to the School Library by Leavers, Staff and Old Sennockians; the vigorously contested House Competitions in Boxing, Swimming, Gymnastics, Tennis, Fives, even in Unison Singing; the first ever victory by our Cross-Country team over Blackheath Harriers; the establishing of an O.S. Overseas Information Bureau to tell boys of job opportunities abroad; the reading to the Headmaster's Society, in a single term, of papers on the Jacobite Rebellion, Probability, Galsworthy, Shaw as Historian (by Higgs-Walker) and Oswald Spengler. Though there were still too few boys staying on into the Sixth, and too many leaving at fifteen without a Lower Certificate, even the least gifted must have felt the exhilaration of a School that passionately believed in itself.

C. P. Johnson had invited his old friend "Q", Sir Arthur Quiller-Couch, King Edward VII Professor of English Literature at Cambridge, to speak at the delayed Speech Day, on October 15th, 1930. Since this happened to be the Bimillenary of Virgil's birth, "Q" took the opportunity of drawing a parallel between the "soil-based" patriotism of the poet and the strong loyalty owed to a School so firmly rooted in its locality. We should make the most of its phoenix-like growth, for "there are tears in things, and a human sigh for all that is mortal. Of men and women and the short lives allotted to them on earth Virgil would say:

> But, oh, the very reason why
> I clasp them is because they die".

CHAPTER THIRTEEN

Some Good Years

My first formal tea at School House, where I was invited with other wives, was very stiff. The door was opened by the Butler who proceeded to announce me . . . I was a bride from the north and petrified by Mollie, that gracious and confident woman . . . but she was a great conversationalist and wonderful hostess. . . The H-Ws always dressed for dinner which was a very formal affair.   (Gwen Robinson, who joined Jack at the school in 1937).

In 1931 the Prizes were distributed by Ernest Barker, Professor of Political Science at Cambridge, who had taught Higgs-Walker at Repton. Praising the School for its pioneering and successful efforts to bring a Public School education within the reach of families who could not afford the larger schools, he said that he was delighted by the co-existence in one School of 100 boarders and 150 day boys; that this "mixture" was a genuine one was clear from the fact that both the Prefect Body and the undefeated XV were drawn in roughly equal proportions from the two "sides". He concluded with the ringing declaration that Sevenoaks School "seemed to conform to what he saw in his dreams as the best example of the type for boys from twelve to nineteen".

Fired by this extravagant tribute, Higgs-Walker responded with a passionate defence of the Greek ideal of Balance in all things, and poured scorn upon those post-war educational theorists who "tended to look for easy ways and short cuts, semi-magical formulae, and cheap panaceas, with the result that the world today was suffering from a lack of well-informed, well-balanced judgment, and from the influence of popular states of mentality which he did not hesitate to describe as the mentalities of the race course tipster or the sweepstake enthusiast".

Despite his evident distaste for the "progressive" methods then fast gaining ground in elementary education – the emphasis, for instance upon self-regulated learning and a variety of informal techniques adapted to the different stages in the development of a child's language and understanding – Higgs-Walker remained supremely confident that Sevenoaks had got it right, and the following year he made the Quincentenary Speech Day a very grand affair. Eight hundred guests had been invited, far beyond the capacity of the Assembly Hall, and speeches were delivered in a Marquee, with the overspill of boys listening outside. Apart from the Archbishop of York, once Higgs-Walker's Headmaster at Repton, the platform party included Sir George Truscott (representing the Lord Mayor of London) and the Headmasters of King's School, Canterbury, Sutton Valence School, Seaford College and Cranbrook School. A massive oak chair for the use of the Archbishop arrived just in time, donated by N. C. Stenning, President of the Anglo-South American Trust Company of New York, who had been at Sevenoaks under Heslop.

The School Captain, R. J. Martin, opened the proceedings with a Declamation in praise of the Founder and Benefactors. Then, C. P. Johnson rehearsed the history of the School, paid grateful tribute to the Sackvilles, to Francis Swanzy and to the Kent Education Committee, and called upon the Archbishop to present the Prizes.

Dr Temple, in a fairly light-hearted mood, mocked the fashionable "scientific outlook": inappropriate for choosing a wife, it "tends to make people unable to enter into the most important things in life, for scientists want everything defined in precise terms". He recommended poetry with its atmosphere of infinite suggestion, declared that Character and good citizenship were the true aims of education, made a strong plea to parents to keep their children longer at School, and finally asked the Headmaster to grant the boys an extra week of summer holidays.

One momentous benefit of that celebratory day was revealed just a year later when, in a dramatic Speech Day announcement, Charles Plumtre Johnson promised that within a year the School would possess a Hall worthy of its growing reputation. This took Higgs-Walker completely by surprise, for though there had been general acknowledgement of the embarrassing inadequacy of the old Gym/Hall, he had no idea that Johnson's discussions with the architect of the Sanatorium, C. J. Cable, were in fact almost complete, and that he had already made arrangements for the necessary funds to be transferred to trustees. While Lord Stanhope, Under Secretary of State for War, was speaking and distributing prizes, Higgs-Walker was frantically scrapping his prepared speech and improvising another, in which he listed the multiple uses and advantages of the new Hall, and reiterated the depth of the School's gratitude to Charles Johnson – and to his brother Edward, who now had not only supplied a roof to his Fives Court, but promised to equip the new Hall with all its necessary furniture.

By December of that year the walls of the new Hall were already six feet above the ground: they were rising under the close personal supervision of C. P. J., frequently to be seen checking the quality of the ragstone, carefully chosen to harmonise with the old buildings. An Old Sennockian recalls his first view of the great man:

> There he was, in elegant clothes, picking up the dressed stones and instructing the workmen. A friendly master stopped beside us and said CPJ was making sure the stones were laid 'with the grain running the right way'. Grain in a stone! I reckoned the master was pulling my leg. Later I was told it is so with Kentish rag; laid the wrong way the rain gets in and frost flakes it away. CPJ, as exacting as he was generous, made sure in person that his gifts were not wasted.

That the completed Hall did not, despite its great size, appear grossly out of place or scale may have been due to the fact that C. J. Cable's design was partly inspired by a plan for an Assembly Hall in York, drawn in 1720 by none other than the architect of School House, the Earl of Burlington. The Hall was 110 feet long and 40 feet wide. Beneath the stage in the apse-like curve at the east end was the new Library; small side-rooms at both levels were to be used for Sixth Form work and private study, or as dressing rooms during the School Play. Stage lighting equipment was partly paid for by parents and other keen admirers of the School's dramatic traditions, partly by proceeds from the last production, Shaw's *Saint Joan* (in which Joan was played by D. Pal, later foreign correspondent for the *Observer* under his father's name, Bloodworth). Edward Johnson's furniture consisted of 350 Bennet chairs, benches to seat 250, a platform table and three platform chairs; the Governors contributed Honours Boards; oak shelving for the Library was given by Mrs Constant.

Higgs-Walker's only criticism of the new Hall was of the three tall windows in the apse, "so essential from the outside . . . a hellish nuisance inside (see a letter in the Mag. complaining of the strain of looking at black blobs on the platform). The middle one was temporarily blocked after we had had difficulty trying to stretch a cloth in a curve to provide a cycloramic background for *Richard of Bordeaux*". During the coming war, he was to use black-out restrictions as a pretext for blocking off the others, and "the Governors, though year after year they sat there, never noticed the disappearance of the windows – this I know because when I pointed it out they admitted it, and blessed my crime".

Despite the departure of three outstanding all-round cricketers – Martin, Jago, and Cavell – from the unbeaten Eleven of 1933, the following year's team under B. C. Fay did even better, while Fay played a large part in winning for School House the Senior Cricket Final. There was now a new Day House, Hardinge, created in 1933 by transferring six Seniors from each of the other three, then filling up from below. The official reason given was that "it is easier to maintain an efficient corporate spirit in a Day House of forty rather than of fifty boys"; however, one Old Sennockian, who remembers being "volunteered" to transfer from Fenton to Hardinge, says that among the day boys it was believed that Higgs-Walker was worried that if the Day Houses became as large as School House and Johnson's they might begin to threaten the dominance in games of his beloved boarders! This is probably unfair, for though it is clear that the Headmaster believed boarding to be the type of education most likely to benefit a boy's all-round development, he regularly found many of his most trusted Prefects among the day boys, and sometimes rewarded them with privileges envied by boarders. Martin and Jago, for instance, were the only boys in the School allowed to use cars: another O. S. remembers "these young swells roaring up to Solefields for a cricket match at the wheels of sports models with straps over their bonnets".

The Death of C P Johnson

These were good years. The list of names lengthened on the Honours Board; John Longmire composed the music for "The Song of Sevenoaks" (words by Peter Warwick), which Head of Classics George Rich judged "manly, strong and singable"; Charles Page designed a patent mechanical time-table; up at Keble, J. D. Bates was chosen to box for Oxford, while R. J. Martin was soon distinguishing himself at St. Catherine's, Cambridge, winning the Freshmen's Quarter-Mile, playing for the Crusaders, Captaining his College XI and playing in the University Orchestra; the acoustics of Johnson Hall were found to be excellent, and when the Higgs-Walkers and John Parks put on their first big production there, *Richard of Bordeaux*, Rollett's Orchestral Preludes to each Scene were hugely enjoyed; membership of the Old Sennockians' Club was soaring towards four hundred, and in 1935 *The Sennockian* began to carry a special section devoted to its activities, including those of its two XVs; when Herbert Chase was Captain of the O.S. 1st XV in 1935, team members' names appeared every Saturday in the *Times* and *Morning Post*; in 1936 Lord Plender, a Governor from 1935 to 1944, presented a magnificent eighteenth century "Parliament Clock" to be placed in Johnson Hall. The following year he presented the Prizes, and in his address extolled the virtues of "a school where personal contacts between the Masters and the boys are close and possibly more intimate than in many of the larger schools".

That was to be the last Speech Day attended by C. P. Johnson, for in 1937 his health was failing, and Lord Sackville read the Chairman's valedictory address. As if in sympathy, Higgs-Walker had fallen quite seriously ill and had been confined to bed for fourteen weeks. During that time Jockey White had been Acting Headmaster. Johnson was typically warm in his praise of White, of Groves as Senior Housemaster, and of Mrs Higgs-Walker, all of whom had had to take on a lot of extra work and responsibilities. Lord Sackville took the opportunity of saying a few words about Leadership and Courage, aware that in these dangerous times the School had an unusually large number of candidates for the fighting Services. "The Prefects of this School", he concluded, "start as leaders, and I hope they will continue their leadership until the end of their days". As if he too had a premonition of the dark days ahead, Higgs-Walker rejoiced "that this School is producing a sufficient number of boys like its adventurous Founder, who are not satisfied with the office desk, but who are going out determined to exercise as fully as possible their capacities for leadership".

Charles Plumptre Johnson, after attending one last Governors' Meeting that winter, died on May 9th, 1938. It is impossible to exaggerate the School's debt to him. Lord Plender declared: "Well might he be proud of the School, for it is largely his School, and the name of Johnson is to Sevenoaks – though in different ways – what Arnold was to Rugby and Thring to Uppingham". Different ways indeed, though Johnson gave far more than money and buildings to Sevenoaks. Over his years as Governor and Chairman he took a close interest in the smallest as in the most important matters affecting its daily life, and the warmth of his support for Higgs-Walker was crucial. The two men shared a belief in the country's urgent need for leaders of Character, and a deep conviction that the best nursery for that quality was the kind of education offered at Sevenoaks, where day boys as well as boarders could grow within a small, close-knit community which demanded great commitment in terms of time and loyalty, and which offered the greatest possible variety in terms of intellectual, artistic and sporting activity. Johnson had been a keen rugby player in his youth, a fine yachtsman all his life: a member of the Royal Yacht Squadron, he had twice won the King's Cup at Cowes in his beloved "Moonbeam". He was also a dedicated collector of books and pictures, a recognised bibliographical authority on Thackeray and Dickens, editor of the Victorian edition of *Pickwick Papers*, and a member of the Atheneum. He was on the Managing Committee of several hospitals, including the Great Ormond Street Hospital for Sick Children, which benefited largely under the terms of his Will.

His financial bequest to Sevenoaks was princely: £75,000 was to be held by his Trustees for the eventual benefit of the School; in addition, £3,000 was to endow a Scholarship, preferably at St. John's College, Oxford, which had been founded by a member of his mother's family. At the Memorial Service held in Johnson Hall on May 12th, attended by Governors and by the whole School, Higgs-Walker spoke of "twelve years of friendship and work with him –

sometimes involving interviews daily, seldom less than three or four times a week", and paid tribute to our Second Founder's great qualities: "We pray that their example may guide and inspire the lives of all in this School".

Writing in 1957, Higgs-Walker thought that the First XVs of 1937 and 1938 were the best by far in the School's Rugby history, better even than those of 1929 and 1930. Points scored in 1937 were: 101 For, 60 Against. Many First XV members gave up time to coach other teams, and both the Second XV (106 For, 62 Against) and the Under Fifteen side (36 For, 16 Against) had successful seasons. Among the new First XV Colours was a tall young three-quarter, L. C. Taylor. Since there will be much to say, sixteen years later, about this promising young man, it might appear unseemly to give too much attention to his schoolboy years. In fact it would be impossible to ignore him; a doubtless seductive *Renée de Cocheforet* in *Under the Red Robe*; *Captain Absolute* in *The Rivals*; *Dorante* in an adaptation of Molière's *Le Bourgeois Gentilhomme*; Secretary of the Headmaster's Society; Sub-Editor of *The Sennockian*; Captain of Johnson's; Second XI Cap; First XV Cap; Captain of Gym; Captain of Boxing; Captain of Rugby; Captain of the School. At least the Vice-Captain of the School, Editor of *The Sennockian* and his life-long friend, D. J. Holroyde, beat him in the High Jump on Sports Day, 1939; moreover, having scraped into the First XI and scored only 20 runs in 7 innings, he was advised, "with his long reach, to play forward whenever feasible."

Earlier in that fateful year, Taylor had proposed to the Headmaster's Society "That compulsory National Service is desirable in this country". He was seconded by R. Coigley, who was to die in the coming war, and opposed by Stanley Berwick and Mr Bennett of Toc H. The motion was defeated by 40 votes to 20. One month later Taylor and Syms (also of Johnson's) moved "That the foreign policy of the National Government in the last five years is worthy of the strictest censure", condemning the lack of any constructive policy as the dictators advanced unmolested. The opposition argued strongly that continued appeasement was best, since the German Empire must soon disintegrate though internal disorder, but the motion was narrowly carried, by 23 votes to 21.

Speech Day, 1939, was a cheerful occasion. The Headmaster quoted judiciously from the Inspectors' Report. He supported their judgment that the Masters were "exceptionally zealous and pleasant young men" with his own warm praise of "the zeal and comradeship with which Masters entered into the community life of the School – incidentally, no less than eight Masters had played in a Rugby, and nine in a Cricket team, got up against the School – a token of both zeal and youthfulness!".

Dr Cyril Bailey, C.B.E., (School House 1882–84), was the Guest Speaker.

The previous week, as Oxford University's Public Orator, he had presented P. G. Wodehouse for an honorary degree, addressing him in Horatian hexameters. Now he entertained his Sevenoaks audience with some jokes of positively Woosterish implausibility; then, more seriously, he congratulated the School on its growth and development, and particularly on having retained its mixture of day and boarding pupils. "I think one of the troubles about England at the present moment is the division between different types of education . . ., between the day school and the boarding school, between the public school and the secondary school. I believe that these local schools, mixed boarding schools and day schools . . . will show us the type of education that England has got to evolve".

The Old Sennockian Club, now nearly 450 strong, held their annual Dinner at the Holborn Restaurant; toasts were proposed by Major H. G. Brackley, D.S.O., D.F.C., and by Darrel Bates, Assistant Commissioner Tanganyika Territory ('loyalty to the School is something which no other occupation or interest is able to shake'); responses came from the hard-working Hon.Secretary and Treasurer, H. R. G. Gear, and from the President, J.A. Higgs-Walker, who reiterated his belief that the future of the English Public School system lay with the smaller and the less expensive of the old foundations. The Headmaster's Society debated whether "Corporal Punishment should be abolished", and decided that it should not.

> During my first year at Johnson's I remember the whole of the Senior Common Room (6 House Monitors, Sub-Prefects etc.) – with the exception of Paddy Taylor, then head of the house – being beaten for skipping off games and going down town to see – I think – "The Wind in the Willows." They were taken by E.G. to find Mr Parks to 'execute'!"   (J.H. Verrall, 1939–46).

CHAPTER FOURTEEN

Into War Again

A number of first-year sixth form boys in March–April 1940 helped (the Home Guard?) to fill and test Molotov Cocktails to be used against possible German invaders. We tried out various mixtures of petrol and paraffin and tested them by throwing them against a wall at the top of Seal Hollow Road. (D. Bennell, 1936–40).

I remember one night a German bomber dropped sticks of incendiary bombs, some of which landed in the school grounds next to Johnson Hall and the fives courts. They were light cylinders about 14″ long and 2″ diameter made of a very light shiny silvery metal – perhaps magnesium – and containing a flammable powder. A fellow boarder and I found several that had not gone off. We unscrewed the bottom of the canisters and removed the detonators which were discs about the size of a half-crown. Probably a bit rash given our ignorance! I'm glad to say we weren't caught in possession.

(G. Bingham, 1940–44).

In April 1939 Higgs-Walker sent a Memorandum to the Chairman of Governors concerning three special subjects due to come up for discussion at their next Meeting: the Headmasters' Conference proposals for a Royal Commission on the state of Public Schools; the recent Inspection of the School; and the K.E.C.'s proposal that in the event of war all their own schools – and, they hoped, all their Aided Schools too – should receive as many evacuated pupils as they had on their present rolls.

The 1938 Inspectors' Report has already been touched upon. Higgs-Walker did not at this point discuss their reservations about the School's ability to meet the needs of local Elementary School-leavers, but was content to submit to his Governors a few statistics indicating the very satisfactory progress made since the 1928 Inspection: 16 Scholarships and Exhibitions gained in the past three years (4 in 1926–28); 34 School Certificates in 1938 (4 in 1928); 6 Higher Certificates (none); numbers up to 255 (183); a Sixth Form of 36 (12); and all the new buildings provided by the Johnson brothers.

He had no sympathy at all for H.M.C.'s request for a Royal Commission, made after a discussion that had been "extraordinarily rambling, and no credit to the intellectual ability of the Head Masters present". He was convinced that the request was occasioned solely by the serious decline in numbers of boys at the larger Public Schools. "I trust the Governors will authorise me to oppose the Scheme . . . I do not see how a Royal Commission can increase the birth-rate or the dwindling number of parents ready to pay £200–£250 a year per boy". He believed that many of the larger schools had only themselves to blame. Some now charging high fees had been founded during the short boom period of the Twenties, and had since built expansively on borrowed money. "Some of us, Head Masters of smaller, less expensive and therefore solvent schools, fear that *some* of the hard hit larger schools are hoping that a Royal Commission can be used to reduce our power to compete against them".

One of the things C. P. Johnson admired most in Higgs-Walker, and which most encouraged his generosity to the School, was the determined attempt made to keep fees as low as possible, and to this end to make maximum use – to the point of strain – of all the human and material resources available to him. This was why Higgs-Walker was appalled at the thought of numbers being *doubled* by the arrival of evacuees from unsafe areas. "It is implied, though not stated, that work and games would be carried on in shifts by night and day. Teachers evacuated with the children are to teach them, but the Governors, Masters, and Caretakers etc. of the Receiving School are to be responsible for their *general* discipline, safety, hours of work, equipment, stationery, fuel and light, finance and maintenance generally. Criticism of any A.R.P. Scheme may seem unpatriotic. But my experience of the last war taught me that easy-going acquiescence in futile plans can be more unpatriotic".

Apart from his genuine concern about his ability to offer proper protection to large numbers of new boys, Higgs-Walker knew that the inevitable dilution of the facilities, teaching time and care available in his already fully-stretched school would lead to the removal of many fee-payers. "Personally, I think that it would ruin the Boarding side of the School – and that would destroy Sevenoaks as a Public School". Even bribes were rejected. One of our good "feeder" Prep Schools offered to send us, after the war, many more of their boys if we would accommodate their School when hostilities began. Higgs-Walker rejected this admittedly tempting scheme because "I felt that I could not risk serious overcrowding or the absence of A.R.P. shelter for the extra numbers".

Yet the December, 1939, issue of *The Sennockian*, though already reduced in size in the interests of economy, was far from gloomy. It bade farewell to Ron Wheeker and Jack Mills, both off to France, and it mentioned the trenches, recalling "the terrifying din along the upper and lower corridors as some seven or eight leather-lunged Masters competed with the concrete-mixer"; but it also recorded the marriage of Higgs-Walker's daughter Bridget in the School Chapel – the Lady Chapel – in St. Nicholas' Church, and the defiant birth of a Fine Arts Society, "to discuss subjects connected with the arts of Literature, Sculpture, Music, Painting and Architecture".

In *At Honour's Game* Higgs-Walker recalled those anxious years:

Our war really began more than a year before Munich, when I tried to discover the intentions of the Authorities in Whitehall, Maidstone, Tunbridge Wells or Argyle Road, Sevenoaks: what were the proper A.R.P. and how could they be constructed? By September, 1938, I had collected a hugh pile of correspondence, and a considerable disillusionment about so-called experts; but nothing else. Finally, Lord Sackville and Mr Knocker bravely sharing the responsibility with me, I got hold of a friendly builder who . . . put up windows and gas barricades which at least comforted us.

By September, 1939, the K.E.C. had been induced to accept responsibility for all "Precautions", but without practical results. A few scratchings by a builder's labourer were all I found when I bustled back from Switzerland a few days before Chamberlain declared war on Hitler. Fortunately, our first evacuees, 200 of Dulwich College, together with our stalwart Day Boy volunteers, did the job in a way which astonished and gratified the contractor; . . . and so, by January, 1940, we had got outside shelters, 15 feet down, while in School House the ancient beams of dining Hall and Kitchen were hidden by steel ceilings. When we think how nice it would be to see the old wooden beams again, we remember gratefully how glad we were to be under the steel in the blitz, and even more in the Doodlebug Summer. In both Blitz and Doodle-Blitz Johnson's used the phenomenally strong wine-cellars which the first owners had in 1870 so thoughtfully constructed.

It is not generally known that School House was earmarked for a defensive strongpoint if the Germans landed; machine guns were to be sited from its windows; there were trenches and wire in the lower garden and in Plumptre Meadow, and, quite unsuitably, there was to be a hospital in the basement while fighting went on above; this was a war secret that worried me considerably, especially as I could never learn where the boys were to go. Some photographs show the sliding steel shutters on the lower windows.

In mid-September, 1939, Dulwich was succeeded by Shooter's Hill – about two hundred strong. Till December we used Class Rooms and fields in turn . . . But by January, 1940, our Governors wisely persuaded L.C.C. to provide a separate establishment . . . and thenceforward they came to us for labs. and workshop periods only, though they used Solefields when we were at work.

In theory the outside Trenches – or, as they were called from their proximity to the Labs, "Jockey's Maginot" – were to shelter the whole school in Daylight raids, but in practice we found that the appalling waste of time was not justified by the risks, and after a few weeks of the September-October daylight air-fighting we went from Class Room to Class Room as usual.

Doodlebugs brought the most trying phase of the war. When the balloons obscured most of the sky and seemed only too likely to succeed in bringing down a covey of doodles we decided to revert to our Blitztime custom of sleeping below – half the House under our ceilings, the rest in Jockey's Maginot – so that nightly in July you could see them disappearing down the steps by the Pine Trees – "the night shift going down the mine" someone christened them.

Firewatching became a routine part of boarding life from 1941, as indeed it did for many Senior Day Boys. From 1943 an all-night watch was compulsory, and all old enough had to take their turn. During raids steel-helmeted watchers were on duty outside – sometimes flat on the ground under the Archway! It was from there (when I had resumed a standing position) that I saw the contents of a canister of incendiaries – 500 of them – blazing and banging round Knole House: only one landed in a Courtyard, but one set the timber-yard on fire and produced so much smoke that with the glare of the incendiaries reflected from the ancient windows a horrible illusion was created that the whole building was on fire. Another near-miss was the Parachute Bomb which hung itself on a tree between us and Knole, and broke windows all over the town, including 160 panes at the school and some of the oldest glass in the West windows of Knole.

The open trenches at Solefields were useful in October, 1940, and much more so in June and July, 1944. But they were hard work to dig and troublesome to keep in order – Simmons had to do a lot of draining and revetting of the 1914–18 variety.

The Price of War

Higgs-Walker later claimed that "if standards declined (for they did, in Sevenoaks as in every other School, even in those which never heard a bomb), nothing of importance was allowed to die. By 1941, half the pre-war staff had gone to the Services; the remainder – despite the heavy demands on the Home Guard and in some cases A.T.C. – carried most heroically the burden of organising and coaching games, and guiding the many other activities of which the School has been proud and which, once dead, it might provide impossible to revive".

Though he put a brave face on it, it is clear that for Higgs-Walker it was little short of agony to watch the rapid erosion of athletic, artistic and intellectual standards, as many of his best Staff and Prefects went off to the war. While publicly praising the valiant efforts of "our temporary colleagues, male or female", he privately admitted that "the rest of us had the ghastly job of trying to preserve essentials, in the simplest sense of the word, and to stop the temporary staff doing positive harm!".

There were no big School Play productions between December, 1938, and December, 1945, though W. Davies' "Follies" provided light entertainment in the first two winters, and in 1943 and 1944 the Sixth Formers did *Julius Caesar* in modern dress, and Drinkwater's *Abraham Lincoln*, for the School only. A. P. Rollett's Orchestra, and Desmond Pakenham's Music Club and the Choir, all suffered badly.

Apart from running, all the pre-war games were played, though inevitably at a lower standard, for more and more Sixth Formers left early – particularly after the lowering of the call-up age in 1942 – to take Short University Courses into the Army or the R.A.F., or to sit the Navy's Special Entry Exam. Cross-country all but disappeared, partly because a Lorry Dump monopolised the best bits of Knole Park, more because of the shortage of gym shoes.

Typically, just as he had discovered redeeming character-forming opportunities in the 1926 General Strike (when some boys had walked sixteen miles to and from school each day for three days), and in the bracing belt-tightening of the Depression, Higgs-Walker praised the way in which Staff, Prefects, Gardeners, Housemen and "rank-and-file" boys responded to "a host of problems which never troubled their peace-time predecessors". These included trench-digging at the School and at Solefields, gardening at Kippington Grange under the supervision of E. G. and the Johnson's gardener, volunteer groups working on farms or in the Food Control Office during their holidays, the organisation of A.R.P. rotas, all-night fire-watches and air-raid practices.

In 1938 it had been decided not to start an O.T.C.; that decision, after a serious debate between Prefects and Sub-Prefects, and consideration by the Governors, was made on the grounds that the military value could not justify "the burden upon the energy, time, and even the pockets of those boys over the age of sixteen who were already responsible for organising and leading a number of activities, intellectual, aesthetic and athletic, which was remarkable for a School of this size". But in 1941 there was no resisting an Air Ministry appeal, and in March No. 604 (Sevenoaks) Flight of the A.T.C. was formed. In charge was the ever-willing "E.G." – Mr Groves, already in charge of Johnson's, School Rugby and war-effort gardening. Assisted by A. P. Rollett and Jack Robinson (a fine young cricketer now teaching Chemistry and destined, like E.G., to become Second Master one day), he quickly secured the voluntary enlistment of all boys of the required age. One half-holiday, and one evening after school each week, were devoted to parades and to lectures on Aerial Navigation, Morse, Drill, Anti-Gas, Aircraft Identification and Armament. In the Easter holiday 30–40 cadets – including boarders living close to Sevenoaks – had four hours of instruction each week in the town Drill Hall, and in the summer holiday several attended an A.T.C. Camp. Recruiting Officers arrived to interview boys intending shortly to enter the R.A.F.

That same year, several senior day boys and a number of Old Sennockians, having attended a Youth Rally in the Cornwall Hall, helped set up the Sevenoaks Youth Movement, known as "The Oaks", which attracted considerable attention from the local Press. The aims of the Movement were: "To provide opportunities for people aged from 14 to 21 to lead a full and useful life; to develop in body, mind and spirit, and to enrich the life of the community". Football and hockey teams were raised; folk and ball-room dancing were popular; a dance band was formed; a "Community Service Group hoped to collect waste paper and dig for victory". Just how great was the School's contribution to this patriotic version of the future Voluntary Service Unit is not clear, but Rollett and J. M. C. Parks gave lectures to the Science and Literature groups.

Among the early O.S. dead was Lieutenant John Wilson, R.N., specially picked in 1927 to help start Johnson's, placed second in the Navy's Special Entry Exam in 1930, given command of a destroyer at the early age of twenty-nine, lost with most of his ship's company by enemy action in December, 1940. Increasingly, such news was to darken the ever-slimmer issues of *The Sennockian* over the next few years, though there were a few things to celebrate. For instance, the Cricket XI of 1941 was one of the best the School had ever had, thanks largely to the exhilarating batting of C. B. Gibbons (434 runs at an average of 62) and R. K. Crocker (370 runs, average 41): the School lost only to the Vine C.C. (by one run) and to St. Dunstan's College, but Dulwich College and Tonbridge 2nd XIs were both handsomely defeated (by 9 wickets and 7 wickets respectively). Meanwhile, humbler exploits were performed by gangs of boys working on the allotments – Johnson's in Lord Hawke's garden, School House and the Day Boys each in a field in the dip beneath Duke's Meadow. All boys save those in School XIs now gave one afternoon a week to agriculture instead of cricket. By 1943 the gardeners had three acres under the spade, and proudly reported a crop of three tons of potatoes, two thousand cabbages, five hundred cobs of sweet corn, "and an unassessed assortment of beans, sprouts, beet and curly kale".

In 1943, Flight-Lieutenant Groves' A.T.C. Flight became a Squadron, and Flying Officer Robinson formed a Spotters' Club: tests and quizzes were conducted, using cards and an epidiascope, and model aircraft swayed on strings in the upper corridor; Old Sennockians on leave returned to talk about their work in various branches of the Services; J. M. C. Parks came back to judge the Harold Smith Elocution Competition (three Macbeths, three Malvolios, two Lady Macbeths and one Viola); Sevenoaks' Wings for Victory Week raised £500,000, of which the School contributed £303 10s. 6d.; a much loved Governor, Colonel Rogers, resigned after serving for forty-one years, three of them as Chairman (1910–13) and seven as Vice-Chairman; *The Sennockian* published a full O.S. Services List, showing those killed, missing or taken prisoner, as well as many awards won in action; Ivan Cole arrived from Queen Elizabeth's College, Guernsey, to help C.G. Rich on the Classical side.

Classical Studies in schools were in serious decline during the war. In 1944 the Editor of *The Sennockian* hoped that this was due to National Service and not to the "materialistic dry-rot which is attacking our educational tradition at a deeper level". Under threat, he felt, were "things of the so-called non-useful variety, such as the appreciation of fine sights and sounds, the cultivation of intelligent interests in things outside one's own subject . . . These things – Culture seems to be their generic term – are those which give life its richness, and which do not proceed from the curriculum of a Technical School or a Secretarial College. But they have never been foreign to the atmosphere of the English Public School . . .".

We may take leave to doubt the extent of the high-minded Editor's knowledge of what went on in Technical Schools and Secretarial Colleges, but his defensive tone serves to remind us that throughout these years discussion was raging about the future of education. The Fleming Report of 1944 had revealed passionate feelings for and against the Public School. The W.E.A. told the Fleming Committee that "the position of the Public Schools is anomalous in a modern democratic society", while in many broadly sympathetic quarters it was felt that something must be done to bring the Public Schools into a closer relationship with the state sector. As it happened, the Fleming Report recommended something very close to what was already happening at Sevenoaks: the reservation of 25% of places at independent schools for children from primary schools, maintained with public funds. In 1942, when the "Times" had carried an acrimonious correspondence about character and intelligence, Higgs-Walker had declared that "so far as the Public School system was concerned, he did not consider there was anything to apologise for in the form it had taken at Sevenoaks. Up till 1939 Sevenoaks had been given, and had used, exceptional opportunities of trying out a type of school which would be of national importance, and, he believed, they would make even better use of those opportunities after the war". The words "up till 1939" betray his dismay at war-time Sevenoaks' inability to sustain the high standards of such life-enhancing activities as drama, music and debate, which he had worked so hard to establish. Early in 1944, he was all the more delighted to welcome to Johnson Hall the Boyd Neel String Orchestra. Invited by Sevenoaks Music Club, they played to an audience of over five hundred, including many Sevenoaks schoolboys. The highlight was a performance by the well-known tenor, Jan van de Gucht, of the *Dies Natalis* by Gerald Finzi, with words by Thomas Traherne. *The Sennockian*'s knowledgeable reviewer enthused that "the work has an almost classical unity – strings and voice, rhythm and timbre are completely at one, and the result is a Cantata of exceptional beauty".

The Headmaster was known as Jimmy and his wife usually known as Mum or Ma Higgy. She had the habit of sitting in the Head's study near the fire smoking through a long cigarette holder. She would press the bell and a fag would dash upstairs to her bidding. This might be an instruction to walk the dog, change her books at Boots library or buy cigarettes from the Tuck Shop.

A typical day for a School House boarder would start with cold baths at 6.50, then Prep till breakfast at 8 a.m.; lessons were from 9.00 till 1.00, with a quarter of an hour break to drink our third of a pint of milk; lessons from 2.00 till 4.00 on Tuesdays, Thursdays and Fridays, compulsory cricket or rugger on the other three half-days; tea at 6.00, Prep 7.00–8.30, evening prayers with the Head at 9.00, lights out at 10.00. Every Sunday we went to St Nicholas or to Johnson Hall for a sermon. On a Sunday afternoon we had to go for a walk. One day it would be a "free" walk. This meant going where you wanted (except to anywhere out of bounds). It usually meant somewhere in Knole Park for a quiet smoke.

We had curious customs in School House. One was that on the last night there would be a supper during which all boys new that term had to stand on a table one by one and sing. They had bread, etc, thrown at them.

J.A.H–W. was a stern but kindly Headmaster who believed in the ways of the Victorians. . . He had little time for anyone who was interested in science believing that only historians were fit for anything. . .

(G. Gatling, 1941–47).

144

CHAPTER FIFTEEN

Peace – and Independence

On VE-Day, Tuesday, May 8th, 1945, for the first time since 1939, School House and Johnson's took their old places in the Chantry Chapel of St. Nicholas', for a brief Thanksgiving Service. That night seventy lights floodlit School House, a great bonfire was lit on the allotments, Hitler's effigy was burned, and there was some lusty singing of the School Song, "Auld Lang Syne" and the National Anthem.

In terms of physical damage the School had been very lucky. In November, 1940, bombs had fallen on our playing fields; one of them destroyed the Pavilion which had once stood on our ground near Walthamstow Hall, before being lovingly dismantled and re-erected at Solefields. This time the remnants were used to build a much smaller one which had to serve until 1949. Another bomb had fallen within twenty yards of Mr Groves' study at Johnson's, breaking windows and damaging a chimney. Two incendiary bombs had fallen on School House without exploding, and were not found until 1945.

At Speech Day, 1945, Old Sennockian Servicemen were represented on the platform by Squadron Leader Frank Cleaver D.S.O., D.F.C. Of the eight hundred who had gone to war, eighty were dead or missing, forty had been decorated, and three hundred and fifty commissioned. Lord Sackville congratulated the School "on the way in which it had upheld its traditions and

145

maintained its standards throughout the war", particularly praising Mrs Higgs-Walker and Mrs Groves for their valiant efforts in the Boarding Houses.

The year 1945–46 must have been one of the most challenging and demanding of Higgs-Walker's life. After the exhausting, frustrating and grief-laden years of war, he had to summon up all his reserves of courage to begin restoring his School to its pre-war state. Though immensely grateful for the wise counsel and support of his distinguished Governing Body, he was saddened to lose three old friends from his Staff: White, Rollett and Rich. The Second Master, "Jockey" White, retired after 36 years, 22 of them under Higgs-Walker, who remembered with deep gratitude his early help and guidance. A. P. Rollett, R. E. Tanner and C. G. Rich had been Higgs-Walker's first appointments twenty years earlier. Tanner had gone in 1935 to become Headmaster of Bishop Field College, Newfoundland. Now Rollett left to become an Inspector of Mathematics at the Ministry of Education (later the country's Chief Inspector, and President of the Mathematical Association), and Rich was appointed Headmaster of the Cathedral School, Bristol. "These three mean a lot to me", Higgs-Walker was to write later, "for they had faith when a lot was needed". Rollett had arrived soon after the opening of the Swanzy Physics Laboratory in 1925, and had developed it until it rivalled a university Laboratory. As Head of Physics, Director of Mathematical Teaching and Tutor of the Science Sixth, he had helped many boys win their places on the Honours Board. A first-rate Housemaster of Hardinge, he had also created the Orchestra, coached the Colts cricketers, and for some years master-minded the complex School Time-Table. Rich, in Higgs-Walker's words, had "made the Classical side, organised the School Library, vitalised every kind of Society and debate, cultural and political, been a devoted Housemaster, until he had become an Institution and almost a legend".

Seven of Higgs-Walkers's 1939 Staff had gone to war. Two had given their lives: Captain Jack Mills (P.T. Instructor 1934–39) and W. D. Davies; two, A. A. Smith and Desmond Pakenham, were remaining in the Navy and the Foreign Service respectively; but Ron Wheeker was back, John Parks was returning, and so was Hankin as Director of Music and a full-time member of staff. With the arrival of Wenham, Rutter, Hopkins and Bate, there would be a permanent Staff of pre-war standard.

Yet things would never be the same again. For in that year, 1945–46, a year which Lord Stanhope thought "might prove the most important in the School's long history", Sevenoaks School became independent. Even before the 1944 Education Act had been passed, its likely provisions had been known, and our Governors had been alert to its dangers. This was largely due to the invaluable presence on the Governing Body of Sir Charles Innes. In 1943, at a meeting in

London of the Headmasters of schools likely to be adversely affected, Sir Charles had been unanimously elected Chairman of their Committee.

The educational reforms were intended, as Lawson and Silver put it, "to remove some of the stigmas attached to lower-class education, provide a new pattern of opportunity, and set education in a framework of improved welfare and social justice". The Beveridge Report had been published in 1942, and by 1948 national insurance, family allowances, national health and the improvements in old age pensions would all be in place. "The principles of the new Act have been rightly praised", said Higgs-Walker on Speech Day, 1946, while his guest speaker, Canon Day, agreed that they were "in cordial agreement with a policy of educational opportunities which would give us what we had long badly needed, men and women really fit to fill the Country's responsible positions". Though this emphasis upon the responsibilities of the educated, rather than upon the rights of the uneducated, would not have been entirely to the reformers' taste, he went on to praise the admirable "mixture" achieved at Sevenoaks – of boarders and day boys, of local boys with those from all over the world – "for one boy reacts against another, and that creates character. Such a mixture . . . is a safeguard against snobbery, and against a possible danger in the new Act unforseen by its designers, the danger of a gulf between a limited number of very expensive Independent Public Schools and a large number of others controlled by the State".

The Governors and Higgs-Walker had no quarrel at all with a very enlightened and friendly Kent Education Committee, but they were determined to preserve that "mixture" applauded by Canon Day, Ernest Barker and so many other distinguished visitors. They feared that the new Act would compel the Committee to do things that would "injure our traditions, cripple our independence, and jeopardise our future". Consequently, fully supported by the K.E.C., they applied for Direct Grant status, entailing financial support from central rather than from local government. The School's application, along with 32 of 36 similar applications from other Governing Bodies, was rejected by the Minister, Miss Ellen Wilkinson. Direct Grant Status would have provided an acceptable, and secure, measure of public support. The Minister's decision faced the Governors with a disturbing dilemma. Independence with no support from public funds ran the risk of financial collapse and the end of the School's life. More public money, on the other hand, would entail greater public control, thus diminishing the Governors' independence to act in the best interests of the School as they thought fit.

Such were the depth and intensity of Higgs-Walker's conviction of the rightness, the irreplaceable value of the relatively cheap, relatively small Public School in producing responsible citizens and leaders that, patriot though he was, he believed the Government wrong, during the war, to strip such schools of their eighteen year old Seniors and all their dynamic young masters. For him, these schools were living organisms, each part of which was vitally dependent upon and responsible for every other part: the balance was delicate, but the finely tuned organism was uniquely resilient, creatively responsive to the needs of its pupils as no other school could be if bound by patterns of organisation imposed from outside. "Unfortunately", he told his Speech Day audience, "certain parts of the new Act threaten these vital organisms: there is the danger of a uniformity clamped on by County Control".

The Governors decided first to appeal against the rejection, and Sir Charles Innes made out a strong and lucid case. He pointed out that the Fleming Committee had recommended granting Direct Grant status to schools aided from public funds which had "like characteristics and resources" to schools already on the list, and that Sevenoaks would soon be better endowed than most schools; its scholarship record had been pronounced "outstanding" by the Inspectors just before the war, and its case was fully supported by the K.E.C. There was a real danger, he said, that if Sevenoaks were forced to accept County control, the Trustees of the Johnson legacy would divert the School's promised "moiety" elsewhere, and this would be a calamity for education in Sevenoaks. The boarding side of the School would probably collapse, for though L.E.A.s were empowered by the Act to support boarders in their own schools, they were not required to do so, and there was no guarantee that the School's excellent relationship with the present K.E.C. would always continue so; moreover, Counties could only support boarders living in their area, and 37% of Sevenoaks' boarders came from other Counties and from overseas. Boarders, Sir Charles declared, are "the making of the School", for they are the boys who tend to stay on after the age of 16 and encourage day boys to do the same. "They are the mainstay of the school societies and generally to that side of the school which is devoted to character-building as opposed to mere instruction. It is chiefly to them that the school owes the Sixth Form and its scholarship record". He reiterated the educational and social advantages of having a "mixture" of boarders and day boys, and of local boys and others from further afield.

The Governors urged the Minister that, "if she will open the door just a little wider, she will earn the gratitude of a numerous class which does not usually get such sympathy or consideration . . . the professional men of small means who have been brought up in the idea that it is their responsibility to educate their own children, who dislike the idea of this responsibility being taken off their hands by the Local Authority but who cannot afford the fees charged by an independent school". Sir Charles assured the Minister that, if the School were to be granted Direct Grant status, it would undertake that no boy suitable for a grammar school education would be debarred from admission by reason of poverty. The Act allowed the K.E.C. to support 50% of admissions: this should be ample for the area, but if it were not the School would be quite prepared to admit an even higher proportion. Finally, the Minister must not believe that Sevenoaks existed "to serve a narrow privileged class". It never had done. Even now it drew the great majority of its day boys from the Elementary Schools and from the sons of tradesmen and other people of small means in and around Sevenoaks. "Nor is there anything in the argument based on 'parity of esteem'. Quite frankly it is the ambition of the Governors to improve the school in every way, but in the first place there is no grammar school with which comparison could be drawn nearer than Tonbridge, and secondly, seeing that the school is ready and anxious to admit every boy of the right type in its area, there can be no validity in the argument".

Friends gave Sir Charles advance knowledge of Miss Wilkinson's rejection of this appeal. By the time it came the Governors and Higgs-Walker had already begun detailed discussions with the K.E.C. about the School's future and independent of any direct grant from central government but, it was to be hoped, with the continued readiness of the Authority to pay the necessary tuition fees of pupils selected for free places. Sir Charles had calculated that replacing the earlier deficiency grants with higher tuition charges would entail increasing day boy fees from 12 guineas (£10 for boys from the privileged area) to £50 (£20 for privileged area boys); for boarders the new tuition and maintenance fee would be £140. The K.E.C. were agreeable, but approval had also to be obtained from the Board of Education. When this came, the County Education Officer, Mr Woodhead, rapidly worked out with Higgs-Walker the details of a five-year agreement: the K.E.C. would pay the full fees of Free Place boys, give assistance to others, and make certain other allowances for such things as books and stationery; for its part, the School would undertake to pay Burnham Scale salaries, provide and maintain accommodation and all other facilities at a standard acceptable to the Committee, make proper provision for day boy lunches, make available regular Statements of Accounts and consult the Committee when appointing a Headmaster. Parents were given a term's notice of the fee increases: surprisingly, only one objected, and he was told to apply to the K.E.C. for assistance as in the past.

The Finance Committee, composed of Lord Sackville, Sir Charles Innes, Major Pym and Messrs Judd and Rogers, agreed to meet more frequently. It is unlikely that they realised just how hard they were going to have to work over the next few years, though they knew that planning for the future was dependent upon too many imponderables. When would inflation stop climbing? When would the Johnson bequest become available to the School? How many parents would in future be deterred by the new fees? How heavy would be the burden of Burnham Scale salary increases, and of the associated superannuation and pension arrangements? Immediately, they had the problem of taking over the Boarding Houses from the Headmaster and drawing up a new agreement with him. As part of the latter, they agreed to purchase from him the furniture and fittings of School House: the agreed price was £1,124:1:6, but since no funds were available it would be paid over a period of several years, with interest of 6% until payment had been completed.

It is not clear whether, when the Governors made their bold decision, they had any inkling of an imminent windfall, but shortly thereafter they were told by the Johnson Trustees that the Park Grange Estate would in due course be made over to the School, and that through the kindness of Edward Johnson, the present occupier, it was to be given immediate access to part of the grounds, sufficient to provide Rugby pitches for 100 boys. "Here, in this Estate", exulted Higgs-Walker, "we have all that a School needs, buildings, room to build, room to play – a great thing for the School, a great thing for the Day Boys as well as the Boarders, and therefore a great thing for the town". Later, he recalled the background to this new act of generosity. It seems that the U.D.C. had plans to build a housing estate on Edward Johnson's meadow. This provoked strong opposition from the Civic Society, who called a public meeting. At this a Sevenoaks Sixth Former, George Gatling, made an impassioned speech, and Mr Johnson "was so pleased that he said the School could start playing at once and have the land after his death if the U.D.C. would drop their scheme – which they did, making a covenant with him and the Governors".

Restoration Begins

The task of restoring the School's pre-war standards was no easy one. Though the fee increases necessitated by independence were kept as low as possible, some parents of boarders turned to Cranbrook, now a Maintained School, where tuition fees were paid by the County, or to Tonbridge, where fees were higher than ours but where facilities, thanks to the backing of the Skinners Company, were considerably superior to those at Sevenoaks. Not that there was a lack of applicants, for demand rose rapidly after the war as the town of Sevenoaks expanded; but the bounds of our day boy "catchment area" were drawn so tightly that many good boys were excluded. That day boys should live close enough to enable them to play a full part in out-of-school activities was central to Higgs-Walker's philosophy, and clearly sensible if the "mixture" so often praised was to be generally operative in all areas of school life. Nevertheless, it did mean that when, in response to local pressure, and in the knowledge that further boarding accommodation would become available in Park Grange, a third "stream" was added, a number of boys came into the School who would not previously have found a place. Increased numbers would require more building, more classrooms, more Staff accommodation; so that despite the anticipated cushion of the Johnson legacy it was imperative that all places should be filled. Yet the system for selecting fee-paying day boys – a simple pass examination without interview or school record – was hardly likely to ensure that all boys admitted were really able to take full advantage, or even make sense of, a grammar school education.

However, Higgs-Walker and his strengthened post-war staff were determined to put the School on its feet again. Though few new names were for some years added to the Honours Board, and school teams were slow to start winning matches, enormous efforts were made to revive the rich variety of Clubs and Societies that had flourished before the war. The charismatic Ivan Cole took over the Fine Arts Society, the Music Club, and soon the Orchestra too; John Parks inherited the Young Farmers Club; the Debating Society got going again, considering among weightier matters who should first be thrown out of a sinking balloon basket containing Sir Thomas Beecham, Einstein, Dr Joad, Joe Louis and Frank Sinatra. Joad was expelled first by 15 votes, followed by Sinatra (10), Einstein (4), and Beecham (2), leaving Louis (0) in charge – perhaps benefiting from the news that Taylor had boxed for Oxford against Cambridge (albeit "briefly", as the new Blue modestly admitted).

The 1946–47 Rugby season was redeemed only by the performance of the Colts, given a full fixture list for the first time: Won 5, Lost 3. The 1st XV lost heavily to Tonbridge and Dulwich College 2nd XVs and to H.M.S. Worcester and Caterham, narrowly to St. Dunstan's and King's School, Rochester. The 2nd XV lost seven of their eight games. In cricket the 1st XI had their worst ever season, winning no matches at all, though here again the Colts showed promise. Certainly there was no lack of willing and skilful coaches: one of them, Jack Robinson, who had played for Yorkshire, unfortunately suffered a serious injury to his eye while coaching in the nets at Solefields, but Higgs-Walker and Ronnie Bate were both excellent cricketers, and they were enthusiastically aided by Ron Wheeker and by a newly appointed linguist, Tom Mason.

Mason's more lasting claim to fame was his major role in developing, and for many years directing, The Digweed Devastation and Mason Development Company. A Sixth Former, A. D. J. Digweed, initiated the scheme in 1948, under which non-A.T.C. members and other volunteers could undertake useful work about the school. Under Mason's skilful guidance they rapidly moved from devastation – demolishing the wall between Jockey's Platch and Plumptre Meadow, pulling down the old bicycle sheds – to more constructive work: building new bicycle sheds, laying a water pipe 250 yards long and two feet underground to the playing field, and erecting brick pillars at Solefields to receive the eighteenth century Main School gates, knocked down in 1942 by an army lorry. In 1956 the H.M.I.s were full of admiration for what the unit had achieved.

Ivan Cole worked hard to revive the Orchestra; George Hankin persuaded the whole school to give a Choral Concert performance of Handel's *Acis and Galatea*; John Parks, from 1948 running Park Grange as a "Waiting House" for thirty boys between the ages of 10 and 14, laboured with the Higgs-Walkers to re-establish the tradition of a major School Play instead of the war-time

"Follies" put on in alternate years by School House and Johnson's, (Higgs-Walker had considered them "invaluable in maintaining morale . . . but useless for the preservation of the slightest acting technique') and the 1948 production of *Arms and the Man* was compared favourably with that of 1928; school teams started running again in Knole Park.

> We were beaten regularly. . . Jimmy was the ultimate sanction and I remember that he always used a cane with a green cord wrapped round the handle. I remember on one occasion having administered "four", he said to me "Well, Holly, have you anything to say?" I replied "No, Sir, only thank you". He told me not to be insolent and gave me two more. . .
>
> There were alternative punishments: one master who subsequently took Holy Orders used to give you the option of either going to the Headmaster or being kicked up and down the corridor. We always opted for the latter. . .
>
> Chippy Page used to take Workshop. If you ragged he would ring a bell and then make you stand against the wall. He would then knock your head against the wall, before marking the spot where your head touched with your name and the date. The wall was covered with such items.
>
> (D. Handley, 1946–51).

And yet, despite all these efforts, it is impossible, thumbing through the pages of *The Sennockian* covering the late 40s and the very early 50s, to avoid the impression of a bravely dissimulated weariness, an underlying lack of the high-spirited confidence and pride of the pre-war years. It is difficult to pin this down, and difficult to explain why, if the impression is justified, Sevenoaks seems to have suffered more than many other schools from a kind of post-war depression. Entry was buoyant, numbers were rising; the Governing Body, though wrestling with financial problems, was as caring and supportive as ever. It has been suggested that the strain of the war years, watching the winding down of so much that he had built up – the Prefect and Monitor system, House Competitions, the Orchestra, the Debates, the prestigious School Play, the strong 1st XVs and 1st XIs – took a lot out of Higgs-Walker, and that the man who had to confront the difficult early years of independence without his close neighbour, friend and unfailing stay, the great C. P. Johnson, was not quite the inspiring force he had once been. Perhaps it was hardly surprising: many of his old colleagues on the Staff had gone, and in 1947 the loss of his faithful Secretary, Miss Lockyer, "who had for twenty years prevented his making many mistakes, corrected those he had made, or even taken the blame on herself, was a matter of the deepest personal regret to him". It may be that, at a deeper level, he sensed that society had changed irreversibly, and that he was going to find fewer and fewer people prepared to share his unashamedly "old-fashioned" ideals – his belief in courtesy and honour, in character, and in the respect due to those prepared to take on the responsibilities of leadership.

But the change, if change there was, must not be exaggerated. His energetic devotion to the School remained intense. At Speech Day, 1947, after one year of independence, he spoke proudly of "the psychological renaissance of the school" which its new freedom from control had made possible, thanked the Governors "for really governing", and declared his faith in the ability of Public Schools to resist interference by Church or State, standing together as members of the Headmasters Conference and of the Governing Bodies Association.

He was delighted when one of the outstanding "products" of the School's golden age, R. J. Martin, a natural leader and a fine sportsman, was invited to become a Governor. Had he not played for the Kent 2nd XI while still at school? Higgs-Walker's passionate love for the queen of all games certainly showed no signs of decline. In 1948 Edward Johnson died, and in the last of his many acts of generosity left money for a new Pavilion at Solefields, in which the Headmaster took great joy: "The enclosure was instituted in my time with suitable rules for its use by the privileged. . . The chains were given by my father; they were made in the family factory by the men who also made chains for the "Queen Mary"; the curl in the links is a special feature. The posts are carved with the names of the boys who made them". Tom Mason remembers "Jimmy H-W" strolling round the boundary, "a striking be-plusfoured figure complete with stick, and accompanied by Titus, that dog of uncertain temper . . . Well into his fifties, he could still bowl a very useful off-cutter . . . If the First lost, there was a distinct nip in the air in School House". If they won, Molly Higgs-Walker said irreverently, "it was a joy to see his little rosy, beaming face".

The Governors had little to beam about. Within two years of Independence they had been forced to ask permission to make a further increase in fees – to £55 for day boys (£25 for "natives") and £100 for boarders, and by 1950 they were contemplating another. The Boarding Houses were losing money. Park Grange had been bought for £10,000, and though £9,332 of this sum had been lent by the Johnson Trustees on the security of a mortgage on the estate, the loan had to be paid off in thirty equal annual instalments of £311.1.4d. Necessary alterations to the House were being met by a bank overdraft, already nearly £3,000. Negotiations to sell Park Lodge to the existing tenants were dragging on interminably, as were discussions with the Inland Revenue about the amount of Death Duties to be paid on the C. P. Johnson estate, the exact value of which was still not known. The Burnham increases expected in 1951 were likely to add £2,800 to the annual salary bill. And now they had a new worry: their latest acquisition, the lovely eighteenth century Manor House, was proving a liability, its beauty expensively flawed.

The Governors had decided to allow numbers to rise to a maximum of 400, and in 1948 had investigated the possibility of putting up pre-fabricated buildings in Park Grange grounds. Already disgusted by the name ('Pre-fabs!'), Higgs-Walker recoiled in horror from the photographs, and wrote to Lord Sackville asking whether the School might lease Manor House. The Sackville Trustees replied that they could not let, but might consider selling it to the Governors. In 1949 they bought it for £6,000: £2,000 was paid in cash; the rest, loaned to the School by the Sackville Trustees at 4% interest, was to be repaid in thirty annual instalments of £231.

Alas, the lovely eighteenth century house was no longer the jewel it had been when Mr and Mrs Hay were lavishly entertaining there between the wars, with the help of six maids, a woman to scrub, a butler and four gardeners. Those days were vividly evoked in *At Honour's Game* by Lilian Shepherd, who with her husband lived in Manor Cottage from 1921, looking after the House when the Hays and their staff were wintering in Bude:

> The big house looked very beautiful in those days, especially the hall and staircase. The hall still had the stone slabs, but they were scrubbed white and polished until they looked like marble. Priceless Persian rugs were laid right through; these were in soft subdued colourings with specimen pieces of furniture at each side. At the foot of the staircase was a very fine bronze group of classic figures, "Flautist and Pan", signed A. Coyzevox, 1709. These stood on a square red marble base.
>
> The Gardens were very lovely. White Muscatel grapes, Black Hamburgs, peaches, nectarines, green figs, mulberries, choice pears, apples, raspberries, gooseberries and currants . . . Masses of flowers, and a giant tree of mimosa, a wall of yellow bloom, covered the walls on the long conservatory in winter . . . the lawns were like lovely green velvet. . .

The garden was a jungle when the Governors bought the House, and it was to be many years before it recovered any of its old charm. Writing in 1957, Mrs Shepherd saw that "the Digweed boys have only just pulled down the little stable (where the cycle sheds are going to be) where the fat little black pony, who pulled the roller and lawn mower, lived". The Army had requisitioned the House during the war, and left it in a deplorable condition. In 1947, girls billeted there were so excited, when lorries arrived to take them back to Chatham to be demobilized, that they threw all their black iron bedsteads down from the top of the exquisite spiral staircase, cracking many stone slabs in the hall. Much more serious than this was the discovery of extensive dry rot, which had to be dealt with before any alterations could be begun. The bills mounted alarmingly. Meanwhile a "long battle of licences and permits" raged between the Governors and Whitehall, and it was not until the Spring Term of 1951 that four ground floor rooms were available as classrooms – just in time to cater for the third stream "bulge" as it rose through the school.

   In public, Higgs-Walker displayed no apprehension. Indeed, there is a new belligerence in some of his speeches. When an old Oundle pupil of his, Geoffrey Crowther, Editor of *The Economist*, came to distribute the Prizes, and spoke passionately in favour of "levelling up" the State system to the standard of the Public Schools, Higgs-Walker was no less outspoken. He condemned the new Minister, Mr Tomlinson, for not allowing children to sit for the School Certificate before the age of sixteen, presumably to discourage "cramming" in exam-orientated schools. Indignantly rejecting such "pseudo-egalitarianism", he declared that "School Masters were perfectly capable of deciding when it is advisable to hold a young boy back". At Sevenoaks the aim was "to train for life and not for some particular vocation". He realised that parents choosing independent schools were now having to make sacrifices, but assured them that they were "performing an invaluable service by enabling us to educate future citizens in the principles by which they may live their lives in liberty, and find happiness in work well done for others and for themselves". Perhaps in discreet illustration of the value of a Sevenoaks School education, he congratulated two Old Sennockians on their recent appointments: Air Commodore Brackley, C.B.E., D.S.O., D.S.C., as Chief Executive Officer of B.S.A. Airways, and Rear Admiral McLintock as President of the American Institute of Navigation.

In January, 1951, there were 208 day boys and 132 boarders in the School. Parents were warned of a new increase in fees (Tuition up £20 to £75, Boarding up £5 to £105). Only four objections were received: in each case concessions were made. Sir Charles Innes' Finance Committee had secured a bank overdraft of £7,500, which would have to be reduced annually by £1,000. One year later the Tuition Account showed a small surplus, but this was balanced by a loss on the Boarding Account. In that year feeding costs per boy per week had risen from eleven to sixteen shillings, and the price of coal, coke, gas and electricity had all risen steeply; Johnson's had last been repainted in 1938. There was nothing for it but to increase the boarding fee by £15, despite the danger of withdrawals: in the event, only two boys were withdrawn. Meanwhile, the bank had raised its rate of interest on our overdraft from 3½ to 4½, the Masters' Common Room had had to be improved, and though £357 had been received in respect of War Damage to the Pavilion, it was clear that frugality would be essential.

   In 1951, thanks to the kindness of John Vizard, Lord Sackville's farming tenant of Duke's Meadow, the school gained some desperately needed playing space at no cost to itself. With Lord Sackville's blessing, he granted us the use of land sufficient to provide two full-size rugby pitches, which were duly named

"Dorset" and "Sackville". The following year he not only provided a third pitch and the gift of free rolling, but thoughtfully put his sheep in to keep the grass down.

Academically, the School's performance was hardly outstanding, though the Sixth Form was slowly building up. Higgs-Walker explained that the "three-ladder" organisation into A, B and C Streams grouped boys roughly as Linguistic, Moderately Linguistic and One Language at Most. It would not, he assured parents, "prejudice a boy's general examination chances; it would make it easier in fact to decide whether he should by-pass the first stage of the new Tomlinson examination on his way to the Sixth; and it would certainly not deprive any boy of the best available human or material aids to progress".

Since there were now nearly seventy boys in the Sixth, it was decided to raise the qualifying standard for admission to the Honours Board: a boy must have at least a Higher Certificate before an Award could be gained. This condition was written into the regulations for the new Plender Scholarship of £60 a year, endowed in his will by Lord Plender but not into the C. P. Johnson Scholarship of £80 a year: consequently, names of winners of the latter Award were inscribed on a Special Board. The first Plender Scholarship was held by Robert Noakes at Lincoln College, Oxford, while R.B. Hussey took up the Johnson Scholarship at St. John's. In 1953 another valuable Leaving Award was added, when Mr J. Lingner left £5,000 to endow a Scholarship at Gonville and Caius College, Cambridge. The School now subscribed to the Public Schools Appointments Bureau; Carol Forder was appointed Careers Master and was in frequent contact with helpful Old Sennockians.

In the early 1950s there were several important Staff replacements and additions, and whilst Higgs-Walker was keen to recruit first-rate intellects he was also on the look-out for sportsmen to help raise the standard of our games. Harry Morley, who came to teach English, had been Captain of Cricket and Rugby at Leeds Grammar School and at St. Peter's Hall, Oxford, and had played Rugby for Yorkshire, Northampton and Rosslyn Park. Duncan Townson (History) was a Cambridge Crusader and had captained the Selwyn College XI. Colin Saunders (Classics) was a member of Oxford University Aquatic Club. G. M. Saul (Science) had won a Cambridge Blue for Long-Jumping. Harry Talbot had had a brilliant university career at Peterhouse after winning an Open Mathematical Scholarship when a boy at Sevenoaks, where he had been a fine sprinter and a member of the Rugby XV.

Mary Lees was now installed in the new Art Room in Park Grange; Geoffrey Gilbert, a fine craftsman, had taken over the Workshop, Charles Page having died suddenly in mid-term in 1950, shortly after completing a handsome case to hold the Memorial Book; George Hankin had left, leaving Ivan Cole in sole charge of the Orchestra, and Brian Townend, who was to be such an influential figure in the development of School Music, had come to teach the Classics which Cole had had to give up. In 1952 all music lovers, and many others, mourned the deaths of Sister Buyers and Claude Hunter. Sister Buyers, once School House Matron, had left in 1938 for Ambulance work in wartime London, and had then joined the Embankment Mission. Claude Hunter died at 79, within days of retiring after fifty-three years as Organist at Kippington Church. A brilliant musician and a taciturn, intensely private man with no living relatives, he had taught piano and singing in the School several days a week over all those years, and had seldom missed a School Concert whether as accompanist or dazzling soloist. The warmth of Higgs-Walker's tributes to him and Sister Buyers, as to Charles Page, reveal the intensity of this "remote" Headmaster's attachment to those who had loyally worked with him in the vibrant pre-war years. He was now very happy to welcome back George Tester, another great cricket-lover – as Director of Choral Music.

By now, most of the old Clubs and Societies had been revived, and some new ventures reflected the interests of new Staff. Forder conducted the first of many Geographers' Expeditions to Malham Tarn, produced two of his own one-act plays and worked with the Higgs-Walkers on a full-scale production of Molière's *Miser*; Morley started the Thursday club, a self consciously elitist group of twelve Sixth Formers and Masters, meeting fortnightly in Morley's rooms to read ambitious papers on Literature and the Arts (Townson was an early contributor with "Great Operatic Singers 1910–50"); a Danish Exchange had been initiated between the School and the Oregaard Gymnasium, which had led in 1951 to a visit by His Majesty Prince Georg. Invited to lunch by the Higgs-Walkers, together with Lord Sackville and Sir Charles and Lady Innes, Prince Georg inspected the A.T.C. on Jockey's Platch and addressed the assembled School in Johnson Hall. This was our first visit by Royalty since 1778, when George III and Queen Charlotte, staying overnight at Montreal with Lord Amherst, had briefly paused to hear a short speech by the Master, Dr Whitfield.

The Last Years

Governors' Meetings during Higgs-Walker's last four years as Headmaster were almost exclusively devoted to financial matters. As yet uncertain of when the School's "moiety" of the Charles Plumptre Johnson bequest would become available, and of the amount of annual income it would eventually provide, they were inclined to be cautious. Yet demands for further expenditure were insistent, and in many cases irresistible: dry rot in Manor House, where new classrooms were essential, was much more extensive than anticipated; Park Grange had urgently to be equipped and adapted as a full-size Junior boarding house; increases in the Burnham Scale salary awards, and in the Governors' contribution to superannuation and special responsibility allowances, had to be met, and if good staff were to be attracted more staff houses had to be provided; inflation was rampant, and the costs of providing books and stationery for growing numbers of boys, as of feeding the boarders, were soaring alarmingly; many of the school buildings were in desperate need of repair and repainting. Inevitably, fees had to be raised if standards were to be maintained and facilities improved, but only by the smallest possible amount, for Governors were determined that Sevenoaks should continue to offer a good public school education, "marvellously cheap" in comparison with its grander competitors, yet sufficiently "rich" to attract parents who might otherwise choose the state sector.

Perhaps it was a recognition of the near-impossibility of pursuing for long this noble ideal, at a time when parents were beginning to pay rather more attention to exam results, staffing ratios and pupil comforts, and rather less to vaguer Arnoldian concepts of character-formation, that contributed to Higgs-Walker's decision, in July, 1953, to announce that he would be retiring the following summer. However that may be, there is a certain irony in the fact that, almost immediately after the announcement, Arthur Cowdry broke to Governors the very welcome news that discussions concerning the distribution of the C. P. Johnson Residuary Estate had at last been concluded, and that the approximate gross annual income available to the School would be over £3,700. Though this would by no means solve all the school's immediate financial problems, it was to provide – alike for bankers, Governors and a new young Headmaster – a platform of confidence upon which bold decisions could be taken.

However, Higgs-Walker was far from a spent force during his last few years in the School he loved so much and served so devotedly. In 1952, he and his wife directed their last School Play, The *Importance of Being Earnest*, and the Times Educational Supplement pronounced it, "as school drama goes, something of a collector's piece". He continued to encourage his teachers and senior boys in the hard work they put into maintaining a wide diversity of Clubs, Societies and minor sports and activities, defiantly resisting any temptation to "cram for exams". His love of sport was undiminished. He was delighted that so many of his staff shared his passion for cricket, and followed with great interest the fortunes of the Sevenoaks Orbilians, a team composed of masters and a few friends: formed in 1949, and named by Ronnie Bate after Horace's schoolmaster – *plagosus Orbilius*, "the swiper Orbilius", by 1953 they were playing six or seven matches a season against local teams, some on very rough village pitches. That year Higgs-Walker posed proudly for a photograph of the Headmaster's XI which, thanks mainly to Townson, Bate and Morley, defeated the School First XI: not since 1925 had a Master's team, unaided by strangers, managed to do this.

He still believed passionately in the importance of the House system – "the guidance of House Masters and House officials is all important in every side and phase of a boy's life" – and deplored "the threats, as ill-natured as they are ill-informed, even now being made against the Independent Schools". A loyal supporter of the Old Sennockians, a witty speaker at their London Reunions, he was delighted to applaud their adult achievements and to link these with strengths acquired at school: in 1953, when J. D. Bates was appointed Colonial Secretary at Gibralter, Higgs-Walker recalled that he had been one of the boys selected to form the nucleus of Johnson's when it opened in 1927, later becoming a Prefect, a Cap in both School teams and winner of an Open Scholarship to Keble.

☆ ☆ ☆

After the death of George VI in 1952, praised by Higgs-Walker as "more than a great King, he was a good King", he must have sensed, and can hardly have welcomed, the coming upheaval of social patterns and habits. What would he have made, one wonders, of the fashion for co-education, and of the subsequent utopian visions of a sexless and classless society? Writing in 1982, Paul Clark (1945–1951) remembered both that a few Walhamstow Hall senior girls had used our chemistry laboratories since theirs had been bombed and that a few Sevenoaks sixth formers were taught biology amongst the girls:

> School policy generally viewed any association with girls with the deepest misgiving, so much so that by 1949 it had become a beatable offence to be seen talking in public to a girl. One boy, apprehended in flagrant conversation with an attractive young lady in the High Street, was given an extra stroke for his impudence in alleging her to be his mother: subsequently it proved that, Iolanthe-like, she was. However, in 1951, six boys, carefully selected and briefed by the Headmaster personally, were sent to the annual dance of Walthamstow Hall School, hitherto an exclusively female evening.
>
> Were we then driven to homosexuality? I think not. Statistics suggest that there may have been a degree of carefully hidden homosexuality, but I am aware of none, except that two boys were generally known to make advances to those of their own age (though not to each other) and I believe received no takers. Generally, the subject was unpopular and not discussed.
>
> This was still a period of acute class-consciousness . . . It is hardly surprising, therefore, that a policy was followed (with some success) of trying to elevate the social status of the school. This endeavour took various forms, and included firm encouragement of middle-class attitudes, speech, manners and dress. Accusations of snobbery were occasionally made against the Headmaster – unjustly, since, at a time when many schools were carefully selective as to the background of entrants, our school for various reasons accepted all competent comers who could either pay the fees or win a free place. Boys occupying free places then, unlike now, always came from families

without much money: but not infrequently they were, in terms of social class, apparently up-market of some fee-paying day boys and boarders.

Not all Old Sennockians share Clark's belief that "at the time, as boys, we were entirely indifferent to each other's social background", but most would agree with him that "generally speaking, we liked each other and we liked our masters. We enjoyed some of our work and most of our play . . . We liked our distinctive uniform of straw hats, walking sticks, special sports caps and scarves. We were, in short, proud to be members of so fine a school". "Jimmy" Higgs-Walker would surely have known the value of this tribute, and been content.

CHAPTER SIXTEEN

Taylor Arrives

"Great Things May Soon Be Expected"

Kim Taylor, having rejoined his parents in India when he left the School in the summer of 1939, was commissioned when nineteen and served as an Intelligence Officer with Southern Army. After the war, he took a "First" in History at New College, Oxford, and was then awarded a Commonwealth Fellowship to Chicago University. After a spell teaching at Repton (of which he was later to become a Governor) he was appointed Headmaster of Sevenoaks in 1954, a month after his 32nd birthday.

Even if it were desirable, it would be quite impossible to deal with the next fourteen years in the more or less "linear" manner adopted hitherto. Henceforth ideas will almost invariably precede, precipitate and shape events. A stream of projects initiated by Taylor and his astonishingly supportive and courageous Governing Body, swept away the cautious "reactive" habits of more than one lifetime, and thrust Sevenoaks School boldly into an era of rapid reform and innovation. However, these reforms and innovations were not introduced, neatly, one after the other, and not all of them were immediately successful. Many were introduced simultaneously, sometimes with unforseen effects upon each other, some beneficial, others not. Sometimes two giant steps were taken forward, followed by one sideways to avoid an obstacle, one

backwards to allow another innovation to squeeze past, then another leap
forward to make up for lost time. This is not to say that confusion reigned.
Taylor reigned, bursting with ideas and ideals, but communicating to his
occasionally bewildered Staff much of his own tremendous energy, excitement
and confidence.

Higgs-Walker's brave and patient stewardship of the little school's "renaissance" under the princely patronage of Charles Plumptre Johnson has been
rightly honoured; nevertheless, like the historical Renaissance, it had been in
many respects backward-looking, concerned to preserve the old values of
thought and decorum threatened by the rising tide of materialism and "pseudo-
egalitarianism", so that, despite increasing numbers, an expanding campus and
a growing local reputation, the School had made no serious attempt to come to
terms with the enormous social changes in post-war Britain, nor to harness the
new forces released. Its philosophy had remained basically that of the great
nineteenth century Headmasters who had striven to create small "city states" in
which privileges had to be earned by effort and retained by increased
responsibility, where group loyalty was more important than individual success,
where the qualities of leadership were fostered by a Spartan frugality of
comfort and the exercise of firm discipline, where all-important character was
formed by strenuous efforts on the playing-fields for one's House or for the
School, but also on the stage, in the orchestra and the choir, and in all the other
civilising clubs and societies largely run and supported by Sixth Formers.

An early photograph of Kim and Sue Taylor with their Prefects, set beside
a pre-war picture of a group of stern-faced young men more like Masters than
boys, vividly illustrates at least one of the sea-changes precipitated by the
arrival of this bustling young phenomenon and his clever, vivacious American
wife. Neither of them had much time for the reverential observance of empty
ritual, nor for the exaggerated respect due to mere rank. Not that Style was to
be jettisoned, far from it: Taylor was no iconoclast. For instance, though the
sacred cow of Speech Day, with its solemn ceremony of processions, hierarchi-
cal seating-plans and noble rhetoric, was before long to perish upon the much
jollier altar of Open Day, with boys and their activities firmly at its centre, the
new style was if anything more emphatic than the old. Taylor had genuine
affection and admiration for Higgs-Walker, but when invited as Headmaster-
elect to say a few words at his last Speech Day in June, 1954, the warmth of his
tribute was perhaps less revealing than the informality of its expression:

To very many of us, Sevenoaks is personified in the Headmaster. Say
Sevenoaks to me suddenly – and the image that springs into my mind
is of a stately, yet spritely figure, a round jolly face, all amiability, and
gestures: a flick of the hand, a tongue in the cheek which generations
of boys have delighted to imitate. Add a yapping Cairn terrier and an

162

ancient Rolls . . . and you have a symbol as distinctive and indestructible as John Bull or Mr Punch.

And then, as if aware that some among the audience, if not his old Headmaster himself, seated upon the platform, might find this inappropriately familiar, Taylor moved smoothly into a higher gear, heaped generous praise upon both Higgs-Walkers, and concluded:

We in this hall are a privileged few who by our words and applause must testify for a great cloud of witnesses their gratitude and affection for all you both have done for them and for this most ancient school.

☆   ☆   ☆

A man to whom creative thinking and talking were an almost sensual delight, and who was brilliant at both, Taylor was also capable of tackling complex and intractable practical problems – especially if, having remained unsolved for many years, they were no longer regarded as problems but as permanent if unfortunate features of the school's landscape. The first to which he turned his attention – or at least, the first to be described here – was the dangerously wide ability-range of boys entering the school at different ages. He found that all eleven year olds went through the school at the same pace, sitting 'O' Level after five years when they were sixteen or seventeen: after Taylor's arrival the brightest were admitted into a higher form and sat 'O' Level after four years. The rigid system of "streaming" boys – 'A' stream taking Latin, French and either Greek or German, 'B' stream taking French, 'C' stream no foreign language at all – had made transfers across the streams impossible; the 'B' stream was usually very large, the other two very small; boys reaching the Science or History Sixths by way of the 'B' stream lacked the Latin required by the older universities; and a late developer trapped in the 'C' stream was doomed to years of frustration.

In 1955, after long discussions with the staff, radical changes were made: up to the Lower Fifths all boys now took the same curriculum, including Latin; in the Lower Fifths they were setted for Maths, and in those sets were also taught Science, English and "form subjects" such as Divinity and Gym; they were setted separately for French; in addition each boy had to choose two optional subjects from seven offered (Latin, Greek, German, History, Geography, Art and Mechanical Drawing), Biology and Russian to be added as soon as possible. Great care was to be taken, in discussions between boys, masters and parents, to see that options were chosen wisely. "The system has its snags", Taylor admitted to the Inspectors in 1956, "but they seem less serious than those of the streams".

Streaming and Trawling

One very obvious snag was that, unless the qualifying standard for entry to the School was raised, the weakest boys were going to find some parts of the new curriculum beyond them. In 1955 the eleven year old entrance examination was made competitive, and the qualifying mark for thirteen year olds entering via Common Entrance was raised from 45% to 55%. At the same time the Governors agreed to offer fewer Boarding Scholarships – which in recent years had sometimes not been awarded for want of suitable candidates – at both eleven and thirteen, but substantially to increase their value. This move bore immediate fruit: in 1955 there were 17 entries for the Junior Scholarships, 5 for the Senior; in 1956 the corresponding figures were 27 and 16.

Turning to the fee-paying day boys, Taylor was surprised to discover that, though many of them were very able, quite a few were academically no stronger than the boarders. The reason was not far to seek. Demand for places had been brisk after the end of the war, and the bounds of the "catchment area" had been drawn in so that boys admitted would be those living close enough to the School to play a full part in the vitally important out-of-school activities. However, the adding of the third stream in 1948, and the financial necessity of keeping all forms full in the rapidly growing school, had resulted by 1954 in a sharp depression of the standard of entry. Clearly, the bounds of the day boy area had to be extended. The Governors agreed to do this in terms of travelling time rather than by Parishes: any boy living within forty-five minutes of the School by Public Transport was eligible to apply for a day boy place. This made little difference to the boundaries to the south, east and west of Sevenoaks, but to the north lay large centres of population such as Orpington (which was still waiting for its Grammar School to be built), from which many children travelled to the big London day schools. Within a year or two, many of them were preferring to come south, against the run of morning and evening traffic, towards greener hills and a purer air. As for the out-of-school activities, they were moved from early evening to late afternoon, so that none of the new "commuters" would be deprived.

There remained the problem of the County Place boys. Why, Taylor asked, were some of them, awarded places at Sevenoaks, so weak? Why were boys from local Primary Schools putting Judd School and Skinners' School, in Tonbridge, as their "first choice'? To find out, he visited these schools, and concluded that "one thing was abundantly clear: that if we were to get good boys from the Primary Schools, then at least the same efforts had to be made to keep in close touch with them, and with parents of boys in them, as were made to keep in touch with the Preparatory Schools". Several members of Staff began an energetic campaign to make those parents think of Sevenoaks as the local Grammar School. Again, the effects of trawling in this way were well nigh immediate. By 1955, the number of boys seeking, as their "first choice", one of the twenty-six County Places at Sevenoaks, had risen in one year from 58 to 105. In 1956, of all the boys in the area awarded Grammar School places, only one put Judd as his first choice.

All these moves may look obvious enough, once the long-standing problems had been clearly identified and analysed. In fact, they were the result not only of Taylor's extraordinary ability to bring a fresh and decisive mind to bear upon the central issues, cutting through a mass of *idées reçues*, but of an enormous amount of sheer hard work. Governors, Staff, local parents and the Kent Education Committee had to be convinced or reassured that this new broom was not being wielded fecklessly. His success in this respect, now and later, was due to the fact that his most "outlandish" proposals, argued with infectious passion and persuasive eloquence, were always supported by papers revealing a hard-headed mastery of detail: all possible objections and difficulties were foreseen and answered, the financial implications squarely faced. This goes a long way to explain the County Authorities' remarkably generous sympathy and support whenever Taylor approached them. Learning, at the end of his first year, that the Boarding Houses were losing money due to the rapid rise in wages and the cost of food and power, he agreed with his Governors not only to raise the boarding fee by £10 a year to £140, but to substitute for the 50% reduction hitherto granted to boarding brothers one of a little over 10%. At the same time the 50% exemption from fees allowed to boys from the privileged area was reduced to 20%. The K.E.C. raised no objection: moreover, they declined to take advantage of the concession themselves, and continued to pay full fees for the boys they were supporting.

Several of these important changes were put forward at Taylor's very first Governors' Meeting on October 15th, 1954. If some Governors were feeling twinges of unease, they were perhaps comforted to hear him announce the restoration of the mark system to encourage boys to work harder. The alpha, beta, gamma grade system introduced in 1950 had been, he thought, a thoroughly worthwhile experiment, but one which had "many snags when practised in a School in which a considerable proportion of the boys are not so intelligent as to find academic work in itself stimulating and rewarding, and one in which boys continue to be taught in the traditional class manner". Grades tended to shroud a boy's progress in "genial obscurity". Marks could be added up as grades could not, and could produce a "form order" more likely to enable teachers to identify boys specially in need of attention. After each three-weekly "order" staff meetings were held, and at these the name of every boy in each form was read out and comments invited, so that staff would no longer be tempted to ignore the unobtrusive majority quietly ticking over between the admirable Top and the wretched Bottom. Twice a year, each boy had to endure "Headmaster's Collections" – a substantial interview with Headmaster and

Housemaster – at which his reports and progress were discussed. Some new "Carrots and Sticks" were introduced. The Sticks included Detention for individual pieces of bad work; Satisfecits for generally poor work (boys awarded Satisfecits were seen by the Headmaster the following morning after Prayers); Prep Books for badly done Preps or for boys on General Satisfecit. For consistently good work, Prize Essays and so on, boys were given a "Copy" which they took to the Headmaster; a boy with three Copies won a 7s.6d. Book Token. Naturally enough, this "shameless bribery!", as Taylor disarmingly called it, did not find favour with the Inspectors in 1956, but the Staff were delighted. Taylor did not hide from Governors the fact that examination results had in recent years been distinctly poor: two years later he was able to report a modest improvement, with 'O' Level Passes up from 43.4% to 54.5%, 'A' Level Passes up from 51.0% to 67.7%.

Changing the Inheritance

It is not easy to find a unifying theme running through the pulsating Taylor years. It is far from certain that he himself had at the outset a clear vision of the future he wanted for the School. At his first Speech Day, in 1955, he praised "the immensely strong foundations" Higgs-Walker had laid, which had made possible certain "minor conversions and modernisations". He felt that the School, "in its richness and complexity as in its age and constitution . . . was thoroughly medieval", but that having survived virtually unchanged the upheavals of Victorian times, it now seemed in its constitution very modern. "Being a bit of everything", it reflected, the Headmaster concluded, the rapidly changing society of today and was particularly well fitted to move with the times. Not that Taylor was temperamentally inclined to revere anything simply because it was new – as witness his unfashionable but hard-headed restoration of the mark system. In him, as in the School, there was in fruitful conjunction "a bit of everything", a love of tradition together with a delight in original thought, and a recognition of the invigorating effects of discovery. In dinner-table conversation, he had been known to defend brilliantly, if only half seriously, the virtues of Change for Change's Sake, arguing that *anything* is better than torpor, and that minds not seeking to improve the world are quickly enfeebled.

Of course, Sevenoaks would have had to change, whether under Taylor or another Headmaster, for it was already caught up in the inexorable logic of its own fight for survival, subjected to many apparently irreconcilable pressures. It was growing in size in response to local demand – *had* to grow, if it were to produce a decent Sixth Form capable of respectable academic results, (and later, *had* to go on growing, if it was to respond positively to the County's demand for more places, failing which the County might build its own Grammar School in the area). More pupils meant more classrooms, more buildings, more teachers, more staff houses. How were the Governors to finance all this? By higher fees? but Sevenoaks had always prided itself on keeping these lower than those of its rivals, particularly those whose boarding facilities were superior. By taking in yet more pupils? but that would mean either more buildings, or classes unattractively full. Clearly, fees would have to be raised, but simultaneously there had to be an urgent attempt to make the School more attractive to fee-payers.

That the School not only survived but triumphantly overcame these pressures was in large part due to the courage of the Governors and to the shrewd manoeuvres of the Finance Committee led by Sir Charles Innes. With the invaluable help of Arthur Cowdry, invited on to the Governing Body to represent the Johnson Trustees, buildings were mortgaged, substantial over-drafts granted and the builders called in: for the next several years they were seldom to be absent from the premises. In addition to two new Staff houses recently built in the grounds of Park Grange and first occupied by Harry Talbot and Brian Townend, the Governors bought Red Lodge, a large Victorian house beyond Johnson's in Oak Lane, and set about converting it into three Staff flats. Four new teachers were appointed in 1955, including Geoffrey Hoare (Head of English) and Brian Scragg (French and English) in an attempt to improve the unacceptably low staffing ratio of 1:18. In September, the Red Lodge conversion not having been completed, Hoare, Scragg and another newcomer, J. Applegarth, were temporarily – and expensively – found accommodation in the sedate Ormiston Hotel, destined seven years later to become the International Centre. Here, the average age of residents being about seventy, and where one charming old lady told of cycle rides in her youth with Thomas Hardy, the Applegarths found that their very boisterous young child was attracting too many disapproving glances during the hitherto silent meals, and soon moved into a caravan hired for them by the Governors.

Faced with this flurry of activity, and in anticipation of grave financial difficulties promised by the new Burnham Scale rates for teachers' salaries and Responsibility Allowances, the Governors decided that a full-time Bursar was needed. For the past forty-one years Mr A. Clive Knocker, head of the firm of local solicitors, now seventy-five years old, had loyally acted as their Clerk, as had his father for twenty-eight years before that, at salaries inadequate even to cover their expenses. It was hoped to find the new Clerk, Mr A. Tutte, an office in Manor House; there, further classrooms were being rapidly prepared, for in the Michaelmas Term, 1955, there were to be an unprecedented 435 boys in the School.

☆　☆　☆

In the following year Taylor gave an early indication of his remarkable talent for locating and exploiting sources of financial support. Approaching the new Industrial Fund for the Advancement of Scientific Education in Public Schools, he elicited a promise of £18,600 towards the probable £30,000 cost of new

Science Laboratories. In London meetings with the Directors of the fund Sir Charles Innes and Stanley Berwick were told the daunting conditions: work must be completed by the end of 1957, and before that time no money at all would be paid over, which meant that the School had to find, urgently, a great deal more than the £12,000 balance. Due to the credit squeeze, the bank was unable to increase our overdraft facilities. Would the K.E.C. help, since we were educating 130 of their boys? They were sympathetic, as always, and thought that they could either make us a grant of £10,000 or lend us the money, provided that the Ministry would give its approval. The Ministry refused to do so. Fortunately, Barclays Bank now relented, and agreed to support the scheme up to a maximum of £10,000, while Cowdry was prepared to advance a similar sum from the Johnson legacy on the security of the buildings.

Scarcely allowing his relieved Governors time to draw breath, Taylor laid before them, in January, 1957, two proposals with far-reaching financial implications. First, supported by the recently departed Inspectors, he proposed the creation of a new form of brighter boys entering at 13 by way of the Common Entrance examination: they would be kept together and would be expected to sit 'O' Level after only two years, then strengthen the Sixth Form. Unaware that by the summer of 1959 these boys would contribute to the pressure for a second Science VI, and thus for an extension to the brand new Laboratories, the Governors agreed. Second, he presented his draft proposals for an International House at Sevenoaks: the British Council was interested, and believed that industrial sponsorship might be forthcoming. Would the Governors agree to the scheme in principle? After questioning the Headmaster at length as to the possible benefits of this House to the School, and insisting that all funding must come from outside sources, they did so, unanimously. It is probable that few other Governing Bodies of schools in similar circumstances would have been prepared to consider such a bizarre proposal, and much credit is due to Lord Sackville and Sir Charles Innes for their exemplary support. They did, however, insist that the statues Taylor wanted to place in the niches in front of the Almshouses must cost "very little indeed".

While her husband was busy spending, or planning to spend money, Sue Taylor was doing her best to save it in the Boarding Houses. Convening weekly meetings of the Housemasters' wives, she presided gaily but very effectively over a concerted economy campaign. For instance, arrangements were made to buy meat from a local butcher, Radbone, at the same rates enjoyed by the K.E.C.: the meat was excellent, the saving considerable, and two second-hand refrigerators were bought for £180. The meetings were held in rotation in the Houses, where it was soon realised that the Headmaster's Wife, for all her exuberant friendliness and lack of side, had a very sharp eye for a grubby mirror or a coffee-cup ring on a table.

Meanwhile, the carpenters and painters were hard at work reclaiming for use the spiral staircase and the top floor rooms of Manor House. In the garden behind, Digweed were building new cycle sheds, while in the little courtyard to the north, above two old garages, a new, bright Art Room was being prepared for Bob White, the absurdly young-looking and richly talented Art Master appointed in 1956. The Library, too, was moving to the ground floor of Manor House, and the old library premises under Johnson Hall stage became, rather grandly, the Music School.

Her Majesty's Inspectors, during their November 1956 visit, thoroughly approved of these changes and of the enterprising spirit informing them. They understood that the need to grasp the opportunity of Industrial Fund support for new Laboratories had forced the postponement of a new Gym (whose old location was to have provided the sorely needed dining space and common room for day boys). They thought highly of the young Headmaster: "The Governors are to be congratulated on all that has been done so far and on the backing which they have given to a new headmaster, who, with his wife, can look back on two years of remarkable achievement. Inevitably much remains to be done; but if the school is able to continue on this present course great things may soon be expected".

Some of the great things to come were signalled by small but significant things, such as a greatly improved design and type-face for *The Sennockian*, and the inclusion of much more poetry and creative material, written and drawn, of a steadily rising standard; Geoffrey Hoare had joined the Editorial Board; there were delicate "end-piece" pen drawings by one of White's talented pupils, Richard Reid. Later, as an internationally recognised architect and author, he was to be responsible for the controversial "transparent cubes" flanking the Froy Gates, and others adorning the watery Piazza behind School House. Such splendours were still far away; for the moment, the Taylors – for Sue shared Kim's belief that one worked better, indeed lived better, in harmonious and when possible beautiful surroundings – had to content themselves with damage limitation as the omnipresent workmen gutted and transformed rooms, and long lines of boys with downcast eyes carried valuable scientific equipment or books from old to new premises. But the New Library in the Manor House was far and away the most graceful sanctum the School had ever known, created with loving care and discrimination, in defiant disregard of the alleged destructiveness of all schoolboys. Taylor remembered his own attempts to work, as a pre-war member of the History Sixth, in the Library beneath the Johnson Hall stage.

> Deep shelves from floor to ceiling on three walls, and frosted glass in small panes on the fourth, made for gloom and claustrophobia; and the rain hurled by high winds from the Park had penetrated the porous

ragstone walls and stained the window surrounds with a combination of moss and rust, and a musty air better suited to beer than books, pervaded the room. . . One generation of Six Form historians developed an initiation of tribal ferocity: a tenderfoot had to cross the library swinging hand over hand along the girder supporting the roof, while subject to a book bombardment. One table bore chalk markings for shove-ha'penny,; another witnessed the elaborate and esoteric skills of tuppeny-ha'penny football. . .

Things were going to be different in the Manor House. A matching pair of beak-fronted mahogany bookcases were up for auction at Cobham Hall – miraculously, at sixteen and a half feet, exactly the right size. Exhausting searches through City wholesale warehouses finally produced something pleasing to Taylor the aesthete and historian alike: "Excellent copies of the great 'hanging lantern' carpet, considered by many to be the greatest ever made, filched by rapacious hands made bold by bigotry from the Mosque at Ardebil". The great D-ended central table, veneered, cross-banded and inlaid, was a fine Victorian copy of an early Georgian original; there was a Georgian pedestal table in the window bay, and a solid Victorian 'rectory' table over toward the Church end. The Librarian's table came from Chartwell. The chairs were Victorian dining chairs: "Solid, circular, generous in proportion, padded to give a little, yet to sustain, they seem to us admirably suited to Library use; beside which they were constantly coming up in sales at anything from five shillings to a pound". The beautifully crafted built-in bookcases were the work of Mr Gentry from Knole, and the ceiling decorations, appliqué strips of papier-mâché in a variety of fruit and flower and ribbon designs, were elegantly composed and neck-crickingly applied by Geoffrey Hoare. "To those who question such embellishment in a Library", wrote Taylor, "we would reply that we regard this as strictly functional. We wanted our library to be a place demonstrating the respect and affection due to books, an attractive place and even a civilising one". Two fully-trained librarians, Mrs Hoddle and Mrs Sturton were engaged to share the job part-time.

The Inspectors Return

In 1956, when there were 451 boys in the School, including 88 in the Sixth Form, the Inspectors had foreseen "a slight further rise to a figure of about 500". They felt that, "while it would be ungrateful not to admire the combination of individual munificence and careful planning on the part of the Governors which has achieved so much in so short a time . . . yet much remains to be done; the very expansion which recent provision has made possible has in its turn imposed severe strains upon the school premises". At their follow-up visit in 1960, they found that "this is no longer the same school . . . four years have seen a transformation". There were now 557 boys, 196 of them in the Sixth Form. At first view the staffing ratio had improved from 1 in 19.1 to 1 in 17.4, but if the normal practice were to be followed of counting Sixth Formers twice, it had in fact *worsened* from 1 in 22.9 to 1 in 23.8. With 580 pupils expected the following year, national staffing averages in independent schools (1:12 for boarders, 1:18 for day boys) would require a staff of 38, instead of the 35 expected at Sevenoaks. "It is certainly encouraging that the school can count on a general good will and reasonableness in dealing with its teaching problems". Nevertheless, the astonishingly rapid expansion was inevitably stressful: many of the Sixth Form groups were much too large, and here and elsewhere in the school there was too great a reliance on "passive learning" in cramped surroundings, too few opportunities to experiment with newly discovered forms of group and individual study. Taylor, always a strenuous opponent of the more passive forms of classroom learning, must have read this part of the Report with gritted teeth.

Had he forced the pace too early, too hard? What neither he nor any one else could have foreseen, in his desire to build up the Sixth Form and establish high standards of scholarship, was the rapid increase in the third- and fourth-year Sixth: none in 1954, 12 in 1957, 40 in 1960. At the same time more boys were staying on for just a single year in the "Geography Sixth" to pick up a few more 'O' Levels, perhaps to enjoy one more season of cricket or rugby. The Inspectors took no exception to this: on the contrary, they were pleased that "the school remains a community in which less able boys too can find a secure place and do useful work",and they were no less sympathetic about the difficulty of enlarging the staff in a school with such an "excellent tradition of frugality and low fees. . . The school seems very much aware of its local responsibilities, and would be reluctant to raise its fees to a point at which these might seem unreasonably high to local opinion".

Despite their reservations, the Inspectors in 1960 were lavish in their praise of a school which "needs, and is receiving, leadership of a high order. The headmaster knows how to combine three virtues which are not always found together: lucid, long-term planning, careful working out in detail, and, most important of all, a profound concern for the individual boy. In all three he owes much to the support and understanding of his Governing Body". In 1959 Lord Sackville, in his eighty-ninth year, had felt unable to continue as Chairman, after more than twenty years in office. His interest in the affairs of the School, his support of Higgs-Walker and Taylor during momentous years of decision, had been consistent and generous. Sir Charles Innes now took over, and his son, also Sir Charles, was elected Vice-Chairman; a local resident and future historian of the Town, Sir John Dunlop, was invited on to the Board. Sadly, the elder Sir Charles died, at the age of eighty-four- within six months of assuming office. The School's debt to him was immense. A former Governor of Burma,

Chairman of the Mercantile Bank of India from 1938 to 1952, he was one of the ablest Indian Civil Servants of his day. For twenty years a Governor of Sevenoaks School, his outstanding Chairmanship of the Finance Committee had been invaluable during the difficult years of independence and expansion. Taylor said that to know him was an astonishing experience. "A schoolmaster habitually moves among people of tolerably quick and accurate minds. Sir Charles, when over 80, was able to sort out complex problems to get to the heart of a matter, in a way that I have never experienced in anyone else".

Change, Growth and Diversity

Between January, 1957, and September, 1960, more than forty projects were undertaken affecting the school grounds and buildings; eleven more were under way, and a further six had been authorised by the Governors. Some had been done by Digweed, notably the conversion of garages under the new Art Room into pottery and printing rooms, and the design and erection in Manor House garden of a cedar building housing five music practice rooms. Some were relatively minor, but indicative of a new concern for the environment: the hideous fire-escapes which had disfigured the front of Burlington's original school house were removed; four beautiful eighteenth century statues and some urns, tracked down by Taylor, were set in niches along the school and almshouse front. Sir Graham Savage, Chairman of the Industrial Fund, had agreed a further grant of £7,000 towards two additional laboratories. A separate Headmaster's House – the need for which had been most strongly urged by the Inspectors, who considered that both boarders and day boys must suffer from the Headmaster supposedly doubling as a Housemaster – was being built in the vegetable garden of Claridge House: two acres of this garden had been bought, allowing the extension of The Cottage eastward over an arch to provide new classrooms and two tiny administrative offices; the rest had been leased, and a path laid to gates giving safe access to Manor House, across the lane leading to Knole, away from the dangerous main road. Nos. 7 and 9 High Street had been purchased, together with the lease of the ground floor flat in No. 2, to help provide accommodation for the growing academic and domestic staff. Improvements had been made in all three boarding houses; a new staff house was being built in Park Grange grounds, to which it was hoped to attach an annexe for eighteen junior boarders; when this was completed, Park Grange would become a "full-size" third senior boarding house – urgently needed, for boarders too were staying on longer than expected: in 1960 only twelve were leaving, while entry lists, made up several years earlier, had "promised" thirty new places . . . .

This by no means exhaustive list must serve to give some idea of the extent and pace of the School's physical growing-pains in the late fifties; it may also explain the Inspectors' admiring comments: "At a time of exceptional expansion new building and rebuilding have been planned with judgment and skill; a

172

fair balance has been kept between finance, building priority, and human beings. Though the fees have remained relatively low, surprisingly little debt has been incurred; the Johnson Trust seems to have been most skilfully administered".

Playing fields and other facilities for games, as well as classrooms, were desperately needed. A squash court in the grounds of Garden House was acquired, behind Knocker and Foskett's, but there was still no gymnasium, no tennis court, only one fives court and a minute swimming pool. Before his retirement from the Board of Governors, Lord Sackville had come to the rescue. Not only had he given the School two acres of land in order that its view of Knole House and the park might be preserved, but he had granted it the main lease of Duke's Meadow, so that in future it would be available during the spring and summer terms as well as in the autumn. Meanwhile, the lease of some six acres of school ground in the Park Grange estate had been recovered, and part of it was being resown to make a cricket pitch. Thanks to the generosity of the Old Sennockians, who in 1956 presented a Firefly dinghy, and to the kind welcome of Chipstead Sailing Club, E.G. and Scragg were able to divert twenty or so boys onto the water, and to lay the foundations of a School Sailing club destined for great things.

Living conditions were spartan but improving thanks to Carol (Forder). A new boy had only a small wooden locker, but probably by the time one reached the Fifth Form – and certainly by the Lower Sixth – one had a cubicle. Dormitories were still iron bedsteads with red hospital blankets – and all windows open at night even in snow. There were at first no lavatories available to boys in School House: one had to walk across to the Day Boy loos through Sennocke Close. Fagging had been abolished, but bullying by senior boys was frequent: I was once taken into a room and shouted at for twenty or so minutes – I can remember crying and being very frightened. Cold showers were abolished after my first year but, for some reason, warm showers were not offered as an alternative; rather, three baths were filled with warm water and, under the House Tutor's eye, we had to submerge ourselves, soap and rinse in about twenty seconds, and allow the next boy in line to take our dirty water.

There was more *time* to do things . . . Sevenoaks was like an allotment only part of which was cultivated: if you wanted to grow new plants (Focus, University nets, etc.) there was always untilled land available; now, every inch is planted and specimens crowd each other. . . I did work pretty hard, but I remember as a Sixth Former going up to London on weekday afternoons in a manner that would be more difficult now – you would have to get off something.

What amazes me is how much we achieved in an academic sense with so little in material terms; perhaps, if you have only classrooms, a teacher must find in himself the wherewithal to teach well, rather than retreat behind a video. . . Possibly, also, we worked harder and in a more disciplined manner at the syllabus and thus had time to explore beyond it.(J.B. Guyatt, 1956–61).

☆   ☆   ☆

Amid the roar of generators, the grinding of concrete-mixers, the sawing and the hammering, Taylor and his staff were doing their best to stimulate the intellects and broaden the interests of their charges, hoping to encourage more to go on to university, and to hone the minds of the best to Scholarship standard. New staff were encouraged to found new clubs and societies to exploit and communicate their "secondary passions" for philosophy, poetry, opera, chess or whatever. The Gutenberg Society was formed around an ancient printing press presided over by Geoffrey Hoare, whose own elegant graphic skills were setting new standards for a profusion of internal magazines, and for concert and play programs. The latter were handsomely praised in 1957 by the *Times Educational Supplement*, which reproduced some of Bob White's "suave drawings". The same Supplement, which had said that drama productions when Taylor first arrived showed "as high a dramatic standard as any school in the country", now declared that Carol Forder's production of Pinero's *The Magistrate* was "unfailingly delightful", while Brian Townend's mould-breaking Summer Concert – an Entertainment illustrating various themes such as Work, Innocence, Wine, Women and Experience – "displayed a widely ranging musical intelligence", despite the inclusion of Bartok folk-songs and "a mercilessly academic palindrome by Machaut". Presented with an 8 mm. cine-camera, Brian Scragg and half a dozen enthusiasts were trying to learn how films are made. Clubs were urged to form links with town clubs, whether the Knole Golf Club or the Bolebroke Beagles. The academic pick of the Sixth Form were recruited into something called "University Nets": about sixty of them divided each week into groups of five or six which were taken by volunteer masters to discuss a wide variety of topics; tea was provided, and every fourth week the groups went to London to hear lectures, visit galleries or museums, the law courts or great industrial institutions. Cross-fertilisation between the Two Cultures was strongly recommended. "I deplore", said Taylor, "the foolish division in our education system between the Sciences and the Arts. There is no other country in the world which imposes so arbitrary and artificial a division upon boys still at school . . . Sputnik has underlined equally the importance of the humanities and sciences". Significantly, there was no reluctance among staff to be involved: on the contrary, a few were hurt not to be invited, fearing that they must lack the required intellectual bite and infectious zest.

Not to be outdone, Sue Taylor founded "Focus", an at first forbiddingly serious-looking Society for the Fifth and Sixth Forms, intended as an alternative to a traditional debating society, in which a fascination with the pompous rhetoric of parliamentary formality tends to obscure the subject under discussion. In Focus, a single major topic was chosen for the term, a relevant book prescribed and two lectures announced; a day of visits to appropriate places in London was arranged, in preparation for a final debate, when two outside speakers were supported by boys: members had to agree, on pain of fierce retribution and shame, to attend all four termly meetings. In the Lent term, 1959, they focused on India, and the programme was devised with the help and participation of the Taylors' old friends, Derek and Peggy Holroyde. The first meeting ended with a demonstration of Indian dancing by a young Indian lady, and *The Sennockian*'s reporter, David Gibbard, was quite won over: "It is doubtful whether the old Manor House has ever throbbed to such powerful rhythms. The magic of the bare feet and bells, tapering fingers and flashing silks still lingers".The second meeting welcomed Dr Gopal, an author and son of the Vice-President of India; the third took them to India House and later to dinner at Veraswamy's Restaurant; a fourth was a debate with Indian students invited through the British Council.

Sue Taylor's brother, Peter Kane Dufault, an excellent minor American poet, had agreed to judge entries for the Dufault Poetry Prize. Over one hundred and sixty poems were submitted, the best of which were included in *Numbers*, a beautifully produced anthology of Sevenoaks School poetry published in 1960. Designed by Taylor and his brother, with decorations by White, this attracted such favourable critical attention that the Headmaster and one of the poets were invited to a Foyles Literary Luncheon. That year W. H. Auden gave the first annual Sackville Lecture in the Manor House Library, and though his partly inaudible talk disappointed some, those fortunate enough to share the dinner-table with him that evening were properly dazzled. In 1961 the Sackville Lecturer was to be Earl Attlee. There is no doubt that young minds were being opened and broadened as never before, and though Taylor was not fooled by the "freak" score of 92% 'A' Level passes in 1958, he was pleased to see standards rising steadily despite the difficult working conditions, and growing numbers of confident young "culture vultures" in the Sixth flexing their wings. The Hay and Laurie Travel Scholarships, now augmented by one endowed by John Parks, were also encouraging exploration throughout Europe.

Taylor's policy of diversifying games, in order to give all boys the opportunity of enjoying at least one of them, did not find favour with everybody. In 1957, hockey, boxing and (scandal!) even rugby were dropped from the Lent term, to give a better chance to cross-country and athletics. Ironically, though during the following winter over 200 boys were laid low by "Asian 'flu", the 1st XV had one of its better seasons under Stuart-Smith and the promising Under 16 Colts (227 points For, 15 Against) won seven of their eight matches and drew with Tonbridge. The Games Fund provided the sailors with a second Firefly, "Plumtre"; fencing was started; beagling had its loyal supporters; and squash, despite a floor capable of turning the tamest shots into winners, was in great demand.

CHAPTER SEVENTEEN

The Great Experiments

Those who worked with and for Kim Taylor at this time tend to remember him, most of them vividly, for what he was rather than for what he did, as a remarkable *force de la nature* rather than an efficient leader clocking up one solid achievement after another. The many innovations which attracted so much attention in the sixties, and gained for "medieval/modern" Sevenoaks School the reputation of daring pace-setter among independent schools, seemed to most of the staff to flow as it were *naturally* from a man capable of making Staff Meetings occasions to be looked forward to. He worked very hard, and those about him were expected to do the same, but they were also expected to share his excitement, his restless refusal to believe that things couldn't be better. A few muttered about "gimmicky stunts" and deplored the strains imposed by constant change upon staff and pupils alike; many more were infected, more or less gravely, by the man's irresistible intellectual optimism, and convinced that his idealism and humanity were above suspicion. Certainly, Taylor was not averse to taking, now and then, deep draughts of the oxygen of publicity, but self-promotion was not his aim. One of his great qualities as a headmaster was his ability to delegate confidently to a member of staff the working out and implementation of a "Taylor Scheme", and then refuse to meddle; if, later, the project was praised, the chosen "man at the

THE GREAT
AND THE GOOD

48. Left, Sir Ralph Bosville, a governor from 1603 to 1637, grandson of Ralph Bosville who secured Letters Patent in 1560 changing William Sevenoaks' School into Queen Elizabeth's Grammar School

49. Below left, Thomas Farnaby, the first of many Farnabys serving as School governors

50. Below, John Frederick, 3rd Duke of Dorset (d. 1799) who sent his Chinese servant and one of his illegitimate children as pupils to the School

51. Left, William Pitt, 1st Earl Amherst, c. 1830. His family served as governors from 1783 to 1924

52. Below left, Elijah Fenton, Headmaster 1708−10. He may, through family connections, have secured the architectural services of Lord Burlington

53. Below, Lord Burlington who provided a design for the new School House and Almshouses (1722)

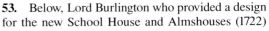

54. Above, George Heslop, Headmaster 1898—1919

55. Right, J.A. Higgs-Walker, Headmaster 1925—1954

56. Below, Higgs-Walker, Taylor and Geoffrey Garrod, Headmaster 1919—1925

CHARLES PLUMTRE JOHNSON

The Johnson family have been the most generous benefactors of the School since William Sevenoak. Their gifts include Park Grange **(16)**, Johnson's Boarding House **(29)** and the Johnson Hall **(30)**

57 & 58. Charles Plumtre Johnson **(57)** was Chairman of Governors from 1926 to 1938. He presided over the Quincentenary Celebrations in 1932. The photograph below shows him on that occasion with the Headmaster and the Guest of Honour, Dr Temple, Archbishop of York and later Canterbury

RECENT BENEFACTORS

59. Right, Jack Aisher, Governor 1964—1986, whose company, Marley Tile plc, donated the Marley Sports Hall

60. Below right, Mrs Eileen Aisher, donor of the Aisher Music Centre

61. Below, Frank Warwick, Governor 1964—1984, in the language laboratory donated by the Worshipful Company of Pipemakers and Tobacco Blenders

62. Kim Taylor, Headmaster 1954–1968, his wife Sue and the School Prefects in 1955

63. Above, Lord Sackville, Hereditary Governor and current President

64. Right, Gerd Sommerhoff, the moving spirit of Vista

65. Below, the Duke of Edinburgh meets some veterans, 1966. (l to r) Brian Townend, Ron Wheeker, John Parks, Ernie Groves

66. Alan Tammadge, Headmaster 1971–1981 and Robert Froy, Chairman of Governors 1983–91 welcoming the Queen Mother, 1980

67. Richard Barker, Headmaster since 1981, his wife Imogen and two recent School Captains.

coal-face" was allowed to take the lion's share of the credit.

The Voluntary Service Unit

At Speech Day, 1960, to which he had invited the Director of the British Council, Sir Paul Sinker, Taylor announced, with something like embarrassment, the launch of an Appeal to provide better facilities for minor sports in general, and a new swimming pool in particular, for which Lord Sackville had kindly granted a beautiful site in the valley between School and Duke's Meadow. These "pleasant amenities . . . which I cannot myself regard as an essential part of education", would cost, with a great deal of self-help from Digweed, about £10,000, half the sum it was hoped to raise. As to the other half, "we have been anxious . . . that any appeal that we make should not be simply for yet more privileges"; the Appeal Brochure set out two ways in which the School hoped to be able to serve others: a Voluntary Service Unit and an International Sixth Form Centre.

Taylor had always keenly supported Voluntary Services Overseas: he and Robert Birley of Eton were the two schoolmaster members of Alec Dickson's original committee. Dickson had come down and fired boys with his own missionary zeal. The previous school captain, Julian Blackwood, had just completed a year in charge of a remote settlement of Amerindians in British Guiana, and Tim Berry and Colin Ball had just been selected for service in Nyasaland and Malaya respectively. It was now proposed to set up a Voluntary Service Unit at Sevenoaks to help prepare boys for such service overseas, particularly in education – "by far the most desperate need, and the key to a better future in all under-developed countries". At the same time, Taylor realised that only very few boys would have the opportunity of working for V.S.O., and "wondered whether we could find a way of making the notion of service more normal in schools . . . If such remarkable things could be done by boys who had so recently left school, then plainly what could be done by schoolboys was much more extensive than had previously been supposed". Kurt Hahn, the founder of Gordonstoun, had come to Sevenoaks and spoken movingly of what young people could do to arrest "the decay of care and skill, the decay of enterprise and adventure, the decay of compassion". Lacking Gordonstoun's opportunities for beach and mountain rescue, could not schools in ordinary, town, suburban or country settings find other ways to help those in need? After the best part of a year of local enquiries and visits, twenty worthwhile jobs were identified, suitable for school-age volunteers and each requiring at least two hours' work a week. This, Taylor decided, was enough for a start. He had a first-rate young man in mind to run the scheme: Neil Patterson, just appointed to teach History, agreed to take it on, and the first volunteers were called for. Nineteen came forward: a pause for reflection . . . the School

Captain added his name, the Voluntary Service Unit was born, and school-based community service of the active, everyday sort began to grow.

A Governor, Stuart Chiesman, had just set up a permanent Trust, the proceeds of which were to go to the new Unit. In the event, the law, proving itself a more than usually egregious ass, forbade the use of Trust funds – or indeed of County Authority grants – on the grounds that the direct beneficiaries would be the people helped, not the schoolboy helpers: thus the Unit was not strictly educational. As Neil Patterson put it: "Buy spades and cultivate school allotments – that's education; buy spades and look after an old person's garden – that's not".

Nothing, however, could dampen the growing enthusiasm, nor obscure the fact that a hitherto concealed source of energy and idealism had been tapped. The Unit first concentrated on the needs of the old and the handicapped young. Patterson recalled that volunteers for the first twenty jobs came forward, "even after a fierce and deliberately off-putting account from the Headmaster of the likely difficulties and demands of regular social Service". At the Headmasters' Conference in 1962, Taylor eloquently urged upon other schools the value of such a unit, however small:

> First, it is a fresh assertion of the values I imagine we all hold to but which somehow are not reflected very clearly in the institutions and arrangements of our schools. Second, such a group or unit provides a rallying point for many decent boys, nervous perhaps about organisations that require uniforms, oaths and promises. Third, a Voluntary Service Unit helps to give boys an understanding of the society they live in. It is a society which in a most extraordinary way manages to sweep the crumbs under the carpet. The not very beautiful processes of growing old are carefully shut away from our eyes; the difficulties of the deformed, the spastic, the blind, we scarcely ever come across, for we have provided separate institutions for them. This is a shoddy way of meeting the needs of such people.
>
> A great many boys feel that for far too long they are barred from doing anything useful or practical. It is as though, having extended dependent babyhood through years undreamt of by previous generations we have devised compulsory secondary education to help with the baby-sitting. Their clubs, their games, even their studies, must seem at times like taking part in an eternal ritual dance only remotely, symbolically, related to the hunt they will take part in – one far-distant day.

It was no good urging young people to do good, to be positive or unselfish: they would recoil with horror and fashionable cynicism from such labels. But put them in a real situation where they can actually do something for someone weaker and less fortunate than themselves, and they will often react very

178

differently – especially when they realise that no glamour is involved, and probably no embarrassing gratitude either.

> The old, the handicapped or deprived young are seldom nicer, easier to deal with than the average run of people. The brats you help across the road lark about and seldom say 'Thank you'. Litter is consistently horrid. It is simply that there is a surprising amount to be done and 'it is better to light a candle than shout at the dark'.

This was to prove an influential address, and many schools sent delegations to Sevenoaks to see the Unit at work and learn about its organisation. Two years later there were 100 boys involved, including some from the Wildernesse Secondary Modern School, and some 80 girls from Walthamstow Hall and St. Hilary's, doing ever more varied, ever more responsible jobs: manning school crossings (after rigorous training by the police); boys and girls, working in pairs, visiting old people to garden, wash up, clean and decorate; helping in local hospitals, in schools for the blind, the educationally sub-normal, the physically handicapped and the emotionally maladjusted; one boy, a talented potter, taught a group in an Approved School; some volunteered to work in the holidays, for instance with the Franciscan Brothers at Plaistow in the East End of London, or with the W.V.S. and 'Meals on Wheels'.

The initiative was welcomed enthusiastically by the town. Under a full-width front page headline, the *Sevenoaks Chronicle* applauded the School's involvement in crossing patrols and the collection of litter:

> For many years Sevenoaks School maintained a certain aloofness from the everyday business of the town and its people, but lately its headmaster, Mr L. C. Taylor, has encouraged, by various activities, a feeling that the school is much more part of the place from which it takes its name. The school's most recent experiment is one which will commend itself to serious-minded people . . . it provides an opportunity for boys to engage in civic duties which are of great benefit to the town.

The Unit continued to expand throughout the 1960s as other schools became involved and the range of its activities was greatly extended. It was the subject of one of London University's open lectures on Education and of a session of the Voluntary Services Conference at Nottingham University.

Neil Patterson, with no previous experience of this work, quickly became one of its most passionate advocates; he was later to write the Schools' Council discussion paper on "Community Service" and to become Deputy Director of Education for Leicestershire. He was succeeded by the hugely energetic David Howie, who was later to be Director of the National Youth Bureau and subsequently Director of Community Education at the Open University. The right hand of both Patterson and Howie was Diana Day, a devoted School Secretary and a remarkable person to whom the Unit, the School and the community owe a great debt. School histories seldom pay adequate tribute to the generous contribution to the quality of school life made by non-teaching staff – secretaries, bursarial staff, matrons, lab assistants, groundsmen, gardeners, handymen, medical and domestic helpers – and perhaps in saluting the career of "Di" Day some small amends can be made to them. Secretary to four Headmasters, as contemptuous of the constraints of her "official" working day as of the comforts of retirement, she cheerfully doubled and doubled again the time she devoted to co-ordinating the activities of the burgeoning Voluntary Service Unit. The list of requests for regular help grew in number and variety, and soon some of the growing army of volunteers had to be transported to and fetched from surrounding villages as well as the town; more and more drivers had to be found; tools, paint brushes, mowers – even a tandem for blind children to ride with a sighted partner – had to be borrowed and returned; sick helpers had to be replaced and those expecting them notified. Eventually all this activity meant each major activity, and each school, having its elected boy or girl committee and secretary, but in the early years nearly all the intricate juggling was done by Diana. When David Howie left in 1972, Kent County Council, recognising the Unit's growing importance, agreed to pay for a replacement, and Malcolm Groves was appointed Youth Tutor, based at what was then Hatton School. At the same time a town Volunteer Bureau was set up, the first in Kent, funded by grants from Social Services. Its pioneering purpose was to encourage volunteer adults to meet community needs, and its first full-time paid organiser, on her retirement from the School, was Diana. Through her house have passed generations of boy, girl and parent volunteers, teachers and their families, and an inexhaustible flow of friends of all ages, hale and handicapped, who come to talk and laugh with her, or to be comforted, and to draw strength from her strength.

The Sixth Form International Centre

The next innovation to attract headlines was the opening in September, 1962, of the Sixth Form International Centre, formerly the Ormiston Hotel in Oak Lane. Taylor had nursed this project for at least six years. At last, with the support of the British Council, the encouragement of the Headmaster of Eton, Sir Robert Birley, substantial financial aid from Shell and British American Tobacco (and later from the Dulverton Trust), and the approval of the Governing Body, the bold decision was taken and another pioneering "experiment" was under way.

Taylor had become convinced, in the course of British Council sponsored tours, that there was an urgent demand from boys in many countries for Sixth Form education in England – and not only from developing countries in dire need of highly-trained people, yet without advanced secondary teaching or universities of their own: some, perhaps from America or from the English-speaking Commonwealth, wanted to spend a year or two in the country from which a significant part of their culture had stemmed; others, perhaps from European countries where English was widely taught, wanted to perfect their English before going on to university, technological or professional training, or directly into business in their own countries. The most important group of all, perhaps, were those who, having completed their school education at home, wanted to get into British universities. They now encountered the odd, indeed unique English requirement that two years of highly specialised work in their chosen university subjects should be done at *school*, not at university as in their own countries, where degree courses were at least two years longer. To achieve the necessary "Advanced Level" qualifications, many applied to English public schools, but only a token few were accepted: apart from the lack of sixth form boarding places, such young people were of an age, and of so different a conditioning, that injecting them into "normal" boarding houses, with their settled hierarchies and curious constraints, seemed to promise trouble for everyone. Many of those rejected ended up living lonely lives in digs in London or some other great city, attending Tutorial Colleges of sometimes dubious merit. Some, future political, administrative or commercial leaders of their countries, returned home with bleak memories of an inhospitable Mother Country.

For all these reasons, and also because he was certain Sevenoaks would become a livelier, more outward-looking school if it could make full use of the talents – and perhaps the constructively critical views – of a group of intelligent, highly motivated young men from very different national, social and educational backgrounds, Taylor decided that the new international boarding house should be structured and administered in such a way as to give them the fullest possible opportunity to contribute to its development.

Thus, though boys in the Centre were full members of the School and subject to all school rules, within the house they and their Housemaster, Brian Scragg, were invited to work out a form of 'self-government', a system of association based on certain optimistic assumptions: that the absence of younger boys would remove the necessity for constant supervision by Prefects or Monitors; that the English members admitted, selected for their intelligence as well for their interest in internationalism, would be sufficiently intrigued to cooperate and not abuse; and that all these young men, for all their differences, would have enough common ground – the need to work towards some academic goal – to enable them to construct and regulate an orderly environment. As the Housemaster recalled in *Experiments in Education at Sevenoaks*, published in 1965:

> We did not lack warnings and sombre forecasts: our society would
> have no coherence; appalling problems of discipline would appear,

especially in the absence of prefects; the house was too comfortable and little work would be done; we would be able to make no serious contribution to school games, would have no 'house spirit'; we would become a charming freak show cut off from the other boarding houses and ultimately divorced from the school; our English boys would be spiritless long-haired refugees from the healthier rigours of other houses, or indolent eccentrics attracted by a novelty that would quickly fade.

The house was indeed comfortable, even when the massive beds and wardrobes had been removed and ingeniously-designed bunk-units installed; and yes, it was cosily small – at first only ten foreign boys, eleven English – but there was a price to pay: such a small house could justify only the bare minimum of domestic help, and boys were responsible for serving all meals, washing-up, bed-making and gardening. This came as a shock to some – one Nigerian boy briefly insisted that bed-making was woman's work – but eventually a virtue was made of necessity, and the organisation of these chores, particularly gardening, not only gave the elected Chairman and three members of the Student Committee a practical challenge against which to measure their success, but was invaluable when they ran close to the rock upon which so many idealistic schemes of 'self-regulation' founder – what to do with the offender against the House Rules for which he himself has voted.

Committees were elected twice a term, and had to include at least one English and one foreign boy. Study-bedrooms were occupied by three to five boys of different nationalities, and the Housemaster was empowered to make termly changes in the "ethnic mix" within rooms. In the first three years boys arrived from America, Argentina, Bermuda, Brazil, Canada, Cyprus, Denmark, France, Germany, Ghana, Hong Kong, Hungary, India, Iran, Ireland, Kenya, Nigeria, Pakistan, Poland and Portugal to join the English boarders and day-boarders (these were local boys sleeping and breakfasting at home, but otherwise living and working in the Centre and providing a valuable link between foreign boys and internationally-minded families). An International Club met at the Centre three or four times a term: a boy or boys would "present" a country by way of a home-prepared national buffet, a talk, a film or slides, then a Question and Answer session. To these meetings came other sixth form boarders and day boys, staff and interested local parents, several of whom became unofficial guardians of boys they befriended, inviting them home at weekends or during the holidays.

Confounding the cynics, house pride was strong from the start. The exhilarating sense of being special was sharpened by a steady stream of curious visitors: British, French and Japanese film crews; Headmasters, Educationalists, radio and press reporters galore. Flattering articles appeared not only in the provincial papers – the *Kent Messenger* was particularly generous in its comments under the headline "Sevenoaks School leads way in unique experiment" – but in the *Times, Telegraph, Guardian, Observer* and even (twice) in the *Christian Science Monitor*. However, the real excitement in the first year came from the weekly House Meetings where complaints were aired – guitars being played during the agreed silence periods, beds being left unmade, washing-up badly done, somebody working too hard late into the night – but where also, painfully, the responsibilities and necessary limits of self-government were identified, the need for sanctions was accepted, a workable Constitution drafted and finally agreed. If the International Centre was to be taken seriously, it had to enter teams for inter-House competitions: after all, it had as many older boys as any other Senior House. First responses to questions about the sporting preferences of the overseas boys were not promising: water skiing, from a Brazilian; polo, from an Argentinian; quail-shooting, from a Greek Cypriot; billiards, from a Portuguese; "walking in high places", from a Hong Kong boy. Yet, amazingly, in 1963, inspired and trained by Edwin Gale, Vice-Captain of the School 1st XV (who was also a Prefect, though of course he shed all power other than that of persuasion once in the Centre), their rugby team, including seven foreigners innocent of all but enthusiasm for the game, managed to reach the House Final, and there were only defeated by penalty kicks awarded against their ignorance of the offside rules. And when, in the Pentathlon, their basket-ball team, consisting of three Americans, one Canadian and a Brazilian, swept the board, one particular cause for scepticism had been firmly eliminated.

An Annexe was later added to the Centre to provide extra study bedrooms. Nevertheless, the House was still too small to be economically viable. Moreover, there was no separate accommodation for the Scraggs and their three children, who were cosily crammed into three bedrooms at the top of the house. In 1966 the Leche Trust offered to make a grant of £10,000 towards an extension, if the other £20,000 required could be found from the Appeal. However, it was decided to call in no more builders until the Dining Hall block had been completed. Thanks to the British Council, and to numerous articles in overseas newspapers, applications were flowing in, and selection was painfully difficult: in one year, for instance there had been no fewer than fifteen applications from excellent Kenyan candidates. A Danish boy, Peter Carl, won an Open Exhibition to Sidney Sussex College, Cambridge, in his second term in the Centre; a poor Nigerian boy, Ashiru Adeleke, was brought to the Centre by the Hugh Goffe Foundation, set up to honour the memory of a fine pupil who had died of bone cancer before he could join it.

The Worshipful Company to our Aid

Amid the chorus of praise for the Voluntary Service Unit and the Sixth Form International Centre, no doubt a few disgruntled voices could be heard asking whether charity ought not to begin at home, and whether Governors and

Headmaster would not do better to concentrate on providing those things the growing school so scandalously lacked: a dining hall and changing rooms for day boys, and a proper gymnasium. For years, day boys had been lunching in the Odeon Restaurant, and the announcement in 1960 that the restaurant was to close led Governors hastily to produce plans to turn the old gym into a dining hall, which would mean using part of Johnson Hall for indoor games and physical training. The crisis was averted, or at least deferred, by the intervention of R. J. Martin, who persuaded the Odeon Circuit to lease us the restaurant premises, where the K.E.C. agreed to provide us with up to 150 lunches each day. Certainly, neither Taylor nor the Governors would have been able for a moment to forget the need for more space and improved facilities. In 1960 the County asked them to increase their intake of Free Place boys from 30 to 34; the demand for fee-paying day and boarding places was yearly more insistent, and the competition for entry Scholarships ever keener.

At this point, new great benefactors came on to the scene: The Worshipful Company of Pipemakers and Tobacco Blenders, who over the following years were unfailingly to support the School at difficult moments – not simply with generous grants of money, but with an invariably imaginative and sensitive response to the needs of Sevenoaks pupils at particular times. The newly revived old Livery Company now proposed to support four Scholars, selected for qualities of character rather than academic excellence – a stipulation welcomed by Prep School Headmasters and particularly close to Taylor's heart; he, meanwhile, was proposing to the K.E.C. that the consequences of "11 Plus mistakes" might be mitigated by awarding County Places in the sixth form at Sevenoaks, not only to his own eligible boys, but to boys at Wildernesse School and Churchill School, Westerham, who obtained four or more 'O' Level passes. The Wildernesse Headmaster, Mr Streeter, warmly supported this idea, as an aid to his own efforts to persuade more boys to stay on to take the exam. Under pressure to meet rising demand, the Governors re-phased their building programme over three years, 1961–63, and contemplated various ways of meeting the estimated deficit of £38,500. For the first and last time in its ill-fated existence, the School's London property at 54, Lower Thames Street, brought relief rather than further headaches: bombed out during the war, it now became subject to a Compulsory Purchase Order, and the £7,500 offered by the Corporation of London was rather more than had been hoped for.

Academic, sporting and other successes in the early Sixties contributed to the School's growing reputation. In 1961, nine Open Scholarships and Exhibitions were won – one by Oliver Taplin, a future Professor of Greek at Oxford – together with three State Scholarships. The 1st XV had their first undefeated season since 1930, and Morgan and Duncan played for the Kent Schools XV. The 1962 Cross Country season was the best ever: all school opponents were defeated, and the School Eight failed by only 4 points to beat a very strong Blackheath team which included their five mile champion: in this race Gevers beat the ten-year-old School record by a magnificent 72 seconds, with Morgan only 49 seconds behind. Herb Elliott, Olympic Gold Medallist miler and former world record holder, came down to run (bare-footed and heavily handicapped) against six Sevenoaks boys – and came fourth! The Film Club surprised itself by winning the senior age-group prize in the Children's Film Competition organised by the *News Chronicle* and the National Film Theatre, with a short 8 mm. version of Prosper Merimée's *Mateo Falcone*: the cheque, handed over by Celia Johnson at the N.F.T., went towards the purchase of a very old, extremely heavy Zeiss Movikon 16 mm. camera. Lunch and Stacey, two brilliant sailors, won the Public Schools' Invitation Firefly Championship at Itchenor: their prize, a brand new Firefly dinghy awarded by Fairey Marine, was the largest non-returnable prize in British yachting, and was to be the first of five boats won by Sevenoaks sailors in future years, much to the chagrin of Bembridge, Pangbourne and Dover College, traditional past favourites.

The Technical Activities Centre

For many years, Taylor had felt that boarders had a great educational advantage over day boys, in that they had access to many school facilities outside the rigid structure of the time-table, which distributes Subjects in a row of water-tight boxes throughout the day. Suspecting that education only really begins when learning becomes self-motivated, he encouraged the proliferation of "minority interest" clubs – even purely recreational ones – in the hope of delaying the day boys' departure as soon as the last lesson was over: new societies catered for keen photographers, cyclists, anglers, jazz-lovers, table tennis players; Eric Toser taught judo; the Astronomical Society was building its own reflecting telescope and Patrick Moore had promised a visit; Hugh Mowat chaired the Young Sennockians, who met three times a week to discuss anything from pop music to mountaineering and had frequent expeditions to London.

And then there was the astonishing Lock-Up Rule, which required day boys to obtain their Housemaster's permission to go out in the evenings. Designed to encourage better homework, but also to lessen boarders' jealousy and discontent, it was fairly widely flouted, and was in any case, Taylor felt, a depressingly negative gesture. He told Governors that he wanted to revise the timetable to provide a little more breathing-space for individual work, and eventually allow the introduction of less rigidly compartmentalised courses: this would mean lengthening the school day, and make all the more urgent the need for a dining hall able to supply afternoon tea and snacks. Even more urgently needed, though, was someone like Gerd Sommerhoff. Better still, Gerd Sommerhoff himself. . .

Arguably, Taylor's greatest coup was luring Gerd Sommerhoff to Sev-

185

enoaks. Contact between the two was made in 1960, at the suggestion of a Sevenoaks Governor, Nicholas Sherwin-White, representing St. John's College, Oxford, where Sommerhoff was doing post-graduate work. Sherwin-White's son was then attending the Dragon School, where Sommerhoff had pioneered a quite new way of teaching science as a creative activity by way of a "Science Club". Taylor had been to see it in action, and was impressed. For the next two years there was much coming and going between Oxford and Sevenoaks. Leaving aside the probably decisive effect of personal sympathy generated by the meeting of two highly intelligent, original and inventive men, Taylor pulled it off by agreeing to build and equip at Sevenoaks a Technology Centre to Sommerhoff's specifications. In this case as in others, one can only admire the confidence and courage of the Governing Body in backing and financing what many Boards would have regarded as a hare-brained scheme quite inappropriate to a school struggling to make ends meet. Even after building had begun, the scheme trembled on the verge of collapse, for the academic world was already taking a lively interest in Sommerhoff's research into "The Electronic Simulation of Brain Mechanisms", working as a Nuffield Fellow with Professor C. Z. Young at University College, London. Professor Medawar wrote to Taylor from Sussex, intimating that it would be a waste of an unusual research talent to take him into schoolmastering. Fortunately for us, he chose to come, so passionately did he believe in the need to reform science teaching by directing it towards engineering and technology. The Governors agreed that he might have one day free each week to go on with his research, and to continue to present the B.B.C.'s distinguished series, "Discovering Science".

During the summer term of 1963 Sommerhoff was at Sevenoaks supervising the construction of the Technical Activities Centre. With a typical blend of scientific rigour and visionary fervour, he introduced himself, and his Centre, in the pages of *The Sennockian*:

> The purpose of the Centre is to provide facilities for all boys with technical and scientific interests, and a chance to pursue these activities in their spare time under adult guidance. But there will also be a year of school-time periods in the centre for younger boys so that they can become acquainted with the range of activities it caters for and perhaps at the same time acquire an interest in new hobbies. The building consists of a spacious laboratory, a reading room, a small machine-shop extension and a combined storeroom and darkroom. The main emphasis is on technical and engineering interests.
>
> In scope and organisation the centre is a new experiment. There are a number of reasons why for some time it was felt that there is a real need for a unit of this kind. First, of course, the centre will supplement the scientific side of the School by an active technological side. The strongest demand for this probably comes from the boys themselves.

Second, we live in an age of staggering scientific and technical advance. But the excitement of this advance, the spirit of innovation and scientific adventure, has little chance to penetrate into the classroom. This is not the fault of the teaching staff who are tied to an exacting syllabus. Nor can we hope for greater flexibility in the syllabus itself. The sheer complexity and inertia of the academic machinery would seem to rule this out. But we hope that to some extent the new technical centre will be able to compensate for this defect.

Then came some tempting glimpses: "a full range of electronic test equipment . . . a small computer-simulator . . . facilities for building boys' own transistor logic circuits . . . We intend to fit all the larger models built in the centre with radio control . . . we shall probably concentrate on boats and gliders or slope-soarers . . . gliders can be launched by catapult on Duke's Meadow and we may get some good slope-soaring on the Downs. To test the boats a pool has been built near to the centre".

We intend to keep invention and development in the foreground of our activities . . . Boys have their own world of science. There is plenty of scope for new ideas in that world, for new inventions or developments, and it would seem only natural that some of this work should be done in schools.

Another aim . . . is to get the boys personally involved in the stuff of science and technology. We hope that in this way many of the scientific quantities they meet in the lessons will cease to be merely abstract symbols and will come to stand for things that, they feel, personally concern them. . . Book knowledge and the ability to pass examinations are not always the things that count most. Initiative, enterprise, practical know-how, and a keen intuition for what paper-and-pencil schemes are most likely to prove successful in practice, are equally important if not more so.

Any boy with technical or scientific initiative will be given the 'go-ahead' . . . given the equipment and materials, and we stipulate only one essential condition: and that is that he should understand what he is doing.

That stipulation was crucial to Sommerhoff's method: the combination of discipline and creative freedom was the secret of the Centre's future remark-able successes – the Industrial Sponsorship Scheme, the many top prizes won in the *Young Engineer for Britain Competition*, the national *Schools Design Prize* for an electronic "Moon-writer" (the first machine that enabled a blind person to write) – and an O.B.E. for Sommerhoff. Not for him a boy wanting to build an ambitious transistor from a kit "with easy step-by-step wiring instructions" –

or at least not until the boy had completed some of the Centre's self-paced standardised courses (in this case probably those on Electricity and Electronics), by which time he would not only have learned how to operate an oscilloscope, become familiar with a number of basic circuits and learned the technique of soldering, but would also have constructed a simple transistor receiver. Each course consisted of a file of 30–50 record cards: a card would probably refer a boy to certain pages in a book in the library, then tell him to do a certain experiment which must be checked by the master before he moved on to the next card. A boy wishing to make a model aircraft had first to take a course on the elementary principles of flight and airframe construction, and learn to use the wind tunnel: here he studied the pressure distribution over an airfoil and learnt with the aid of the 3–point balances to trim an actual model suspended in the tunnel. On the practical side he would build a catapult glider which was tested in the tunnel, then catapulted off outside to compare practice with theory. The courses were followed by boys working singly or in pairs – often a young boy working with one considerably older towards a shared practical goal – and were constantly being amended and improved by the boys themselves.

In the academic year 1965–66, the Technical Activities Centre – now known to the boys by its Club name of "Vista", (Voluntary and Independent Scientific and Technical Activities) – was visited by more than two hundred scientists, industrialists and educationalists. One of Gerd Sommerhoff's heroes, Dr Barnes Wallis of "The Dambusters" fame, came to talk to the boys about the excitement and hazards of being an inventor, and came several times again to chat to boys who were making radio-controlled models from some of his own more radical designs such as his kite-winged plane. The Education Committee of the Federation of British Industries came in force. The Centre figured prominently in the Page Report on 'Engineering and the Schools', and on television in 'Science Survey' and 'Tomorrow's World'. Sommerhoff had addressed the Royal Society, the Institute of Mechanical Engineers, and the British Association for the Advancement of Science: some of his boys demonstrated their work at a crowded session. The Careers Research and Advisory Centre at Cambridge had raised funds from industry to produce a half-hour film about the Centre called "Creativity at School", which was shown to a distinguished gathering at the Shell Centre. A second building was added to ease the pressure, and to provide for work on automation, a place for finishing models, storage and room for long-term projects. The pool was enlarged, and given a "harbour" area with a ramp for model hovercraft and experimental amphibious devices, while the original building was extended to give a larger lathe section and a separate computer room: in the latter a computer programming machine was installed, linked to Marley Tile's big computer, into which the Company had kindly agreed that the Centre's programming tapes might be fed in "marginal time".

In July 1966 the School was honoured by the visit of H.R.H. Prince Philip, Duke of Edinburgh, who came to open the new wing of the Technical Activities Centre. Under lowering clouds his long-rehearsed arrival by helicopter was cancelled, and he arrived at the wheel of his own car in School House forecourt. There, our ebullient School Marshall, George Ball, resplendent in uniform and standing stiffly to attention in his best sergeant-majorly fashion, was somewhat nonplussed to find himself saluting and opening the passenger door to a complete stranger, while the Duke strolled casually away on the other side. Nevertheless, the visit passed off well enough, and was particularly appreciated by some of the outstanding sportsmen with whom he chatted, including sailors Michael Lunch and Robert Laird, and Carol Forder's son James, the Kent trampoline champion; and by boys at the Technical Activities Centre, whose work plainly intrigued and delighted the technologically-minded Duke.

In 1975, the historian Corelli Barnett asserted in the *Times* that public schools were "one of the keys to our decline, turning out by means of curriculum and the moulding influence of school life alike a governing class ignorant of, and antipathetic towards, science, technology and industry". That year, and for the previous seven years, the largest single entry into any profession from Sevenoaks School was into engineering.

CHAPTER EIGHTEEN

Many Kinds of Excellence

On October 25th, 1962, the Divisional Education Officer, Mr Bryant, had been in Sevenoaks addressing the first public meeting of A.S.E., a society formed to promote the Advancement of State Education. He discussed the possibility of the County meeting the increased demand for education in Sevenoaks by enlarging the two Secondary Schools, Wildernesse and Hatton, or alternatively by building a new selective school: this could be done, he thought, for about £200,000 and would in the long run be cheaper than bussing 500 children daily to Tonbridge.

Sevenoaks School Governors listened carefully. At the time the K.E.C. were paying the fees of 239 of the 597 boys in the School. They now asked for, and were granted, the right to appoint six Representative Governors to the Board. Even without their presence, every effort would have been made to keep fees as low as possible. Taylor warned that any substantial fee increase would probably lead to a slight reduction of applications for entry, particularly at eleven: a number of parents whose sons were awarded County Places at Judd or Skinners' were opting instead for fee-paying places at Sevenoaks, but this could change. Yet how else could the remaining essential amenities be paid for? Perhaps the School ought to consider again applying for a Direct Grant, which would allow a big reduction in fees?

There seemed, however, little immediate cause for alarm in those heady days, for the School was beginning to bask in a warm bath of favourable publicity emanating from all parts of the political spectrum. In the Summer of 1963, the *Observer* ran a series of three long articles on "Progressive Schools" by Caroline Nicholson. She argued that most of the gestures towards social integration made by the public schools were empty ones, involving patronising changes in their admissions procedures, "rather than in attitudes of behaviour".

But the truth is that growing-points in education cannot be pinned down to any type of school or to any system. Growth happens when various factors – not least of which is the personality of the head – interplay. Where there is diversity and integration you find progressive education, and you can find this at Sevenoaks School.

Listing the pioneering experiments being undertaken at Sevenoaks in voluntary social service, science teaching, internationalism and self-government, she praised the unbigoted relationship between an adventurous independent school and an enlightened Local Authority.

This arrangement means that all sorts of fruitless oppositions are resolved. Rich and poor, day and boarding, school and town. . .; tradition and progress; old and new (it has won 18 Oxbridge awards in three years and Gerd Sommerhoff is coming. . .).

Thinking and feeling come together here and spill over into many kinds of excellence; of relationship, of scholarship, of art. It is a mistake to suppose that high standards and humanity cannot go together. A sincerely co-operative head can attract and beget co-operation. This one has taught at Repton and at Dartington. Sevenoaks has a composite character that alone would make it unusual; it gets and gives the best of both worlds. This happy situation suggests a line of development, and we are beginning to hear more about co-operation between private and public education; but real marriages cannot be organised. They need the good will of the people involved.

This was all very fine. On the other hand, the recently launched Appeal was not going at all well. It had been launched rather naively, simply by sending out 2650 letters, and there had been only a 7% response. Clearly, professional advice was required: a Dr Hooker was asked to do a preliminary survey. The boarding houses were having terrible staff problems: School House appointed no fewer than sixteen maids in the course of eighteen months; Park Grange and Johnson's were without cooks for a whole term, and meals were prepared by Housemasters' wives and their matrons. The estimated costs of a kitchen in the proposed dining hall were soaring alarmingly. Taylor had read an article in *Educational Equipment* about a method used in Sweden: meals were pre-cooked, wrapped in tin-foil and deep frozen, then merely heated and served at the point of consumption. He had been to Messrs Smethursts' factory in Sydenham and tried one: not at all bad. Sir John Dunlop, Mrs Davis, Mr Chiesman and the Headmaster agreed to sample the meals at a Dunton Green factory, taking along a couple of boys as guinea-pigs: it was decided that the method was "not yet proven". Heavy snow brought down the School House gutters, almost dislodging the recently installed statue of William Sevenoaks, commissioned shortly before his death by Walter Judd, a long-serving Governor, and unveiled by the Bishop of London after a Service of Commemoration.

Despite these minor set-backs and worries, Taylor did not let the pace of change slacken. To launch a new policy of producing unpublished plays by contemporary dramatists, the hitherto sacrosanct School Play was abandoned in favour of a survey of "Trends in the 20th Century" being prepared by the Assistant Dramatic Critic of the *Observer*: this was to have been illustrated by scenes from contemporary plays, and would have given more boys than usual the chance to brave the footlights. In the event this ambitious project was not realised, and the Play was missed. In a perceptive Editorial in *The Sennockian*, Anthony Miles reminded the Headmaster that "the play served to concentrate the attention and energy of the School upon one work. It distracts from the deep-rooted anxiety which comes with the threat of examinations. Without a play this anxiety is left unchallenged, much energy undirected. The pressures remain. The pressure upon those caught up in the university rat-race, the concern of all with the ever-growing statistical importance of 'O' and 'A' Level examinations, the ambition of parents for their sons; all have tended to change the attitude of the pupils ... Schools are in danger of fostering the value of an outer-directed meritocracy, where a boy's only concern throughout his schooldays is the manner of his leaving them". Nevertheless, he conceded that Sevenoaks more often than not swam against this tide: "Indeed, we can be thankful that this School offers so enlightened an education in a cut-throat era".

Another attempt to spread opportunities more widely amongst boys of varying abilities was the Pentathlon, conceived and nurtured by George Alcock during the harsh winter of 1962. This was, with a few reservations from the die-hards, a great success, allowing far more boys to play the game of their choice (the five sports were rugger, soccer, basketball, cross country and shooting). At the same time, Day Houses were broken up into smaller Tutorial Groups to improve pastoral care, and to involve as many teachers as possible in this vital area. Though tutorial Groups combined when they had to produce teams, there were again a few who gloomily foresaw the death of the old

Die-for-the House Spirit, and its replacement by a desire to work hard for nice Mr Bloggs ("who isn't even *keen* on games!").

The Granada Cinema in Sevenoaks closed down. Taylor bought 100 seats very cheaply and had them installed in a Little Theatre and lecture hall, fashioned out of the remaining ruins of the Manor House stables and garages: in 1963 Peter Brook, Arnold Wesker, Malcolm Bradbury and others spoke here for Focus about the position of the arts and artists in society. Our own artists were doing well: in 1963 the work of six boys was chosen for the Children's Art Exhibition in London, and the Art Room continued to embellish the pages of *The Sennockian*, described by the National Association of School Magazines as one of the finest in the country. The Association asked to visit the School, and in their next Newsletter declared the standard of creative writing in the school "unsurpassed" – deserved praise for the work of Geoffrey Hoare and his English Department. Maidstone College of Art wrote to say that two of our boys "were in a completely different category from the other candidates", and to congratulate our art master. The Governors agreed to provide funds for magazines, including some specifically by and for the Lower and Middle Schools. The following year the Summer issue of *The Sennockian* was placed first out of 600 such publications by the N.A.S.M., and *Verve*, produced by N. A. Powell and entirely owned and run by sixth formers, was placed first in the "internal magazines" class and included in the British Council Touring Exhibition overseas.

These were indeed laurels, but there was to be no rest. The Headmaster spoke to his Governors about a project called The New Mathematics: Professor Thwaites was coming in June, 1964, to talk to parents and to Headmasters of Preparatory and Primary Schools; then, they really ought to know about Nuffield Physics and Chemistry and Biology: he was intending shortly to introduce pilot projects with single forms. And what about language laboratories? These were very expensive, and he had been investigating the possibility of using France itself as a "laboratory" by exchanging a whole form of thirteen and fourteen year old boys with a form in a French school for a whole term . . .

Thus the French Link was conceived. Gestation and eventual delivery involved Taylor – with Scragg as aide, and interpreter of some vigorous if villainous schoolboy French – in several visits to France in search of a like-minded school. Since 1956, up to ten sixth form linguists had each year spent a term in Paris, most of them exchanging simultaneously with boys from the excellent Jesuit-run Ecole St. Louis de Gonzague near the Trocadero, academically one of the best schools in the country. But they had no boarders, and only a roof-top set of tennis courts overlooking the Champ de Mars; moreover, their middle school timetable was far too rigidly organised to allow them to contemplate such a scheme. Visits to the British Council, the Quai d'Orsay and the Centre Pédagogique de St. Cloud were not encouraging: the extreme centralisation and standardisation of the French educational system appeared impenetrable to innovation. Finally, a sympathetic ear – and an attractively rural setting – were found in Pontoise, Sevenoaks' "twinned" town.

The Collège St. Martin de France, a school for some 800 boys, mostly boarders, was founded by the Oratorians in the nineteen twenties with the aim of adapting to French needs the best practices of English Schools. There was, by French standards, unusual emphasis upon the importance of creative out-of-school activities and games; the site was wooded and playing fields spacious. The pastoral element is very strong: boarding Housemasters do no formal teaching. The scheme proposed by Taylor – an Anglo-French form of 'paired' boys at Sevenoaks, a Franco-Britannique form at Pontoise, each spending half a term in each country – breached all kinds of French Ministerial regulations. Fortunately, St. Martin's Headmaster, the late Father Dabosville, a distinguished scholar and a man not easily daunted by bureaucracy, responded warmly, supported by one of his Governors, M. Chauvin, Mayor of Pontoise and an influential Senator. Working parties were set up, tirelessly led by Ron Wheeker at Sevenoaks; teams of teachers of all key subjects exchanged visits to compare curricula and discuss methods of selection and 'pairing'; each school appointed a young teacher to accompany its boys abroad. The success of the French Link, its subsequent extension to other age-groups, its popularity with the staff and children involved, were due to this meticulous preparation, and above all to the reciprocal visits of staff, generously supported by Sidney Bernstein, who also – here as always aware of the special value of money available for embellishments rather than for necessities – made possible the presentation to each French boy of a handsome book to make into a diary of his visit, a house tie, and of course the straw boater, le sacré biff.

Both schools insisted that the exchange term was to be no holiday: the boys were to be worked hard, their progress in all subjects – all taught in French in France, in English in England – carefully monitored. But many treasured prejudices were removed, many firm friendships established between *binômes* (pairs) and staff of the two schools. After 1966 there would be reciprocal visits by athletes, rugby teams, orchestras and theatrical companies; before long there were to be exchanges with schools in Switzerland, Germany and Spain. There is no doubt that, together with the International Centre, the Link , and the favourable publicity it attracted in both countries, was a significant early step towards the School's high international reputation, and towards its pioneering introduction of the International Baccalaureate as an alternative to 'A' Levels.

☆ ☆ ☆

In December, 1963, the Governors had produced a new five-year building plan, which was to cost no more than £100,000. Barclays Bank were sympathetic, though Mr Sanders and his Directors politely took leave to doubt "that the

Governors can accept a standstill on all capital expenditure outside the present programme for so long a period". They agreed to grant overdraft facilities to enable the programme to go ahead, but hoped that "no opportunity will be lost of finding further sources of capital finance as time goes on, whether by appeal or otherwise. Having said all this, I am asked to assure you that the bank watches the dynamic growth and development of the School with great interest, and we are anxious to support this so far as we are able".

The big item was the dining hall. The Governors had at last decided against the Top Tray method – foil-wrapped deep frozen food – and the architect of the Headmaster's House, Mr Lerche-Thomsen, was asked to produce plans for a hall with a conventional kitchen, and with four classrooms attached, one of which would be a specially equipped "English room" as recommended by H.M. Inspector George Allen. Lerche-Thomsen had already submitted plans for the three dormitories to be attached to the master's house in Park Grange, to accommodate junior boarders. By the spring of 1964 new covered lavatories for the boys had been completed, and masters had moved into their new Common Room in the old workshop above Swanzy Close.

In the summer, that year, two sad events occurred: Digweed's lovingly constructed Music Rooms were destroyed by fire, and John Parks retired after thirty-five years. He had been house tutor at Johnson's when Kim Taylor arrived there thirty years earlier; since then at various stages he had run the rugger, produced school plays, been senior English master, and with his wife Joanna had run Park Grange boarding house. Since his ordination he had been the first School Chaplain, and now moved 'just down the road' to become Vicar of Seal St. Lawrence. A tall, deliberate man with a sardonic turn of phrase, he had loved and taught English Literature in an unashamedly "old-fashioned" way, and felt little sympathy – though no contempt at all – for the more analytic Leavisite approach of the Cambridge moralists. Typically, when he learnt that Taylor was appointing a very bright young Cambridge English teacher, he had immediately offered to hand the department over to him (Hoare). No less typically, when the idiotic (and thankfully short-lived) Burnham ruling appeared, that sixth form teachers should be paid more than others, he had very quietly refused to accept the "differential" and asked that it should be used instead to fund travelling awards. A firm disciplinarian but deeply humane, he had lifted a quizzical eyebrow at some of his former pupils' "experiments" since 1954, but had been, like E.G., rock-steady in his loyalty.

Three years later he was to have the sad task of preaching at a Thanksgiving Service for Ernest Groves himself, who had retired in 1966 after forty-two years at Sevenoaks, thirty-four as Housemaster of Johnson's and seven years as Senior Master. With his charming, gentle, indomitable wife Marjorie, E.G. had earned the affection and respect of three headmasters and of countless masters and boys. When he joined the staff in 1923 there were 160 boys in the School, including one sixth former; when he left there were 684 boys, with 220 in the

Sixth, yet the memories of different generations of boys he taught or housemastered suggest a figure essentially changeless: extremely hard-working, and expecting hard work from others, whether boys or colleagues; almost fanatically methodical and tidy; as demanding of his beloved House as he was unfailingly kind to individuals in trouble; a fine all-rounder in his time, a gifted coach of rugby and boxing, he learned to sail, and to coach sailing, at an age at which most masters consider themselves exempt from such rigours; as Senior Master, always impeccably dressed beneath his ancient gown faded green, his shoes lovingly burnished, he set standards of courtesy, achievement and general behaviour rarely even hoped for today (*"Sorry* you're having trouble with your feet", he said with frowning concern to a young master, who had ventured one hot summer day to appear wearing sandals); an outrageously implausible raconteur, his steady gaze transfixing his listeners and making any visible expression of disbelief quite unthinkable. The legends that cluster about his name – many of them smilingly denied by E.G. with a deliberate lack of conviction, for he loved to tease – are too numerous to retail here, but he was, literally and metaphorically, a model schoolmaster.

"Experiments in Education" acclaimed

In the early 60s Constable's, the publishers, suggested that the School might produce a book about its current experiments, and in 1965 *Experiments in Education at Sevenoaks* was published, and quickly reprinted. It described the progress of the New Mathematics, the Voluntary Service Unit, the Sixth Form International Centre, the Technical Activities Centre, and the new developments in the teaching of English and Art. Reviewers were generous:

> "A significant contribution to the literature of educational reform" (Seamus Heaney, *New Statesman*); "An immensely exciting book" (Edward Blishen, *The Listener*); "There is every indication that the progress it (Sevenoaks School) has made will guide trends in education in every part of the United Kingdom and almost certainly beyond it (John Delin, *New Scientist*); "Anyone who left school ten years or more ago, and has since lost touch with developments in teaching, will find the book a revelation" (Duff Hart-Davis, *Sunday Telegraph*); "To a retired headmaster it comes as a shot in the arm. . ." (John Garrett, the *Sunday Times*); "This book will certainly have a powerful influence upon the craft of teaching in secondary schools of every kind. If the public schools remain, Mr Taylor (hateful though the idea may be to him) will surely be canonized as a "great headmaster" (D.L. Howard, *Education*).

Visitors flowed in, flattering articles multiplied, praising "imaginative new sculptures in the garden, original and good paintings on the walls, all made by the pupils . . . poetry: real unimitative poetry, with feeling about it". Others were struck by the good relationships between staff and boys: "They like and respect one another, not in the formal distant manner of the 'good public school' but more like enthusiasts working together creatively. They are more dependent on one another than teachers would usually care to admit".

A four-page article in *Where*, by Sonia Abrams, heaped lavish praise upon almost every aspect of the School's rapid development, but emphasised that Taylor was well aware that not every school could be treated as a test-bed: "Believing that Sevenoaks can be what it is only because it is independent and selective, he recognises the social injustice of the public school system, the inhumanity and waste of the 11-plus. Because there is much that is bad about our present pattern of secondary school provision, he is prepared to accept that Sevenoaks too may have to alter considerably".

In the wake of the Crowther Report of 1959 (recommending the raising of the school-leaving age to 16, and the creation of County Colleges for compulsory part-time education to 18), and the Newsom and Robbins Reports of 1963, informed public attention was now focusing upon the secondary educational needs of the average or less than average pupil, and upon the need to broaden the educational opportunities available in the higher sector – for instance by providing, and raising the status of, more Colleges of Advanced Technology. This new impetus was partly humanitarian and idealistic, but partly it stemmed from the age-old habit of seeing education as a defence against social change, not an instrument for moulding it creatively. The alarming increase in juvenile delinquency since the war, the decline in moral standards, the growth of materialism, the increased incidence of divorce, the base exploitation of crime, violence and sex by the popular press and sections of the entertainments industry – all these were loudly deplored, particularly now that the demand for labour was allowing teenagers to earn unprecedented wages. And so, though in the coming years distinguished and discriminating voices would continue to recommend Taylor's "liberating" methods, others, for political or narrowly ideological motives, tended to regard them as appropriate only to a privileged minority, the luxurious indulgences of an independence which might have to be sacrificed in the interests of a fully integrated state system and equal opportunities for all.

In the mid-sixties, however, Sevenoaks continued on its pioneering way, its enthusiasm and confidence undimmed by occasional murmurs of "exclusiveness" in the local press: after all, half its pupils were still paying no fees. "Perhaps", wrote the *Financial Times* in 1966, "if more headmasters had as much radicalism as Mr Taylor, the public schools would not now be embarrassed by Mr Crosland's searching scrutiny". On the other hand, in a long, extremely perceptive and largely complimentary article in *New Society*, Christopher Chataway raised an interesting question:

> Such doubts as one can summon about the school relate to its dynamism. Does it depend too much upon change? In, so to speak, harnessing the 'Hawthorne effect' – producing better results out of the determination to make a new idea work – does the school derive too much of its spirit and momentum from a rate of innovation that cannot go on accelerating?

> It is hard to see in which direction the school is now most likely to develop. If a totally comprehensive system were still the goal when the Kent Education Authority comes to reorganise the Sevenoaks area, there could presumably be no intake at 11 from the maintained system. While Taylor believes that the school could manage a somewhat wider ability range than now, he does not see that it would be capable of dealing faithfully with a fully comprehensive intake.

> These are uncertainties that lie ahead. For the time being Sevenoaks stands as one of the most exciting of post-war English educational growths. It must encourage those who want to bring the best of the independent schools nearer to the maintained system. It may give pause to those who see no future for selective schools. The only certainty is that it will go on changing – with perhaps some move towards co-education as a likely next step.

The Aishers and the Pipemakers

Meanwhile, the Governors were wrestling with the problem of financing their new building programme. At this juncture a new benefactor appeared, whose involvement in the School, both financial and administrative, was to be on a scale unknown since the days of Charles Plumtre Johnson. In 1964, Jack Aisher, a Director and later Chairman of the Marley Tile Company founded by his father, had agreed to join the Board. His shrewd business sense, his no-nonsense wisdom, his growing affection for the School, and his and his family's astonishing generosity in the years to come were to prove invaluable. The long-delayed Appeal was given the go-ahead, and the following year he became Chairman of the Campaign Committee.

At the Committee's next meeting Dr Hooker was asked to report the result of his enquiries, and to suggest a realistic target figure: he thought £50,000, or perhaps a little more. While the Governors were wondering whether – for a school without, as yet, too many captains of industry among their Old Boys, and at a time when many parents were straining to pay the fees – this might not be a shade optimistic, Aisher quietly announced that he and his Company would double any sums donated up to £67,500. Dumbfounded, Hooker and his team withdrew, returning within five minutes to announce that, in these changed circumstances, £150,000 might be achievable. The original dining hall project had grown into a Social Activity Centre and Dining Hall complex, including specialised English teaching rooms, an Art Room with facilities for pottery and printing, studios for film, photography and television, a small Drama Studio – and of course the long-desired Dining Room served by the most modern kitchens. Work had begun before the launch of the Appeal, but hardly more than an enormous hole in the ground had appeared by the middle of 1965, when it was decided to demonstrate confidence and generate public interest by unveiling the Foundation Stone: this was gracefully done by the former Conservative Minister of Education, Sir Edward Boyle, who spoke warmly of the School's remarkable progress, picking out for particular praise the "open sixth form" policy negotiated by Taylor and the K.E.C., which gave a second chance of grammar school education to those who had failed the 11-plus. Open Day gave way to a School Fete that summer, and over £1,200 was raised towards the Appeal, which was eventually to achieve an admirable total of £182,000.

Another great friend and benefactor of the School, Frank Warwick, had recently joined the Governing Body as the Pipemakers' representative, and he heightened the heady atmosphere by announcing,as head of the trustees of the Company's Benevolent Fund, their gift of £11,000 to be put towards a Language Laboratory. The following spring the Company endowed the first of two free berths on the Sail Training Association's great schooners, the "Winston Churchill" and the "Malcolm Miller". Yet more good news was on the way: one evening when the Taylors were dining with the Aishers, Eileen Aisher drew Taylor aside. She had heard, she told him, of the loss of the music rooms, and now wished to give by covenant a sum that would produce £17,000, sufficient, she hoped, to replace them. In the event, to Lerche-Thomsen's design, it provided the school with a handsome Music Centre consisting of a central auditorium, seven small and two large practice rooms, a staff room and a storeroom.

Creativity Rampant

The Art Department was asked to put on an exhibition at the Architectural Association, and had several 'outside' commissions, including graphic work for the Club Méditerrané and Paris-Pullman. A steady succession of boys were now doing their pre-Diploma work at Sevenoaks and moving directly into places on Diploma courses, avoiding the usual pre-Diploma year at a College of Art. The whole school, indeed, seemed to be buzzing with creativity: in 1965 no fewer than eight magazines appeared, representing all levels of the school, and two of them produced by single forms. The English Department was successfully encouraging the production of a great deal of very respectable and some highly original poetry: Richard Tibbets won second prize in the Under 19 Poetry Competition organised by the *Critical Quarterly*. In this respect the Department had been strengthened by the arrival, fresh from detention in South Africa, of the young future Master of Wellington, Jonty Driver, whose novels had been praised by Cyril Connolly. The Head of Drama, Ben Bradnack of the demonic cackle and a passion for variety verging on the indiscriminate, managed to involve more than half the School in drama by way of a junior competition and a senior Festival of short productions. The School Play was *Andorra*, by Max Frisch, but there were also productions of *Waiting for Godot, The Caucasian Chalk Circle, Murder in the Cathedral, The Caretaker, The Tiger's Bones* (by Ted Hughes) and a Chinese folk play. The Music Department, while their new butterfly-roofed home was still rising at the north end of the Flat, had not been idle: the *Echo Mountain Boys* won two sections of the National Folk Music Competition at Cambridge, and played in a session with Bill Clifton at the International Celebrity Folk Concert at the Royal Albert Hall. School jazz musicians put on a concert and made a record in aid of the Appeal, and one of the Christian Fellowship spiritual singers' numbers was included by Donald Swann in his collection of new church music, *Sing Around the Year*.

With all this going on, one may wonder, were boys finding time for any work? In fact, they were working quite well, even if by today's exam-obsessed standards the statistics would not impress. In 1966–67, the 'O' Level pass percentage was 78.5%, the 'A' Level pass percentage 70%, and this was regarded as an academically satisfactory year. Taylor had long battled against the growing tendency to measure a successful education in these terms. It is interesting to see, in this high-achiever, this dynamic accumulator in his youth of academic and sporting records, something like a hatred of competitive exams, or at least a deep suspicion of the narrowing effect, upon the minds and sensibilities of the young, of a concentration upon exam results. He would seldom, if ever, seek to dissuade an academically weak boy from staying on to take 'A' Levels, for in the sixth form there was so much more to be gained than Certificates, in terms of the broadening and deepening of a boy's interests in a whole range of activities, many of them not academic at all. What he was proud of, looking back over twelve years, was the sevenfold increase in the number of 'A' Level subjects taken: 52 in 1954, 93 in 1958, 259 in 1962 and 345 in 1966. He was distressed to notice, on studying the reports written by boys returning from their French Link stay in Pontoise, "their worry about the effect five weeks' absence in France would have on their academic progress. The conventional persuasions of schoolmasters and parents seem to have been accepted all too readily; the anxiety derived from a competitive society and a competitive system seem to be felt even by thirteen year olds, two years from their next serious exam. All rather horrid; their worry is worrying".

The tide of social and demographic change, however, was difficult to resist. The "bulge" had hit the university entrance stage in 1965, and there were now far fewer places available in relation to applications, especially in Arts subjects. In a few years' time doubting voices would be raised, wondering whether a boy could "afford" to spend so much time visiting an old lady, or enjoying himself making music or doing Voluntary Art or Voluntary Workshop, or debating the Future of Democracy. For the moment Taylor pursued with undiminished energy and passion his aim of giving every boy the opportunity to discover his own talents and strengths, by providing as great a choice as possible in every area of school life. Games "options" for boys over 14 were extended to include Athletics, Swimming, Fencing, Rugby, Soccer, Trampolining, Gymnastics, Weight-training, Cross-country running, Riding, Sailing, Tennis, Cricket and Shooting. It was recognised that competitive results in the 'major' games might suffer, but hoped that this would be amply offset by an improvement in the standard of the 'minor' sports, and by a general increase in enjoyment. Combined Cadet force activities were widely diversified: less drill now, but more horse-riding, shooting, motor maintenance, and building and use of climbing walls, with annual camp and arduous training in the holidays.

At the same time Taylor was encouraging his staff to investigate and experiment with new ways of teaching their subjects – by writing new courses themselves, by using more technical aids, above all by replacing the old formula – silent rows of rather passive, note-taking pupils – by others involving boys in the excitement of asking and then answering their own questions. Lord Bernstein's gift of a new Fellowship allowed the appointment of an extra man each year to a different department, thus releasing staff for this kind of research. Ronnie Bate introduced a new method of teaching Latin; a Business Studies 'A' Level course was introduced, in collaboration with Marlborough (where Richard Barker – later to be our Headmaster – had devised it) and Lawrence Weston School Bristol; new 'O' Level English papers were produced by Sevenoaks and Bedales, designed to blur the rigid distinction between English Literature and English Language; in the lower forms, where Geography, History and Divinity were competing for an adequate allocation of periods, an integrated course called "PEB" was devised: the geographical Predicament of a people was studied, and its historical Experience, to see what system of Belief had sustained them; guinea-pig boys were found in quiet corners, sitting in front of teaching machines, working through 'self-paced' courses; by 1966, Nuffield Chemistry and Biology had been running for two years, and Nuffield Physics was being introduced.

That same year Taylor became personally involved in a major national enquiry into teaching reform. The Sixties had seen a review of the content and sometimes the methodology of subjects taught in schools, a task at first undertaken with the support of the Nuffield Foundation, then of the government-funded Schools Council. The Director of Nuffield, Brian Young, asked Taylor whether he would lead the 'Resources for Learning Project'; when he said no, Young proposed a triumvirate in which Taylor would be Experimental Director. This seemed likely to be stimulating, potentially valuable to the School and manageable: Nuffield offered to pay for an extra member of staff so that Taylor could spend two days a week in London on the research phase of the Project, with Scragg (then Under-Master) released to take over the Headmaster's job in his absence. The Governors agreed to this. If they felt any unease, they did not show it, but chose to regard the appointment as "a recognition of the good work in education the masters and the boys have been doing in recent years". His involvement "should involve the school being in touch with the best methods and developments both in this country and abroad".

During the next two years Taylor spent holidays on visits to Sweden, Russia, France, Holland and twice to America, to find out what of interest was being done. In visits to British schools, and by research, he tried to discover why such once widespread and promising educational developments as P.N.E.U. (Parents National Educational Union), the Dalton Plan and Differential Partnerships had foundered. Some preliminary experiments were launched, mostly in comprehensive schools; at Sevenoaks, the Modern Languages department collaborated in devising self-instructional courses in French for younger children.

A Rescue

Despite his always avid interest in new developments in education, Taylor had in fact taken time, in the mid-Sixties, to rescue something from the past. Intrigued by the disappearance of the valuable Boswell Exhibitions, once so firmly attached to "a farm called Hollywell in Burnham in Essex", he discovered that in 1877 the endowments of the Trust had been translated from land into Consols. Rather vague provisions were made governing the award of these exhibitions, culminating in the Charity Commissioners' "Scheme of 1919", by which "the Governors may maintain Leaving Exhibitions for boys who are and have for not less than two years been in the School. . . Two at least of these Exhibitions are to be called Boswell Exhibitions". A sad dilution of a great bequest! No mention of Jesus College, in whose Prayers the Lady Margaret is remembered as a benefactor, and whose Fellows had once regularly visited the School "to prove ye capacities of ye lads . . . (and for want of lads fitting here then from Tonbridge School)". It was understandable that in the nineteenth century, when Sevenoaks had remained virtually unchanged as a little local grammar school, in close contact with its almshouses, its Parish

Church and its Town, the Exhibitions should have become an anomaly and probably a temptation to fraud; for, since Sevenoaks then had no Sixth Form, and since universities were then beginning to expect entrants to be 17 or 18 years old, "lads fitting" were usually obliged to move on to one of the bigger schools which had more fully absorbed the Arnoldian belief in the supreme importance of Prefectorial responsibility, and had thus tended to cut themselves free from their local roots and obligations. But now? Taylor approached the members of the Common Council of Jesus College, found them well disposed to a revival of the awards, and in 1965 a boy called Curtis became the first Boswell Exhibitioner since 1899. To cement the relationship, a representative Fellow of Jesus College joined the Fellow of St. John's, Oxford on the Governing Body.

Tinkering till we get it right

Though he was now doing two taxing jobs, and despite having to plan the School's response to the imminent reorganisation of secondary education in Sevenoaks – not to mention the possibility raised in the Buchanan Report of an Eastern Way driven between the main campus and Duke's Meadow, perilously and noisily close to the new Music Centre – he set about a radical revision of the school timetable with the aim, amongst other benefits, of encouraging the local community's incursion into the school. David Howie was appointed to look after Voluntary Service – the Unit was now over 500 strong – and also the "Saturday Exes", the range of lectures and activities that were scheduled after break on Saturday mornings for parents as well as Lower Sixth boys in mixed adult-boy groups. Other important changes in the timetable were the inclusion for all boys of an afternoon of "Facilities" (art, music, technical activities, workshop, drama and the like), and an arrangement by which, according to the length of a term, every third and fourth Saturday would be a holiday. Over these Long Weekends, which would give scope for Outward Bound type expeditions, boarders could go on leave from Friday after school, and there would be no "lock-up" or prep on Saturdays, when 'Sunday clothes' could be worn after 4.30 p.m. The school day was lengthened a little, prep shortened; to relieve pressure on the playing fields, boys in the Lower Fifth and above found themselves playing timetabled games on Monday, Wednesday or Friday afternoons; on Thursday afternoons older boys did C.C.F., Digweed or V.S.U., while younger boys did games.

Recognising that the school had now grown so large that many boys might lose "a sense of participation and a sense of personal worth", Taylor now proposed sub-dividing it into four Divisions: the Upper School, Middle School A, Middle School B, and the Junior School. Each would have a master-in-charge, responsible for both boarders and day boys within his group. Assembly and, whenever possible lunch – for the new Dining Hall could cater for boarders at midday – would be by Divisions.

Jack Robinson, the School Timetabler, showed no signs of hysteria, merely clenching his teeth a little tighter on his pipe and allowing himself the ghost of a tolerant smile. It should be said that these changes had been widely discussed for over two years, and would have been introduced earlier had not the Governors, alarmed by the requirement for extra staff to implement them, decided that a delay was advisable until the final cost of the new buildings was known.

This was probably wise, for it gave Taylor a little more time to convince the doubters:

> Every surface change implies all sorts of less obvious changes. Every hoped-for improvement must, of course, make sense in the lives of boys and masters: but, in addition, it will involve additional staff and additional building (and that means finding money); and involves change to settled patterns of life, which few of us like. Goodwill is vital: otherwise the best laid schemes can founder on a cleaner's broom. . .
>
> What is proposed is, of course, *experimental*. All sorts of modifications will prove necessary in practice, and all sorts of bright notions will occur to people for improvements. But we need to have something to start with: then we can tinker until we get it right.

As it turned out, the tinkering would have to be done by his successors. It is a measure of the Governors' courage, and of their confidence in the soundness of Taylor's approach, that when they finally agreed to these radical reforms they already knew that he was going: in February, 1968, he had announced that he had accepted the full-time post of Director of the Nuffield Foundation's "Resources for Learning" project. The Governors' Minutes record Lord Sackville's gracious reaction to this hardly welcome news: "They were very sorry that he was going to leave. One always liked to feel that a Headmaster stayed to see through to the end various things the school was doing, but at Sevenoaks there was never an end since something new was always being started. The Chairman hoped that the Governors were going to be able to find a successor who would continue in the tradition that Mr Taylor had started and so ably pushed ahead. . . He wished to record the Governors' appreciation of all the Headmaster had done".

Valete

Inevitably, there was speculation as to why Taylor should choose to leave at this time. Was he perhaps feeling restless, fretting at financial constraints and at the slow progress – despite Jack Aisher's forceful bottom-kicking – of the Dining Hall/Art Room/English Teaching/Social Activities Centre? Was the test-bed becoming too cluttered? With all his "experiments" now flourishing, did he sense that a time of prudent consolidation, alien to his nature, might be approaching? Or was he simply exhausted after fourteen hyper-active years? If so, he gave no sign of it. That Easter holiday he was in Salonika selecting the first two Schilizzi Scholars, who would spend a year at the International Centre before going on to university, one to St. John's, Oxford, the other to Sussex, their fees paid by the Schilizzi Foundation; the first Schilizzi Fellow, a Greek Schoolmaster, Alexis Dimaras, was already on our staff: all the complex arrangements with the British Council and Salonika University and schools had been devised by Taylor on the Foundation's behalf. Nowhere was there any sense of 'winding down': the Pipemakers Company had just endowed a concert in memory of a past Master, Alan Adler, and in June the first memorial concert was given in the brand new Music Centre, now named the Aisher Hall after its donor; thanks to a chance meeting between Taylor and Colonel Moss on a crowded train journey to London, and to the kindness of Lord Sackville, the Royal Engineers carried out 'levelling exercises' on Duke's Meadow – upon which we could lay a quarter-mile track with a rugby pitch inside it, and Mr Chiesman's Trust generously offered to finance the all-weather surfacing of the track; the School bought an acre of land, once the Royal Oak vegetable garden, and hoped to put tennis courts on it.

No, it is very unlikely that Taylor's departure was in any sense negative. He loved the School, and despite inevitable approaches had never been tempted to move on to any of the great 'traditional' public schools. Certainly he had no fears of Government Circular 10/65 and the possible coming of comprehensive education; no doubt he would have relished the challenge. But he had been heard to say that fifteen years was probably enough to headmaster a school, that, after that, there was a danger of losing the ability to see its problems freshly, of too often 'switching to auto-pilot'. Perhaps, at the still young age of 45, he felt that, if ever he was to leave Sevenoaks, now was the time, for the chance of heading a major enquiry into new teaching methods, and of conducting experiments on a national scale, might not come again. His influential Penguin Educational Special: *Resources for Learning*, quickly reprinted and translated into other European languages, was a wide-ranging but refreshingly jargon-free attempt to pierce the fog of conflicting ideas about the real purposes of education, and to find practical ways of reconciling the rival claims of Relevance ("relevance *now* or relevance *forever*?"), exam success, timetable-dominated classroom teaching, independent self-motivated learning, the precision-training of fine minds or the robust nurture of good citizens. In this book he drew deeply upon lessons learned during his extraordinary years at Sevenoaks, for which he declares himself grateful: the School, for its part, must long remain profoundly grateful to him.

CHAPTER NINETEEN

A Clash of Styles
Michael Hinton

It is not proposed to follow the practice of many authors of School Histories, who discreetly spare the blushes – whether of pride or shame – of the more recent directors of a school's fortunes. Important things have been done in the last twenty-five years – by Headmasters, Governors, staff and pupils – and these ought to be recorded, even if final judgment must in many cases be reserved as to their lasting effect. On the other hand, not one of Taylor's successors would begrudge the space that has been devoted to his extraordinary achievement in lifting a decently obscure public school into the glare of national and international acclaim, or expect an equally detailed account of their own considerable achievements: those must await future historians.

Some of the developments of those twenty-five years – some of the new buildings, for instance – were an inevitable consequence (once they could be afforded) of the expansionist policies pursued by Higgs-Walker and Taylor under friendly pressure from the K.E.C. and fee-paying parents. On the whole, Alan Tammadge and Richard Barker thoroughly approved the main thrust of Taylor's reforms and innovations and, while firmly stamping their own personalities upon the School by the emphasis they laid upon some rather than upon others, have been more than happy to pursue the same ideals. The Government's policy of ending the system of Direct Grant schools led to the socially and educationally regrettable decision by the County Authority to send no more Free Place children to Sevenoaks. While Kent was faced with a fall in the local birthrate and the prospect of unused capacity in their own Tonbridge schools, their decision was deplored by the School's Governors, but they had to make the best of it, and in the circumstances a very good best it has been.

There were eighty-five applications for the post of Headmaster. With Taylor's advice Lord Sackville reduced these to twenty, and full details of those twenty were sent to the Selection Board. Ten were invited to be interviewed, with their wives, at the Granada offices in London on May 3rd 1968. The Selection Board had intended to ask three to meet the full Board, but "considered two so outstanding that there would be no purpose in inviting a third." The Governors interviewed the two on May 7th, and after discussion the appointment was offered to Dr. Michael Hinton, who had been for eight years Headmaster of Dover Grammar School. Educated at Bristol Grammar School, he gained a "First" in History at Merton College, Oxford and a Doctorate in early 19th Century Parliamentary History as an external postgraduate student at Reading University. Many of his activities at Dover suggested a close sympathy with much that was being done at Sevenoaks: he had reorganised the timetable to minimise specialisation, encouraged the multiplication of school games and activities, produced plays and Gilbert and Sullivan operas, introduced a School Council with mainly advisory but some absolute powers, instituted a course of General Studies in the Sixth, and had been the first Chairman of the Dover Schools Community Service Unit.

☆ ☆ ☆

Hinton spent his second Sunday at the school helping to mop up after the floods, which had done a great deal of damage in the Aisher Hall, the Dining Hall, the Concourse (the 'milling-about' area on the ground floor of the Dining Hall block) and the boiler house. Quite undaunted, at his very first Governors' Meeting, the new Headmaster showed his readiness to comment confidently and trenchantly upon the conduct of school affairs. Fortunately, the new running track had survived, and he "congratulated the Governors on authorising such an ambitious project." He was fairly polite about the new timetable: "an immense improvement in nearly every respect, but it was stretching staffing and facilities to the absolute limit." The Governors had already authorised plans for new Biology laboratories – two huts and a greenhouse in Manor House garden – but the provision for physical education and games was quite unsatisfactory: Johnson Hall was totally unsuitable as a gym, and in heavy rain or frost boys were getting no physical education at all. What was needed was a sports hall, "a very large enclosed area, furnished in the simplest way." This was hardly news to the Governors. For some time before he left, Taylor had voiced his concern about the inadequacy of his beloved Manor House Library to cater for increased numbers, and had suggested turning Johnson's Hall into a new one. The original plan was to use the gym as a library – thus making the Manor House rooms available for teaching – and to use the Hall temporarily as a gym until it could be converted. Under the new timetable, the whole-school morning prayers had been replaced by smaller divisional assemblies, and when necessary the whole school could still be assembled standing. This was a far from ideal solution, for it would still have left us with an inadequate gym, but it was just about affordable, and in Taylor's view academic needs had to be given priority. Now, concerned at the financial implications of Hinton's demand, Lord Sackville said that the matter would have to be given further thought.

> Dr. Hinton said that first impressions were not necessarily correct, but he would like to comment on how he saw his task in the immediate future. One of the first things that had impressed him was the richness of school life here and the wide range and depth of activities . . . . Secondly, the friendliness which existed amongst the staff and between the staff and the boys was very exceptional; and new members of staff were brought into an atmosphere which immediately encouraged them. The Headmaster's third impression had been one of confusion. He felt this was partly in his own mind and partly due to a situation where inventiveness and creativity had outrun both resources and administration. He thought one of his first tasks must be to try and consolidate a little on the wonderful work that had been done already, and bring it into a coherent shape.

Now this was new, and a little worrying. In the Taylor years, the Governors had become accustomed to regard it as their job to restrain the wilder flights of their Headmaster's teeming imagination by sensible financial stewardship, never suspecting the danger of "incoherence." Were they not now, by implication, being accused of recklessness? And was there not further criticism lurking in the lavish praise heaped upon Robinson, Scragg and Alcock (now Registrar) "who have held the administration together in a period of great difficulty, first, when Mr. Taylor was deeply involved in his Nuffield Project, and, secondly, when a new Headmaster was trying to understand the enormous complexities of the school'? Certainly, there was nothing indirect about his strictures on the "over-extension" resulting from the School's rapid expansion: bursarial arrangements, "adequate for a small and more or less static school, had got to the point of actual breakdown by last term." While he had full confidence in the ability of the new Bursar, Colonel Smart, to put things right, he felt that "we shall continue to run into the problem that a school which does as many special things as we do must constantly find itself short of money for more routine purposes." As for buildings, "while we offer certain facilities

208

quite remarkable in their quality, we are deficient in other facilities to an unacceptable degree." The lack of a gymnasium was nothing short of scandalous, and had to be remedied.

One of the most serious of Hinton's outspoken criticisms was his insistence that "while a boy who is keen has unrivalled opportunities here, a boy who is apathetic can get away with doing very little indeed outside his academic work. A boy who is keen on physical education, but not outstandingly good at it, gets a very raw deal indeed. Because of the flexibility demanded by the richness of our life, close supervision of individuals has become very difficult; and the result has been a good deal of taking of advantage, of petty theft and petty vandalism, of the cutting of school engagements and of the general evasiveness of which boys are past masters." Since only relatively few boys are able to flourish in, say, the rarefied atmosphere of the Art Room or the Technical Activities Centre, "it has become very apparent to me that the school is in danger of losing it's identity as a community." He thoroughly disapproved of the idea of "accelerating" a form of bright boys to do 'O' Level in two instead of three years. "The bad effects of this proliferate throughout school life." What he did not realise was that Taylor's introduction of a "fast stream" had been in part a hard-headed response to the demands of Prep School headmasters and their parents, many of whom preferred a public school where 'O' Levels could be taken after two rather then three years: for the financially hard-pressed, it meant one year's school fees saved; for the academically ambitious, it meant the possibility of a third or even a fourth year in the sixth form. In Taylor's view, the move was at the time essential in order to attract bright prep school boys; furthermore, he believed in the long-term ill effects of "stretching" a boy were less serious than those of boring him.

Finally – and this, quite clearly, was at the centre of Hinton's preoccupations – "our religious and our moral education are not as effective as they might be." While the Chaplain, Ian Ogilvie (now in his new house in the old orchards of Park Grange) is "about as good as a School Chaplin could be . . . .what I find distressing is an alienation from anything that is specifically Christian among both staff and boys; and an antipathy to anything which even looks like religious activity throughout a very large proportion of the school . . . .Hostility and indifference to institutional religion is a characteristic of our time. But Sevenoaks rises so superior to society as a whole in many other respects that I would like to improve it in this respect too; and though I think this may be the most difficult of all my tasks, and the one where I am most likely to make mistakes, it is not a task from which I shall turn away."

For a moment, we seem to hear an echo of Wesley at the School gates in 1746, declaring that "all have sinned and come short of the glory of God! . . . . As we returned a poor Sherrie came to meet us, bitterly cursing and blaspheming; but we walked straight on, even his companions, the mob, neither laughed nor opened their mouths."

☆　☆　☆

There is no doubt that there was truth in many of Hinton's observations, nor that he was sincere in praising a staff who "generate an atmosphere of intellectual excitement unique in my experience . . . .What I say must be seen in the context of qualities and achievements which, I am sure, place the school among the foremost in the country." Perhaps the depth and intensity of his moral and religious convictions did lead him to exaggerate his isolation, and occasionally to assume a martyr's stance unlikely to endear him to an influential, self-consciously urbane and rather arrogant section of the staff; but which Common Room does not contain and tolerate such cliques?

It is clear that, driving himself unmercifully, he tried to change too much too quickly, in a style unfamiliar to many governors, staff, parents and pupils, and in expectation of such immediate acceptance that a sense of frustration was inevitable. Perhaps this merely reflected his unwillingness to adapt his many years' successful experience of the state system – where Governors played a relatively minor role and were used to being lectured, where parents were less critical and demanding, where time-tabled "P.E." was thought to be much more important than competitive games – to the very different ethos and habits of the independent sector. Accustomed to dealing, largely on paper by way of tightly-reasoned memos complete with conclusions, with distant Authorities, he was perhaps unsettled by the much more personal, more relaxed, more argumentative, possibly less business-like approach of Sevenoaks. No doubt, some of this impatience was justified, but at times a certain lack of realism, or of humour, unnecessarily increased his irritation. For instance, establishing a School Council, he was saddened to find their early meetings dominated by radicals demanding the abolition of school uniform, compulsory games and Detention, and the provision of a Smokers' Room; trying to establish by widespread consultation what the school rules and customs really were, he discovered "fundamental disagreements between and among boys, staff and parents"; in an effort to raise funds to improve facilities, he persuaded his Governors to allow him to push school numbers up sharply, and was surprised at the strength of parents' and staff objections to increased form and set sizes: the resultant revision of this policy caused some bitterness among local headmasters, for the demand for places was unprecedented.

In 1970, 94 eleven year-olds competed for 20 day boy places, 30 for 11 boarding places; in the K.E.C. entry, 118 boys awarded 'selective education' had given Sevenoaks School as their first choice, but only 60 Free Places were available there; in the thirteen-year-old day boy entry, 56 boys applied for 25 places. We were now closing our boarding lists two years in advance, and there were 120 applicants for 20 places in the International Centre – newly enlarged that year, thanks in part to an interest-free capital loan of £10,000 from Victoria College Council.

Apart from playing a prominent part in discussions concerning the School's place in a reorganised system of education, Hinton had to deal with several important disciplinary or pastoral matters which divided the Governors and entailed the drafting of lengthy papers. A sixth form boy asked permission to marry: could he remain at school? – since he was an outstanding member of the lst XV, this aroused considerable staff interest; what was the appropriate scale of punishments for boys involved in the use or purchase of cannabis? must one always inform the police? could a school, whose policy was to expel boys for drug offences, be expected to offer a second chance to boys expelled from other schools for the same offences? What does one do with a local parent who, absent from his house all day, was said to be allowing it to be used every lunch-hour by some of our sixth formers and some schoolgirls for advanced biology practicals?

The Parents' Association, the result of discussions in 1968 between Taylor and its first Chairman, Dr. Brian Chapman, was set up "to enable parents to consult with the school on matters of common concern". It had very quickly raised enough money to put three hard tennis courts on the land behind the Tuck Shop. This was splendid, but the interest parents took in Hinton's efforts to clarify and codify school rules hardly made life easier for him, as he reported to Governors in February, 1970:

> It became apparent that both parents and staff felt that co-operation between home and school needed to extend right out of school hours into constant consultation . . . .It had also come to light that there was fundamental disagreement among staff and parents about what the school is supposed to do these days. Some think the school should provide moral and social education chiefly by way of having the right rules; others urge that rules dehumanise and the school should be built on good personal relationships; others are in the middle, but taking up different viewpoints.

Parents agreed that the "Lock-Up" rule for day boys should be abandoned, and Hinton welcomed this as a sign that parents wished to take more responsibility for their sons' behaviour out of school hours; yet he was soon receiving letters from parents of day boys asking the School to forbid smoking in public at any time, as well as outlandish dress and visits to pubs or to 'unsuitable' parties. Some Governors expressed concern about the length and untidiness of boys' hair.

The Headmaster agreed that some boys' appearance was bad, and he was trying to do something about it, but he was handicapped by the fact that various staff were totally unprepared to do anything. [A Governor] said it was not altogether surprising that the boys' appearance left a lot be desired when one saw the example set by various members of staff. [A Governor] said it was a serious thought that the Headmaster was not getting the right kind of support from the House Tutors, and Dr. Hinton said this referred back to the problem of running a school today, and especially a school like Sevenoaks, where there was almost no agreement about anything. . . .

However, not all was gloom: the financial affairs of the School, Hinton informed his Governors – who included the Chairmen of Marley Tile and of Granada Television – were in much better order, thanks to Colonel Smart, though "once habits of financial carelessness and self-indulgence have been established, they are hard to break".

The middle school timetable, he was glad to say, had now been reshuffled, to eradicate "a host of problems which bedevilled the previous one; and in particular it gets rid of the system of express streams which forced staff to take decisions about boys' academic potential on little evidence and when the boys were very young." Streaming had been almost completely abolished everywhere.

"In administration, as in finance, an attempt to produce order has created frictions, as loopholes have been plugged, abuses discovered and an ordered discipline required." Music was getting better: the first Attlee Fellow, Richard Hames, had done outstanding work, and the new Fellow, Roger Brunyate, was hoping to produce an opera; the Pipemakers Company had given £400 to buy an oboe, a bassoon and a flute for the school orchestra, and in addition they were donating a 17-seater minibus for use by the V.S.U. and others; a club house was being erected in Manor House gardens, which Old Boys were to share with the Sixth Form; the P.E. staff had been doubled by the appointment of Viv Edwards, "who will make the best use of inadequate games facilities as Mr. Robinson and I have of inadequate academic facilities"; the revised system of General Studies "gave opportunities for a deeper and more systematic study of religious and ethical problems"; lunch-hour communions had been introduced and were well attended; as for the "biff", (the straw boater), "boys and staff wanted it made voluntary, parents wanted to retain it; I compromised and made it voluntary for senior boys"; a few unenforceable, widely disregarded and unnecessary rules had been abolished: "my personal inclination would have been to go rather further in this direction, but in deference to the opinions of senior staff the rules remain substantially unaltered."

By this time, in September, 1970 Dr. Hinton had already decided to resign, and to leave at the end of the Michaelmas term. The exact nature of his discussions with Lord Sackville and other Governors, which led to his decision, have not been revealed. Some Governors were unhappy about it, and three resigned; some staff would have preferred him to stay. Probably, enough has been said to indicate that stresses had arisen in Dr. Hinton's dealings with governors, staff, parents and senior boys. This is not the place to try to apportion blame. A man of great ability, high ideals and deep convictions had come reluctantly to accept that he and Sevenoaks School were not "right" for each other, that there had been a fundamental clash of "styles" and expectations: those that had worked well in a state school had worked less well in a public school; perhaps both styles have their flaws. What can be said is that the impact of Michael Hinton upon Sevenoaks School was neither negligible nor negative: some large near-forgotten questions had been raised, some comfortable assumptions challenged, some basic beliefs re-invigorated. With a sober sense of their great responsibility, the Governors now turned their attention to the appointment of a successor.

CHAPTER TWENTY

Alan Tammadge

(1971–1981)

Consolidation and Advance

D istance sometimes lends not only enchantment but a spurious clarity to the retrospective view. Uncertain memories and gaps in documentation invite discreet manipulation of events in the interests of a smoothly sequential narrative, while a little simplification of complex issues can add a refreshing touch of drama. On the other hand, when dealing with very recent years, teeming with overwhelmingly documented incident, the amateur historian has other temptations to resist. An unwillingness to offend the living, either by criticism or by a failure to praise or even mention them, urges him towards bland generalisations. The impossibility of doing full justice to everyone involved in the affairs of a large school, particularly a school renowned for the variety and vigour of its extra-curricular activities, encourages him to concentrate on facts, not on people; yet what does one remember of a school if not the people in it, whether as pupils, teachers or administrators? Such inconclusive musings will perhaps be forgiven, offered as they are in lieu of an apology to the many whose achievements, during the last twenty or so crowded years, go inadequately recorded or saluted.

Alan Tammadge arrived in August, 1971. Educated at Dulwich College and Emmanuel College, Cambridge, a wartime naval officer, he was a distinguished mathematician: his teaching posts, prior to his Mastership of Magdalene College School, Oxford, had included that of Senior Lecturer at the Royal Military Academy, Sandhurst, but he was more widely known as a seasoned performer on television and radio, and as a major contributor to countless books and articles; he had travelled widely, lecturing on mathematics in Nigeria, the United States, South Africa and Ceylon. Sometimes thought of as a safe, sound Headmaster, appointed by a nervous Governing Body anxious to slow the breathless tempo of the Taylor years, and to heal any more recent scars, he was very much more than that. He was a headmaster of exceptional qualities, and if he has not always received full credit for the many extraordinary advances made by Sevenoaks School during the Seventies, this is entirely due to one of those qualities: a rare, almost excessive modesty. Quite devoid of arrogance, smilingly suspicious of the autocratic power that intoxicates and unbalances some headmasters, he looked for the best in those around him, gently tolerated and restrained their excesses, and warmly praised those who gave, far beyond the call of duty, their time and energy to the School. Pupils, Staff, Governors, parents and benefactors responded positively, and within ten years most of Taylor's pioneering projects had been expanded, strengthened and where necessary modified: no longer Experiments, they had become part of the familiar fabric of school life, and the excitement and energy they generated came now, not from uncertainty about whether they would work or not, but from a determination to spread their benefits more widely.

Consolidation, then, rather than innovation, was the watchword of Alan Tammadge's years in office (though the admission of girls to the sixth form, and the introduction of the International Baccalaureate, were later to prove crucially important); but they were enormously active years. Very much a "hands-on" Headmaster, there was hardly an area of activity, however modest, that he did not find time to support: cheering on innumerable touchlines, marvelling in the Art Room or the Technical Activities Centre, playing hockey, singing in the choir, congratulating the kitchen staff or the parents running the secondhand clothing shop, chairing the often exasperating sessions of the School Council or attending every one of the sometimes spiky meetings of the Parents Association. Paying tribute to him in 1981, Lord Sackville noted that "under his guidance there has been a tremendous improvement in both academic and recreational facilities. Those who return to the School are amazed and gratified at what has been achieved in the Seventies. In addition, both he and his wife, Rosemary, have cemented the ties of friendship between the Town and the School."

This last achievement was a considerable one, particularly important in a decade when arguments sometimes raged fiercely on issues such as the School's role in a reorganised educational system, its opposition to the proposed Eastern Way and its decision, in 1976, to admit girls into the sixth form. Tammadge had an acute sense of the School's responsibility to the community, and was always glad to offer the use of school premises and facilities to local organisations: by 1973 the list was impressive, and included Age Concern, Rotary, the Spastics Society, the Workers Educational Association, the Decorative and Fine Arts Society, the Sevenoaks Film Society, the Cheshire Home Committee (on which the School Chaplain was the driving force), the United Nations Association, Sevenoaks Squash Club and many others.

Many headmasters grow suspicious when Parents Associations become too powerful, or begin to take too close an interest in school affairs. Hinton had secured for the Association's chairman the right to attend the first part of Governors' Meetings if he so wished, and the right of the Governors to summon the chairman at other times for consultation. In the event, neither Governors nor the vast majority of Sevenoaks parents showed any enthusiasm for exercising these solemn rights, preferring to trust the Headmaster to keep the lines of communication healthily open. Certainly, Tammadge was not convinced of the value of democratically elected watchdogs, whether chosen from the ranks of parents or of Staff. On the other hand, he did believe in parental participation in school life, and in his own duty to keep parents as fully informed as possible of what was going on in school: he increased the number and frequency of Parents Evenings, and encouraged all departments to make Subject Presentations to parents and Governors to explain their "philosophies" and methods; he urged more parents to make use of the Saturday morning courses open to them, to make their expertise available to boys by establishing a Careers Panel, and by volunteering to give one of the weekly Careers Talks on Wednesday afternoons, which sixth formers could choose to attend in preference to talks given by a succession of distinguished public figures, lured to the school by the persuasive charms of a rumbustious young Irish head of Economics and Business Studies, Casey McCann, of whom we shall hear more.

Parents responded warmly in many ways: by inviting interested boys to visit their offices, firms or factories; by offering their time and their cars to take V.S.U. groups to their places of work on Thursday afternoons; by producing and serving cakes and sandwiches to visiting games players, sometimes numbered in hundreds; and, as inflation soared, he warmly welcomed their fund-raising activities, whether these took the form of May Balls or School Fêtes or a School Shop.

A Time of Gifts

Despite these generous gestures, it is hard to see how, in the difficult Seventies, under the looming threat of the loss of our Kent Places, the School could have flourished as it did without the munificence of its major benefactors. Despite the threat of lost Kent places, the Governors had the courage and the confidence to fund the building of the Sackville Theatre, the new biology laboratories, a television studio, a reprographic centre, a property to become the new Girls' International Sixth Form House, the leasing of Claridge House as an administrative centre, and the conversion of the Old Boys' club-house into the Meeting House – another teaching room, but essentially a centre for worship, for weekday Communions, Confirmation classes and for the increasingly popular meetings of the Christian Fellowship. But they knew that, once more, there were to be generous benefactors on other fronts. The Pipemakers and the Elia Salzman Estate financed the building of the new Language Laboratory and classrooms opened by the Master of the Worshipful Company in 1972. Lord Bernstein and many other well-wishers contributed to an Appeal launched in 1973. The Johnson Trust financed the conversion of the Johnson Hall into a new library opened on May Day 1976 by Arthur Cowdry, Chairman of the Trustees, with Sir Desmond Lee, President of Hughes Hall, Cambridge, and former Headmaster of Winchester, the Guest of Honour. But an inestimable debt is owed to the Aisher Family.

Jack Aisher and the Marley Tile Company had contributed hugely in the mid 1960s to an Appeal, and one result was the Aisher Hall. Eileen Aisher later personally provided for its substantial expansion to seat 300, and in February 1976 the School orchestral concert inaugurated its use and that of the Steinway grand piano given by the Parents' Association. As if this were not enough, Jack Aisher announced in December 1972, to a thunderstruck Headmaster and Bursar, that his Company wished to pay for a new Sports Hall to mark in 1974 their 50th Anniversary in Sevenoaks. Alan Tammadge noted the bare facts in his diary – and added three exclamation marks.

That it was not until April, 1977, that the splendid Marley Sports Hall was finally declared open by the Prince of Wales, is a reminder of just how unhealthy the financial climate was in those years, with no political party firmly in control, and with widespread strikes, the fuel crisis, the "three-day week", rampant inflation and steeply rising costs threatening the abandonment of many building projects a good deal less ambitious than our own. Every delay of more than a month or two meant that something had to be "trimmed" to keep within budget. Not until March, 1974, was outline planning permission for the Sports Hall granted by the U.D.C., and by then the architect, Claude Kempton (O.S. 1930-34), after frequent sessions with Aisher and Tammadge, had been reluctantly forced to reduce the overall size of the building and to drop, one by one, several vital features included in the original plans: a swimming pool; a

217

circuit training area; a rifle range; and three squash courts, one of them with a glass wall. Furthermore, the Council now stipulated that the Hall should be erected, not in the walled garden in the grounds of Park Grange, but in the valley below Duke's Meadow; this had been the site originally proposed by the School, but on examination rejected as too expensive.

The uncertain political situation meant that nobody could predict when, or even whether, the County would be instructed to stop taking up Free Places at Sevenoaks. If the axe *did* fall, would it be in one fell swoop? Or would the Authority, recognising that the School's rapid growth had been in large part a response to their own demand for ever more places, phase the reduction over several years to give us time to adapt to the new circumstances? How many parents, previously entitled to expect a Free Place, would be able to pay our rising fees? Relations with K.E.C. remained very friendly despite worries about the part the School would play, if any, in a reorganised "two-tier" or "three-tier" system. At a meeting at Springfield in September, 1974, Tammadge and Scragg were assured that the County would still want places at Sevenoaks – at this time they were taking up sixty each year – and at Walthamstow Hall School, though how many was not known. Clearly, contingency plans had to be made, despite the many imponderables.

A staff committee called SCOPE was set up (Select Committee on Policy and Education). In the Annual Review 1973-74, Tammadge told parents that

> SCOPE has been letting its imagination range widely over the most fundamental facts of the school's structure. They are considering whether day or boarding, single sex or co-educated, selective or unselective, creative or academic, examination-orientated or not, large or small, eleven-plus entry, thirteen-plus entry, nine-plus entry, whether to merge with other schools, and so on, and so on. This is not to say that all or any of these changes are about to take place! But planning ahead for at least ten years is essential, and must rest on agreed assumptions about the nature of our enterprise and our community. These assumptions need looking at periodically and this is what the school is now doing. SCOPE, the Divisional Heads and the School Council are all hard at it and we plan to arrive at some firm guidelines for the future to lay before the Governors by the end of this year.

This was heady stuff, and was to prove somewhat over-optimistic. Evening meetings of SCOPE, with wine circulating, were great fun, often stimulating, but seldom seemed likely to produce "firm guidelines", or anything approaching a consensus opinion; rather, they tended to illustrate one of the great strengths of this school which still prided itself on being "a bit of everything" – the great diversity of its political, philosophical, religious and educational views. With its every sober, passionate or frivolous contribution assiduously recorded in seamless longhand by its enthusiastic Secretary, Willie Bleyberg, it did indeed let its imagination range widely, but invariably shied away from anything as dull as a conclusion.

Nevertheless, some more practical moves were made. The Taylor Fellowship had been endowed by Lord Bernstein to enable teachers to take sabbatical leave to do research or in other ways to "refuel their batteries": it was now used to despatch members of staff to study other, different schools and teaching methods. Tammadge approached the Headmistress and Chairman of Governors of Walthamstow Hall to discuss, tentatively, some form of union. His diary records: "They were appalled". Meanwhile our Governors, their deliberations perhaps sharpened since 1971 by the keen financial brain of Robert Froy, were wrestling with more immediate problems: our Appeal consultants had collapsed and the inflow of money was faltering; the Kitchen Manager had resigned, and Contract Catering had again to be considered; fees had to be raised to keep the building programme going and to meet the rising cost of borrowing, but how much could parents stand?; the case against the proposed Eastern Way had continuously, and expensively, to be put. Such was the volume of work confronting them, and the intricacy of the financial problems, that in 1973 they formed an eight-man Financial and General Purposes Committee prepared to meet more frequently, and react more rapidly to crises, than could the full Governing Body.

Though many parents were doubtless only too aware that times were harsh, life in school, for most of their sons was full, cheerful and expansive. The sportsmen were doing great things. Our sailing team was virtually unbeatable at home or away, regularly defeating Tonbridge, Dover, Charterhouse, Eton, Eastbourne, Brighton, Lancing and St. Paul's, and seldom returning from Itchenor without a prize; thanks to the Parents' Association's new hard courts, and to a successful liaison with Sevenoaks L.T.A., tennis flourished early in the decade: in 1971, our lst V1 won the Kent Cup for the first time, and reached the National Finals of the Glanville Cup, for which 150 schools competed, losing only to Millfield; athletics was beginning to flourish at all levels; support was growing for soccer, and for cross-country (under Peter McGregor, who also inspired great enthusiasm for the Duke of Edinburgh Award scheme; the first four Golds were won in 1974); badminton, golf and canoeing had their devotees. But it was in cricket and rugby that the School, not yet in possession of the magnificent facilities that would allow it, later in the Seventies and throughout the Eighties, to pursue real excellence at depth in a host of hitherto "minor" or "optional" sports, began to attract national attention.

In 1972, fresh from 'O' Level, Chris Tavare made his first hundred for the school; in 1973 he made six more, collecting 1,035 runs in fourteen games; in all, over three undefeated seasons, he made twelve hundreds for the lst X1, celebrating his last appearance with 101 in 76 minutes on the County ground at Hastings. Under the watchful and admiring eye of Alan Hurd, formerly a wily Cambridge and Essex off-spinner – who early predicted not only the Oxford Blue but the England cap – he blossomed into an excellent captain who inspired fine performances by the X1 even after he had left. In his last year his team included three promising bowlers, Guy Durdant-Hollamby and Guy and Mark Spelman, and facing them behind the stumps was a more than promising young wicket-keeper, Paul Downton.

Had Downton gone to Oxford or Cambridge, he would almost certainly have been our first "double Blue", for he was an outstanding full back for the 1st XV over four seasons, 1972-75. In their Jubilee Year – fifty years after "Ernie" Groves had introduced the game to the school – the XV captained by all-rounder Guy Durdant-Hollamby won 15 of their 17 matches and scored 322 points. The newly appointed coach of the XV, Mike Williams, formerly of Rosslyn Park and Blackheath, paid tribute to Downton's "skill, timing and elegance allied to power. When Paul left he had played a record number of 68 matches for the school, 80% of which resulted in victories". Williams did much to raise the standard of the game at Sevenoaks; moreover, by organising a succession of energetic fund-raising exercises and headline-grabbing tours – to British Columbia in 1974 (accompanied by Alan and Rosemary Tammadge), Australia in 1976, Round the World to New Zealand, Fiji, Hong Kong and Oman in 1980 – he no doubt caused many parents looking for a "traditional" school to consider Sevenoaks, which they had been inclined to dismiss as now altogether too experimental to be serious about games. Victory in the Rosslyn Park National Sevens in 1980, Blues for Brian Gilchrist at Cambridge and Paul Brett at Oxford, six England Schoolboy caps, and then the stirring performances of the Thresher brothers and Richard Langhorn for Harlequins, must all have helped resolve such doubts.

Academic standards were improving, too: 'O' Level passes were 76% in 1970, 86% in 1980, while 'A' Level passes rose from 67% to 84%. Over the same period, the number of subject entries doubled at both levels.

Girls At Last

The seven brave day girls admitted to the sixth form of Sevenoaks School in 1976 may have regarded themselves as guinea- pigs, and so they were, and very charmingly and successfully did they fulfil this role. They perhaps did not realise that it was not only their reactions, and the reactions of the boys, that were under scrutiny, but also the reactions of those members of staff – about one third – who were by no means convinced that the School should be even contemplating co-education. This was in very few cases the result of chauvinism, though some involved with the major games feared that any consequent shrinking of the pool of available male talent might mean weaker Elevens and Fifteens. Others were not at all sure that we would be doing the girls a favour – after all, most staff had been educated at single-sex schools, and were used to teaching boys: how would girls react to schoolmasterly sarcasm, what if they *cried*? Would they distract the boys? And what about uniform and games, changing rooms and lavatories?

However, the K.E.C. agreed to pay the fees of properly qualified girls on the same terms as for boys; parents and the School Council were in favour, and only a few of the most senior Old Boys were strongly against. Heads of local independent girls' schools appeared unperturbed, while the Acting Headmistress of Hatton Girls' School told a *Sevenoaks Chronicle* reporter that "I don't think this will make very much difference to us. The studious sort of girl doing 'A' Levels will probably want to continue at a girls' school. Those who want to meet young men will go to college." Care was taken to select, for this "experimental" year, girls sufficiently lively, balanced and resourceful to be in no danger of coming to harm. They conducted themselves admirably, seemed glad to be there and very capable of holding their own academically. Some boys pretended not to notice them, while others tended to be excessively protective, but on the whole they were welcomed warmly and without fuss. Presumably they reported favourably on their experience to friends and parents, for applications poured in for 1977 – some, for boarding places, from sisters of present or past members of the International Centre, others from girls hitherto educated exclusively in single-sex girls' schools, now keen to sample co-education before plunging into the increasingly mixed and decreasingly regulated life of universities and colleges. The experiment showed every sign of being a success, but it was clear that girls would in some respects be at a disadvantage – in games, for instance – while they constituted such a tiny minority of the sixth form. By great good fortune, three houses in the High Street, including the elegant 18th century Old House readily adaptable for boarding, came onto the market: the Governors approved their purchase, and in September 1977 the first girl boarders arrived in the Girls' International Sixth Form House. John and Jo Adams were in charge, having relinquished Johnson's to Peter and Vivian Lloyd. Five years later there were one hundred girls in the sixth form, with inter-school fixture lists in netball, hockey, tennis and squash.

Too many dates and facts, particularly when they concern buildings, make dull reading, but in a school new buildings can lift the spirit of both staff and students – and probably of parents too, particularly if they are paying heavy fees, being asked to answer a School Appeal, and perhaps expected to help their son raise £300 to send him on a rugger tour of Australia! In 1976 the

Financial Times ran a series of articles retailing "the saga of Anne and Peter and their battle with the cost of living." First checking his facts with Colonel Smart, the author vividly evoked the plight of this imaginary couple with a son at Sevenoaks, and a daughter at a state school but hoping to join her brother:

> Peter can justify cutting back his own standards in order to maintain Mark in the style to which he had become accustomed, but is a little worried that Jane too has to miss out on a few things because of the rising costs of keeping her brother at the day school.
>
> The most recent letter from the Headmaster contained the usual news. Although the school had managed to avoid any increase in fees during the academic year, fees would have to go up in September. . . . from £309 to £340 a term for day boys like Mark. Peter is a little more able to look the bursar in the eyes these days after a couple of times last year when he was a little late with his cheques. Last week he strolled around the school trying to comfort himself that what with the new Sports Hall now being built, and the new Library, it was, perhaps, all worth it. After all, weren't the exam results very good?

Yes, they were pretty good, and getting better: in 1975 there were 84% passes at both 'O' and 'A' Levels, with 13 Open and 4 Closed Scholarships to Oxford or Cambridge (which placed Sevenoaks 12th in the whole country in the Oxbridge Awards table). In the Annual Review Tammadge mused:

> Could those 84%s be increased to 86%s? I am sure the answer is that they could. More time could be given to academic studies, bigger prizes for successes, severer penalties for slackness. But more time for classes means less time for V.S.U., games, visits, concerts, C.C.F., VISTA and all the other facilities which exist at Sevenoaks. Apart from simple enjoyment, the reason for their existence is concerned with a second objective, the development of the whole person, his social and personal adjustment, judgment and control.

His predecessors would certainly have applauded these sentiments (though in Higgs-Walker's time "penalties for slackness" had been severe enough: a beating by the Headmaster for any boy doing badly for more than a week). Tammadge knew, however, that the very richness of the academic and extra-curricular diet available at Sevenoaks could impose a strain upon those of average or below average ability. Anxious that all boys, including the less bright, should be able to enjoy and benefit from the many out-of-school activities, he devised an ingenious method of "block timetabling" which, while avoiding the necessity to stream, allowed for variations of ability and interest, so that, for instance, boys in the middle school could now take one, two or three foreign languages without this affecting their choice of subjects elsewhere, or their eventual progress to further education. Thus, boys could be given one or two extra periods in their weaker subjects, but still be taught with their brighter friends at all other times. This system did not find immediate favour with heads of departments when it was introduced in 1977, but there is little doubt that some boys' lives before 'O' Level became a good deal happier. Tammadge certainly had in mind, too, the probability that the imminent removal of Free Places would mean a slight lowering of our entry standards.

Though a gentle man, not fond of confrontations, Tammadge showed great courage and tenacity when dealing with staff he suspected of pulling less than their weight. On his arrival he had been disturbed to find certain heads of departments doing little to earn their responsibility allowances – failing to lead and counsel their younger colleagues or to control their departmental budgets, or to take their full share of teaching throughout the school; one or two had even come to think themselves alone capable of Sixth Form and Scholarship teaching, so that enthusiastic younger teachers fresh from university, labouring exclusively in the junior and middle school, were in danger of becoming disaffected. Typically, Tammadge demonstrated his belief – that the most experienced teachers should deal with the most "difficult" classes – by himself teaching mathematics to a group of "likely O-Level failures", and only when some declined to follow his example did he decree that all heads of departments must teach within at least two of the school's three divisions. Another initiative was the institution of an annual review, by way of a polite questionnaire, of the extra-curricular activities of staff: this was welcomed by the hard-working majority, fully involved in games, V.S.U. or the C.C.F. three afternoons a week, and often running clubs in the lunch hour or after school; a few decried it as a witch-hunt, devised by a mathematician incapable of distinguishing quantity from quality; but it had its effect, and some unfamiliar faces began to appear in unfashionably humble, but essential, places and roles. Tammadge, by no means a charismatic Headmaster, was widely respected and liked, and his staff responded by constantly broadening the opportunities available to pupils both in term and in the holidays.

A Good School?

In February, 1977, a local journalist rang Tammadge in some excitement , and asked: "Are you one of the ten good schools?" "Which ten?" "The ten chosen by the Department of Education and Science! Haven't you seen their book?" Hastily procured, the book turned out to be a D.E.S. publication in their H.M.I. Series: Matters for Discussion. The full title was *Ten Good Schools*: A Secondary School Enquiry, and its declared aim was "to test whether generalisations could be made about the factors that contribute to success in secondary education." Two secondary modern schools, two comprehensive schools in a two-tier system, three "all-through" comprehensives, one special school and two selective schools were examined: one of the latter was a direct grant day school; the other was unmistakeably Sevenoaks, roundly praised not merely for its "numerous and impressive resources", its high overall standards and "outstanding examination successes at university level", but for its lively professional interest in curriculum development; not merely for its pioneering Technical Activities Centre, International Centre, Voluntary Service Unit and French Exchange, but for its "broad aim of developing self-discipline and of encouraging self-expression and self-realisation though creative activity", its P.E.B. integrated course ("the interest of the pupils is lively, the approach is scholarly and the work produced has significance and quality"), its support of new staff, its team work, pastoral care and careers advice. Tammadge particularly enjoyed the closing assertion that: "without exception, the most important single factor in the success of these schools is the quality of leadership of the head . . . the heads have qualities of imagination and vision, tempered by realism, which have enabled them to sum up not only their present situation but also attainable future goals." He wryly admits, with his familiar lop-sided grin, that when emerging from a particularly waspish meeting of parents, staff or the School Council, he was tempted to remind himself that he was one of those whose "sympathetic understanding of staff and pupils, their accessibility, good humour and sense of proportion and their dedication to their task has won them the respect of parents, teachers and taught."

Could this mean, some wondered, that the politicians and civil servants who decide the fate of schools had come to accept that excellence in education had little to do with political or social theories and ideologies? that good schools should be supported and made available to as many children as possible? that really good schools, whether comprehensive or independent, are not socially divisive, produce neither bitter underdogs nor arrogant overdogs but decent, well-balanced young people aware of their own strengths and limitations, with lively minds which may well be turned, one day, to curing some of society's ills? Surely, if Sevenoaks was a Good School, it would continue to be allowed to educate the children of those who could not afford its fees?

One year later came the Secretary of State's ruling: there were to be no further County Places at Sevenoaks School after September, 1978. Tammadge's reaction, in the Annual Review, was uncharacteristically sour:

After the long association between the School and the County this, though far from unexpected, was wounding and brutal. It had been expected that the number would first be reduced, then phased out. Politicians rarely seem able to do things gracefully. Perhaps it was too much to hope that the good of the school would be considered. Generations of Sevenoaks boys have enjoyed a first rate education thanks to the co-operation of past Governors and Headmasters. The school has expanded to its present size largely to accommodate free place boys. A brief word of thanks would not have been out of place.

PUPILS

Buildings, governors, headmasters, staff . . . all play essential parts in the life and history of a school, and it is right that some of them – all too few in the case of teachers when the school is large – should be commemorated in words or pictures. But how to do justice to those who were and always must be the raison d'être and the first concern of any such community – those largely unremembered thousands of young persons who over the centuries have 'come thither to be taught'?

Which of them should we salute? And if pictures are to be chosen, who shall best represent the faceless multitude, and convey something of the spirit of the changing school? Some seem to select themselves: a martyr burned at the stake, a prodigious scholar, a Governor-General of India, a test cricketer, a Young Musician of the Year – or a Chinese servant immortalised by Reynolds. But these exceptional people are hardly representative of the infinite diversity of interests, talents, achievement and failings of their fellows.

Even if we study the faces of all forty pupils in Birkett's school (see illustration (**75**)), or all one hundred and forty of Higgs-Walker's (**76–79**) – but not, for want to space, Richard Barker's nine hundred! – we can only guess at what the school meant to them. The sportsmen look proud enough, but then sportsmen usually do (**73**). The Arnoldian high seriousness, not to say the disdainful complacency, of Higgs-Walker's prefects (**74**), when compared with the unbuttoned cheerfulness of Kim Taylor's (**62**), suggests something of the sea-change that has occurred. The mortar-board, the topper and Eton collar (**82**), the extravagant blazer (**81**), the dandyish postures (**83**), the jauntily angled straw boater or 'biff', all these attempts to stereotype the middle-class English schoolboy have given way, for better or for worse, to the less contained exuberance, the very different preoccupations, of what (for a while) are the 'modern' boys and girls of Sevenoaks School. As they change, so the School changes, for they *are* the school, and its history is theirs.

68. Joshua Reynold's portrait of Wang-i-tong, the Chinese servant of 3rd Duke of Dorset, pupil c. 1770

69. George Grote, historian, pupil c. 1805

70. Henry Hardinge, pupil 1795–1799, Governor General of India 1844–1848, Field Marshal

71. Paul Downton (left), pupil 1968–75, England Test Cricketer

72. Emma Johnson, pupil 1982–4, Young Musician of the Year 1984

73. 1st XI, 1888

74. School Prefects, 1930

75. Birkett's whole school of some 40 boys c. 1880

76–79. Higgs-Walker's whole school of some 140 boys (by houses), 1925

76. School House   **77.** Wordsworth House

78. Fenton House   **79.** Grote House

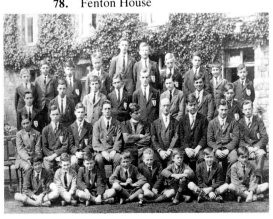 

80. Town (High Street opposite Dorset Street) and Gown c. 1880

81. The Glass of Fashion, 1913

82. Toppers and Eton collars c. 1880

83.   Edwardian Dandies with biffs (1912).

84.   Beauty (Elizabeth Taylor) and the biff, outside Royal Oak Hotel (1945)

85.   Last year of the biff (1967)

86.   At work (exams in Marley Sports Hall)

87. At work and play ('The Importance of Being Ernest', 1930)

88. At play (on Duke's Meadow)

89. His school

90. Their school

The Break with Kent

The Labour Government fell in May, and with it its policy of not providing free places. But by now the School had made arrangements for more fee-paying admissions and more scholarships, and was only able to offer the County forty places. In any case, the reprieve was only brief: a group of Conservative members of the K.E.C. – despite the furious resistance of their Chairman, John Barnes – saw their view prevail, that places at Sevenoaks School were "too expensive." After September, 1979, when twenty free place boys were accepted, there were to be no more. "Is education a commodity that you buy as cheaply as possible?" asked Tammadge in his Open Day address, "Is this the purpose of an Education Committee – to provide the cheapest possible schooling? I suggest that this is far from its purpose, and that quality of education is what counts. . . .

Excellence can be, should be, inspiring and infectious if, as in Sevenoaks, there are good relations between schools."

The prevailing emotion, however, amongst Governors and staff, was sorrow rather than anger: sorrow that, more and bigger scholarships notwithstanding, many bright local boys would in future, for lack of means, be unable to attend the town's own ancient grammar school now riding so high in national esteem. Certainly, the Governors showed no signs of panic, for the demand for fee-paying places, both day and boarding, was steadily rising. They readily accepted Tammadge's recommendation that the School should decline to participate in the Assisted Places Scheme, fearing "a real danger of souring the excellent relations built up over many years with maintained schools, particularly our primary feeder schools." His experience as Headmaster of a Direct Grant School had made him wary of the restrictions and delays that accompany any form of central government control; had taught him that, in a predominantly middle-class area, "much money went to people who did not need it" but who could employ astute accountants, and that attempting to apply a 'Means Test' was "a big and invidious task." He wrote to the Secretary of State:

> What is needed in education is a bipartisan approach. This is equally important to independent and to maintained schools. The Assisted Places Scheme is strongly opposed by the Labour and Liberal Parties, and is far from bipartisan. Coming at a time of severe financial stringency, we regard it as most ill-advised, and likely to increase pressure from the Extreme Left for punitive action against the independent section as a whole.

The Headmaster was now authorised to spend £24,000 a year on Scholarships and Bursaries, and the ever supportive Frank Warwick, a former Master of the Worshipful Company of Pipemakers, for many years a wise and deeply respected School Governor, came forward with more awards for good all-rounders. By the end of the decade, far from having to deal with falling rolls, the Headmaster was politely warned by the Governors that the school was now, at 943, in danger of becoming overcrowded, and was asked to reduce numbers to 875 over the next three years. Certainly, some boys had been admitted who would not have gained places earlier, but Tammadge had been adamant that "we have no intention of reducing admission standards to below that of 'grammar stream', since our school is staffed and equipped to deal with this kind of boy."

On the whole, local parents appreciated the School's genuine regret at the loss of its free place pupils, though a few, inevitably, began to resent its inaccessibility to many who would previously have hoped to join it. Perhaps they now derived less pleasure than before on reading of its many remarkable corporate, collective or individual achievements during the Seventies, generously covered in the local and often the national press, thanks to the efforts of Casey McCann, now not only Staff Tutor but our unofficial press secretary; aged 15, Matthew Best wrote an opera, "Humbug", and later, on his way to a distinguished international career, founded the Corydon Players and Singers even before winning a Choral Scholarship to King's, Cambridge; Lord Bernstein opened the Television Studio, his gift to the school, and the Attlee Fellow overseeing its early development was none other than Old Sennockian Derek Holroyde, once Kim Taylor's Vice-Captain, now Professor of Television at Leeds University (the Attlee Fellowship, endowed by Lord Bernstein, brought each year to Sevenoaks a "practising artist, scientific or other creative or successful person of stature and experience . . . to contribute to the vitality of school life"; Fellows during Tammadge's years included a film director, a dramatist, a musician, a design consultant, a poet, and a brilliant photographer, Ian Gibson-Smith); the new kitchens won a British Steel Corporation Egon Ronay Clean Kitchen Award and a headline in the *Sevenoaks Chronicle*; "School boasts the finest kitchens in the country"; Neil Dickenson beat Boris Spassky in a simultaneous chess match between the National Junior Squad and three Russian Grand Masters; a four-man School Team won the national Schools Challenge Competition – run on the lines of the T.V. "University Challenge" – in which over two hundred schools took part; Jonathan Christie and Clive Waters went to C.S.V. headquarters to talk to Prince Charles about the equipment they had invented to help the handicapped; 'A' Level Design was established, and Roddie Fairweather won a Design Council Prize for a braille teaching machine; Adrian de Souza and Ian Lewis walked 944 miles from Land's End to John o'Groats to raise £2,000 towards the cost of a new minibus for the town's Voluntary Service Unit; Christopher Kirk obtained the highest mark in the country in Nuffield Physics at 'O' Level; Steven Burrows took a cross-country team on a successful tour of Finland, while the annual Knole Run established itself as one of the largest inter-school events in the country, with forty teams competing; Gerd Sommerhoff published his *Logic of the Living Brain*, while industrial sponsorship flowed in to help boys develop their projects, from Page Engineering, I.C.I, Dubilier, Exel Mould, Metal Box, Chubb Electronics and others; three boys produced a microcomputer potentially better and cheaper than anything on the market, and the company developing it retained them as consultants during their final year in the Sixth Form; Sommerhoff and one of them, Chris Thomas , were flown to a European conference in Rome as members of the British delegation.

A World Dimension – the I.B.

Throughout the decade, the availability of sixth form boarding places at Sevenoaks – at first for boys only, for girls too from 1977 – became increasingly attractive to many continental European parents. Some of them were for various reasons dissatisfied with their own national educational system, which they found deficient in pastoral care and discipline, too often subject to politically-inspired changes; many of their sixth forms and universities, they felt, were becoming little more than factories mass-producing certificated articles for consumption rather than rounded young men and women, and operating a ruthless system of "quality control", based solely upon marks, which flung the rejected articles from the conveyor belt without any concern for their future; there was also, for a few very wealthy parents, the fear of their children being kidnapped for ransom, which they deemed less likely to happen among the relatively law-abiding British. Whatever their motives, and whether or not they were justified in their fears and hopes, they came in ever increasing numbers to look at Sevenoaks School.

A few went away quite quickly, disappointed by the absence of beating, fagging and compulsory major games. Others, more seriously, were astonished by the narrowness of the 'A' Level programme, which apparently obliged bright boys and girls of sixteen to "drop" their beloved history or literature or modern languages simply because they wished to study the sciences at university, or to "drop" all aspirations to advanced numeracy or technological knowledge if they were going to study humanities. Had the struggle to bridge the damaging gulf between the Two Cultures been abandoned? They recognised that schools were hamstrung by the universities' insistence upon early specialisation, and that schools like Sevenoaks were doing their best in "minority time" to provide a wide range of "complementary" courses: but were these often loosely-structured courses, without the incentive of a terminal examination, really taken seriously? Not always, it had to be admitted. True, sixth formers at Sevenoaks were already offered an unusually generous choice of subject combinations, so that Art/Biology/French, or Maths/English/Russian were possible, but what of the would-be engineers or doctors or architects anxious to deepen their knowledge and enjoyment of poetry or history or German?

It was largely due to the passionate advocacy of Willie Bleyberg, Head of Chemistry and later Head of Science, that in 1978 Staff and Governors were persuaded, not without reluctance, to allow the trial introduction of the International Baccalaureate as an alterative to 'A' Level. For years he had argued that many 'A' Level courses were overladen with masses of factual information which did nothing to improve a student's understanding of his subject, and much to diminish his zest for it: information which would be forgotten for ever once it had been 'examined', but which by then would have occupied countless hours of study that might have been better spent on something more stimulating. The International Baccalaureate student is required to follow, in addition to a course on the Theory of Knowledge, three Subsidiary and three Higher Level subjects, which must normally include a Humanity, a Science, Mathematics, a foreign language and a national litera-ture, though there is considerable flexibility to suit individual needs. Naturally, considerable doubts were expressed by teachers and administrators: the programme was expensive; numbers would be very small at first, and I.B. students would have to be taught in 'A' Level classes, despite discrepancies in the two syllabuses; how were the Subsidiary Level classes to be staffed?; Heads of Departments feared that this 'dilution' of study would mean fewer Open Scholarships in their subject; would the universities be prepared to respect the credentials of the I.B. Diploma?; would the academic load be too heavy for all but the exceptionally bright?

Many of these reservations were well founded: that they did not prove fatal in the early days was due largely to the unstinting efforts of Bleyberg and his growing band of supporters on the staff, who laboured in lunch hours and after school to teach topics not included in the 'A' Level programme; due also, however, to Tammadges's and the Governors' brave agreement to the need for extra staff, and to the School's patient and ultimately successful attempt to persuade University Admissions Tutors of the merits of the course. Today, fifteen years later, when the availability of the International Baccalaureate has brought hundreds of broadly-cultured and many brilliant young people from all over the world to Sevenoaks, strengthening our international ties, enlivening our teaching and all our school activities, those early doubts may appear unduly timid. They were not: it was a bold, risky, pioneering enterprise, and deserves great praise.

☆　☆　☆

In March, 1977, the unlovely but commodious Claridge House became the school's Administrative centre, inevitably occasioning comparisons with the Kremlin, and accusations that a dangerous gulf was developing between a swelling Administration and the hard-pressed Staff. Some lamented, and movingly evoked, those heady days crammed with vision, when Taylor, with his peerless and devoted secretary, Di Day, ran the school with the help of a part-time Bursar from cramped offices in the Cottage Block, healthily exposed to the clamour of bells and moving classes.

In fact, throughout his time as Headmaster Tammadge remained refreshingly sympathetic to the ordinary problems of classroom teaching – not enough room, not enough light, no blackout facilities, too much noise, a blackboard unreceptive to chalk and so on – and declined every temptation to cut down on his own teaching for fear, precisely, of becoming remote from them. A clear-minded and practical man who seldom wasted words, and tended to suspect those who (however stylishly) did, of not really knowing what they wanted, his laconic style on paper and in conversation did not please everybody, but it enabled him to get through an enormous amount of work very quickly – aided by "the best secretary in the world", Liz Cooper – while anyone, staff or pupil, with a personal problem, was likely to be pleasantly surprised by the warmth and patient understanding shown.

Of course, as in any lively school where talented and energetic staff are encouraged to fight their own corners, there were tensions and squabbles, and towards the end of the decade these were often exacerbated by an underlying uncertainty about the future of the School once it had been forced to become exclusively fee-paying. What should its priorities be? Was it right that the decision to lease Claridge House should have meant the abandonment of George Alcock's proposal to establish a Field Centre in Wales? Was too much money and time being spent on games and the C.C.F. and V.S.U., instead of improving exam results by smaller classes and better teaching facilities? Now that the Appeal, despite the generosity of new parents, had fallen far short of expectations, should the school have a Theatre, or a Swimming Pool? On this last issue Tammadge, eschewing his natural inclination to "hold the ring" on really contentious matters, showed great courage and tenacity in the face of fierce opposition from both Staff and Governors: nailing his colours firmly to the mast of the theatre, over two years he succeeded in convincing both bodies – and, surprisingly, the School Council too – that he was right. One of his most persuasive arguments was that a theatre would further cement the cordial relations between the School and Town, strengthened during the seventies by the growing popularity of the Summer Festival: this, first conceived as a small internal celebration of the end of exams, had blossomed under its dynamic director, Richard Barran, into the second largest Arts Festival in the South East, attracting sponsorship from local industry, support from the Sevenoaks District Arts Council and the South East Arts Association, and enthusiastic encouragement from the local press and public. Though for many years the regular fare remained home-grown – the Adler Concert, Matthew Best's Corydon Singers and Chamber Orchestra, Bob Taylor's inventive drama productions, Fuzz and Friends (Brian Townend and assorted jazz musicians),

229

the Echo Mountain Boys – little by little Barran cast his net wider, hauling in among others Hurwitz and the Melos Ensemble, Benjamin Luxon, Robert Tear, Richard Rodney Bennett, Julian Lloyd Webber, George Malcolm, Digby Fairweather, Swingle II, Prunella Scales, Anthony Hopkins and poets Vernon Scannel, Kit Wright, Dannie Abse, Christopher Logue, Peter Porter and Alan Brownjohn. In 1978 Bob Taylor's production of *Arturo Ui* was staged in Hatton School's admirable new auditorium – which lent more weight to Tammadge's case. Architect Roderick Ham produced exciting plans for a Studio Theatre: the Governors somewhat hesitantly gave their approval, but as the estimated costs soared towards £500,000 over the next two years they dug their heels in and insisted on such substantial cuts that for a while the project was in danger of being scrapped. Tammadge held firm, and despite several sticky meetings with Governors and with staff, fretting at the restraints on other departmental projects, work finally started on May 15th, 1980, with the Vice-Chairman of Governors, Robert Froy, agreeing to keep it under close financial scrutiny.

With inflation rising above 20%, continuing uncertainty about the future of the School, the understandable nervousness of some Governors, and a certain amount of inter-factional sniping in the Common Room over the theatre and other matters, 1980 and 1981 were not easy years for Alan Tammadge. Wryly, he noted in his diary that a meeting of Divisional Heads had stressed the need for "an inspiring leader for the New Age (I'm not one, it seems!)". Change was in the air, which so often in the past had brought exhilaration: now it brought an underlying unease, shortened tempers, narrowed vision, heightened fears. Who would take over the Festival now that Richard Barran was leaving? What would we do without the steadying wisdom, loyalty and geniality of two great pillars of the community, Senior Master Ronnie Wheeker who had joined the staff in 1938, and Bursar Jim Smart? (In fact, Colonel Smart, succeeded as Bursar by Julian Patrick in 1980, was to remain for many years as Clerk to the Governors, looking after the Almshouses and the Old Sennockians, and working as hard as ever). The School Council voted – just 11% short of the necessary 66% – to abolish itself. The system of "democratically" electing Prefects, devised by Michael Hinton, came under renewed fire: sixth formers were alleged to be voting for the prettiest girls and for the boys who gave the wildest parties, rarely for pupils likely to uphold the law, who topped the masters' list.

Even the miraculously sun-blessed quarter of an hour, on a day of torrential rain in June 1980, when the Queen Mother came to hear a Loyal Address from the Headmaster in the presence of Governors, staff, pupils and residents of the School Almshouses, did not go unsoured. Though the occasion was a happy one, the School's well-meant decision to have no press photographers there incensed the professionals, and gave useful ammunition to local critics of our allegedly growing "exclusiveness". Tammadge admitted the mistake (though it was simply an attempt to honour the Palace's request that the visit should be kept as private as possible): "We should not have been so insensitive."

Nevertheless, as he recorded in his last contribution to the Annual Review, he found, in the academic year 1980-81, much of which he and the School could feel proud: the Studio Theatre all but built; six new hard tennis courts completed; work in hand for an Annexe to the Girls International House and a kiln room for the Art Department; Attlee Fellow Ian Gibson-Smith's fine book of photographs, *School – An Independent View*, on sale at Open Day; victory in the Rosslyn Park Sevens and – for the seventh time – in the National Schools Firefly Championships at Itchenor; the honour accorded to the School of convening the first ever residential Workshop for organisers of Community Service in H.M.C. Schools (Mike Bolton, who between 1974 and 1984 greatly extended the scope and effectiveness of V.S.U. activities, wrote: "warm support for the Workshop came from the Headmaster, thus highlighting his ten years of encouragement for community service in Sevenoaks"); the completion of the Cheshire Home at Chipstead Lake and the £1,500 raised by our own rain-swept volunteers in the annual Walk; the second best ever exam results: 86% passes at 'A' Level, 84% at 'O' Level; valuable Scholarships won at Harvard and Princeton by Hemen Shah and Lalith Munasinghe, with ten other places at American Universities (though Tammadge, who had vigorously attacked the Secretary of State over the savage increase in university fees for overseas students, "felt strongly that these young men and women should be attending British Universities both for their sakes and for the sake of our country"); James D'Arcy winning the Fletcher Prize, coming 'by miles' top in Greek in the Cambridge Board 'A' Level examination; many Gold, Silver and Bronze Duke of Edinburgh Awards; Jonathan Lindars and Duncan Simpson becoming the first teenagers to climb the Old Man of Hoy; the nationally and internationally saluted successes of Gerd Sommerhoff's inventors.

Congratulating himself on having had the "great fortune to work under a superb Chairman of Governors and Governing Body", who had unfailingly supported him, Alan Tammadge, looking back with his own special blend of wry humour and modesty upon his years at Sevenoaks, confessed that thinking about his successor was "rather like thinking about your divorced wife's next husband. When you first become a Headmaster the biggest surprise of all is to realise that people have started listening to what you say – talking it over, weighing it up. Shortly, for me, each remark will again be purely private, have no potential energy due to my position. So what did I do as Headmaster? Well, I planted a walnut tree, I wonder how many people know where it is?"

Would that all Headmasters could be so humble! The Parents Association would have none of it, and raised a startlingly generous sum as a farewell gift to Alan and Rosemary, in appreciation of their joint success in serving them, their children and the School so well. At the Dinner given in their honour, one speaker referred to Alan as a Night Watchman, and ruefully in his diary he wondered: "Perhaps that sums it up?" It certainly did not. Far from the clumsy speaker's mind was the image of an inactive man contentedly presiding over a sleeping factory; instead, he meant to honour the courage, vigilance and energy of someone who had kept his nerve, though alert to the many dangers threatening his beloved School at a time of political and social unrest, had encouraged its continued remarkable development, and done a great deal to secure its future.

CHAPTER TWENTY-ONE

Forward with Richard Barker
(1981–)

The closer one draws to the present day, the more difficult it becomes to identify and isolate, amid the ceaseless flow of more or less trivial, more or less significant events that make up the life of a school, those worthy of some kind of permanent record. For one thing, the possibly far-reaching effects of comparatively recent individual or collective decisions, taken by Governors, Headmasters or Staff, cannot properly be assessed and fairly judged, and given their eventual due of praise or blame. For a would-be historian, delving into the memories of those who, as teachers or pupils, were or still are actors on the changing scene, it quickly becomes apparent that the multiplicity of subjective views – however colourful or trenchant – is of little help, for as often as not those views contradict each other, sometimes passionately, and only time will tell which were the most, which the least, distorted by prejudice or by personal successes or failures. Of course, that is as it should be, for life in a school is above all about people and the relationships between them, about their effects upon each other; and no doubt it is a salutary reminder, to one tempted to label periods the Taylor Years, the Tammadge Years or the Barker Years, that such divisions are largely artificial – may indeed appear grotesquely so to the not so Old Sennockian whose one abiding memory is of the day when his or her passion for music, literature, engineering, mathematics, languages or cricket, was first dramatically stirred (or perhaps, occasionally, extinguished) by one particular teacher, whose name is unlikely to figure in a History alongside details of new buildings, statistics and successive Headmasters and Chairmen of Governors. Not that good Governors, Headmasters, new buildings and facilities are not important, often crucially, in the rise or decline of a school's fortunes; but the *texture* of school life, as opposed to its physical structure, is more often than not – like inspired leaks in the popular press – "unattributable" to any one person.

Lest the above be interpreted as unwillingness to comment upon the development of the School in the last decade, or upon the happily uncompleted "Barker Years", we are in the fortunate position of being able to record that during those years the imaginary graph tracing the progress of Sevenoaks School has moved steadily upwards, in some ways quite steeply, and that it is our modest fear of premature self-congratulation, not of critical scrutiny, that is responsible for the comparative brevity of this "unfinished" chapter.

Richard Barker was appointed Headmaster in 1981 at the age of 41. Two other candidates short-listed by the Governors were already Headmasters of comprehensive schools; Barker's background, however, as a Housemaster at Marlborough, was deemed particularly appropriate to the problems and opportunities likely to face Sevenoaks School in the Eighties and beyond. He had read Science 'A' Levels at Repton, Geography and Economics at Cambridge, followed by Management Studies; he had been a founder-director of the 'A' Level Business Studies Project, in which Sevenoaks had been involved, and had done other work on curriculum development. He had taught at Bedales, and chaired the committee at Marlborough considering a move to full co-education. Though admittedly no linguist himself, he was extremely sympathetic to internationalism and to "foreign exchanges": he had already arranged innovatory exchanges for members of his House at Marlborough, whilst Imogen Barker, also a Cambridge graduate and a trained teacher with extensive overseas experience, had accompanied all three of their children to Toulouse for a term, so that they could attend a French school; moveover, he had been actively involved in certain areas of the International Baccalaureate programme. He struck the Governors as both idealistic and hard-headed, full of energy and very much "future-orientated".

Though Barker, on his own admission, spent his first year largely "looking and learning", he was by no means idle. At his first Governors' Meeting, he obtained agreement to the expenditure of £10,000 to improve "the rather clinical administrative atmosphere that is portrayed in the areas of the School used to receive visitors, including parents and potential parents"; obtained the use of a mini-bus to ferry children from the station to the school (as "a marketing exercise in some respects to encourage recruitment from areas in South London"); urged an examination of office administration "with particular reference to our ability to analyse quickly and accurately the facts and figures upon which policy decisions are formulated"; suggested the need for a further internal exam at Christmas for Lower Sixth pupils in order to identify and deal with likely 'A' Level failures at a very early stage; and secured agreement to bringing all terms forward by one week, thus giving more tuition time in the run-up to exams.

This very business-like approach, his insistence upon the need to "market" the school efficiently, to tighten up administrative procedures and to make much more use of the predictive value of statistical analysis, was not, at first, to everyone's taste in the Common Room, where murmurs were heard deploring a "time and motion" approach to the gentle mystery of schoolteaching, and the tendency to treat parents as Consumers and children as Products. This was unfair, for though Barker was unashamedly convinced that, in an increasingly competitive age, schools did have to be seen to give value for money, he was genuinely concerned that Sevenoaks was not attracting enough talented children, and was failing to get the best out of some of its pupils, not simply in terms of examination results but in terms of their fulfilment and happiness. He further believed that, unless public examination results were fairly dramatically improved, the School, for all its acclaimed virtues, would fail to attract very bright children to replace the brightest of the Free Place pupils; if this were to happen, he feared that some highly qualified teachers might leave. He urged upon Governors the need for more and better Entry Scholarships, some of them designed to interest children with particular skills, for instance in Music or Technology. The Pipemakers had already endowed a £1,000 Alan Tammadge Mathematics Scholarship; in 1982, when thirty awards were given at 11, 13 and 16, two new £1,000 Marley Creative Technology Scholarships were offered; by the end of the decade, when 7% of tuition fee income was being devoted to non-endowed awards, the number offered had risen to well over fifty, ever more keenly contested at all levels.

Full Co-Education

There is no doubt that the most momentous step taken by the School since its "forced" choice of independence in 1946, was the decision to become fully co-educational at all levels; no doubt, either, that most of the credit for the remarkably trouble-free success of the operation belongs to Richard Barker. Not that many others did not labour, and labour still, to ensure that success, but without his persistent advocacy over several years when many Governors and Staff were dubious, his insistence upon the widest consultation, upon meticulous preparation and the need to foresee every possible difficulty – above all, without his manifestly deeply held belief that the move was socially and educationally "right", and no cynically opportunistic response to the loss of our Free Places – it could hardly have been achieved so painlessly, nor so quickly have won the whole-hearted support of the doubters.

Though Barker believed passionately in the virtues of co-education, he was well aware of the ancient School's responsibility to local boys, and of the possible harmful effects upon the good independent girls' schools in the neighbourhood. Discussions with the Governors of Walthamstow Hall – about the possibility of a "merger" or of other forms of cooperation – proved unproductive, though of course they were kept informed as our own Governors' deliberations continued. In May 1983, a statement was released to the press:

> The Governors of Sevenoaks School have set up a committee under the chairmanship of the headmaster, to consider the desirability of extending co-education throughout the school.
>
> It is seven years since Sevenoaks took girls, and in September there will be over 100 in the sixth form. The Governors feel that this move into co-education has done much to improve the quality of education in the school.
>
> A decision by the Governors is expected this summer. If they decide to change their admission policy relating to 11 and 13-year olds this could not be before the autumn of 1984.

The Headmistresses of Walthamstow School and West Heath were unavailable for comment, but the response of Mrs Pauline Miles, Headmistress of St Hilary's, formerly deputy head of a state co-educational school, was measured: "I feel that there are parents who will want single sex schools for their children. Certainly a number of my parents would not send their girls to a co-ed school at the age of 11. Each school has its own role to play in the community."

The following week, however, a storm of protest broke. Under a front page banner headline: *"Unisex Plan: Disaster for Sevenoaks"*, the *Sevenoaks Chronicle* published a letter to Barker's "co-ed committee", written by the Headmaster of Sevenoaks Preparatory School – who seemed to weaken his case in advance by declaring that "there has never been any call for co-education in this area" – and signed by six other principals of local fee-paying preparatory and secondary schools. Many of their concerns were natural enough: there would be fewer places and scholarships available, in the face of "crushing competition", for boys from prep schools, whose parents wanted a public school education and could just afford Sevenoaks School day fees but "cannot entertain boarding fees at a 'traditional' public school". . . . "those whom you do not take must either move out of independent education altogether into the already full maintained sector, or travel out of Sevenoaks to achieve it. This generates an appalling level of anxiety for the parents"; girls' schools would suffer from the competition.

The letter went on to question whether, if it did decide to go ahead, the School would be prepared to make the necessary sacrifices: "True co-education means fully integrated teaching and curriculum, games and school activities for boys and girls in the same community. This cannot take place unless the staff are experienced in teaching in a co-educational school and are equally representative of male and female teachers . . . Unless there is to be a mass exodus of male staff by September 1984 a true co-educational environment will not be available to the girls who will attend the boys' school." Perhaps the spectre of redundancy was intended to influence members of male staff still undecided which way to cast their final vote; however, every one of the doubts and fears expressed in the letter had been raised, along with many other considerations, by staff themselves in the course of frequent discussions and debates; headmasters and teachers from co-educational schools had been invited to spell out the dangers and difficulties to be overcome; groups of staff visited Bedales, Oakham and other schools to talk to classroom teachers – particularly women teachers – and to question the boys and girls about the advantages and disadvantages of being educated together; committees explored and costed the "logistics" of the proposed change.

All that summer the public debate raged. An Old Sennockian wrote from London about this "foolish proposal": "Strong male societies – regiments, ships, teams, squadrons and schools – sustain men in hard times, and there are plenty of those to come in this country." Another ironically supported him: "We should ignore any propositions from sullen and discontented citizens that one half of the population might just possibly be entitled to claim equal educational facilities with the other half." A Sevenoaks resident gently mocked the "appalling level of anxiety" suffered by those rich enough even to contemplate paying for independent education; another felt that "the existence of single sex schools is an anachronism in today's society"; the Headmaster of the co-educational Hill School, in Westerham, welcomed the proposal and hoped that it would lead to other schools following suit; the mother of a boy at Sevenoaks, and a girl in a state primary school eager to join him, had visited every independent girls' school in the area, and thought that "without exception, Sevenoaks School towers above them all. If I am to pay school fees I want the best education and value for money for my daughter. If she were able to obtain a place on merit, why should being a female debar her?"; another mother, who had been to a co-ed school, thought that younger girls would do little in class other than pass round love letters.

Fierce opponents of independent education, confident that a Labour

UNISEX PLAN 'DISASTER FOR SEVENOAKS'

Unisex school — the argument rages

GOOD START NEEDED IN HARD WORLD

to the Editor
Dear Sir,

NEWS THAT Sevenoaks School may go co-educational came as "a bombshell" to local independent schools this week.

FACING THE REALITIES OF TODAY'S SOCIETY

Girls at Sevenoaks? What a foolish proposal for this bastion of manhood

OLD SENNOCKIANS everywhere will be shocked and angered by the proposal to make Sevenoaks School co-educational.

Town will suffer

AS a parent of a boy currently in private education at a prep school in the Sevenoaks area I wish to record my concern and that of others in a similar position at the proposed plans to convert Sevenoaks School to

GIRLS IN ALL FORMS AT SEVENOAKS?

by Keith Blackmore

SEVENOAKS School is on the threshold of becoming totally co-educational after more than 500 years as a male-domain.

Welcome to girls?

ASTONISHMENT, outrage and anger, in that order, can be fairly said to describe early public reaction to recommendations to make Sevenoaks School totally co-educational, building on the presence of girls in the sixth form to provide a mix of the sexes in every class. Old Sennockians, if letters published in the Sevenoaks Chronicle are typical, are furious. Equally upset are parents of boys now at prep schools, their futures geared to the hope of a place at Sevenoaks.

SEGREGATION IS NO REAL PREPARATION FOR ADULT LIFE

BOYS — DISTRACTED BY OPPOSITE SEX?

Little sympathy

I READ with interest your front page spread (May 14) on reaction to the proposed changes at Sevenoaks School.

Fig (xxv) Going Co-ed. Some local press comments in 1983.

238

government would shortly put an end to it all, poured scorn upon the whole silly squabble, berated the K.E.C. for failing to make adequate provision of state education in the area, and recommended parents to support Sevenoaks School for Girls, Wildernesse School, and Mascalls School in Paddock Wood.

Though few of the hundreds of letters received by the *Sevenoaks Chronicle* were entirely disinterested, or free of all political or other prejudice, its editorial comment remained on the whole admirably balanced. Recognising that the successful introduction of girls into the sixth form had made the school top-heavy, and that "Richard Barker and his colleagues are rightly anxious to correct the imbalance", it nevertheless urged the governing body to think long and hard about their responsibility to the community.

> Townspeople can be forgiven if they remind those now seeking such a large change that Sevenoaks is still a small public school in a small Kent town that as a consequence of past neglect has no state or state-aided grammar schools . . . If Sevenoaks became much more of a town's school the change to co-education might be less strongly resisted.
>
> We applaud Mr. Barker and his colleagues for revealing their recommendations so frankly in good time for comment to be given free rein. There is a feeling abroad that all has, in fact been decided and that the conversion to a boys-girls school is only a formality. We do not believe this to be so . . . The School's governing body will know that public opinion is a potent factor in decision-making and ignoring it risks perils that may not be apparent in the enthusiasm of the moment.

The *Chronicle* was quite right: all was far from decided. In June, when reiterating to Governors his conviction that the School should become fully co-educational, Barker admitted that he saw great practical problems, and "believed it would be prudent to seek further time to consider and collate the views which were still being received from all parties. Furthermore, this would give more time for the Staff, without whose strong support no change should be made to the present system, to finalise their own views." By the end of that summer, staff support was running at a decisive 85%.

In September Lord Sackville retired after nineteen years as Chairman of Governors: as a mark of personal respect, and in gratitude for his great services to the School, the Board appointed him as their President during his lifetime, hoping thus to secure the continuing benefits of his calm wisdom and his unflagging interest in the school he and his ancestors had served so well. Robert Froy, Vice-Chairman since 1976, became Chairman; a distinguished civil servant, Sir William Pile, became Vice-Chairman, and Kim Taylor returned to school as a Governor. At their first Meeting the new Board, after a long discussion, resolved that from September 1984, girls would be admitted at the ages of 11, 12 and 13, as well as into the sixth form. In a statement to the press, Robert Froy declared that "the Governing Body is convinced that the school best serves the community, in the long run, by offering an environment where high academic standards can be maintained. They wish to afford this opportunity to all pupils, irrespective of sex. We believe that the decision to become fully co-educational will prove stimulating and beneficial for both the school and the community." Though unlikely to have shared this optimistic view, local heads of independent schools accepted the news with considerable grace, acknowledged the Governors' right to do what they thought best for the School, and wished it well.

The Swimming Pool Episode

In the months preceding this historic decision, some of the local wrath had been deflected to a new target: Barker's proposal that the School and the Council should cooperate in building a new public swimming pool on school land. The School was to provide the site on a long lease at nominal rent, and would contribute 20% of the net running costs; in return, it would expect certain periods of exclusive use amounting to twelve hours a week. Just why this proposal aroused such fury is not clear, but within weeks the Conservative Council – whose leader, Colin Garner, was a Governor of the school – was being represented as forcing through a decision to spend £1 million for the benefit of an independent school. "The local Labour Party," said the *Daily Telegraph* in July, "is incensed with the proposal to pour money into a public school and is intent on sabotage." Barker protested in vain that the project was a genuine attempt to strengthen the ties between Town and School, which would benefit both and lessen the burden upon rates. The Headmaster of Wildernesse School, originally considered as a possible site for the pool, told a *Guardian* reporter that "Sevenoaks is divided rather like England into north and south. The south is the haves, and the north is the have nots – and they need it."

So politicised did the issue become, so bitter the criticism, that it was decided to hold a poll on August 18th. The result was never in doubt. The *Sevenoaks Chronicle* commented: "Of the 18% who voted, a predictable majority preferred the county council site. If the ballot proved anything it was that a tiny Labour Party can still rally its faithful for a pointless exercise in pique . . . The deal offered by Sevenoaks School was a good one. It does not deserve to be rejected out of jealousy because a fee-paying school is involved."

☆　☆　☆

In his quest for improved administrative efficiency, for more effective pastoral care, for closer monitoring of pupils' academic progress and for a more sophisticated use of statistical analysis for advance planning, Barker relied heavily upon the willing support of the Registrar, George Alcock, and of Mark Pyper, the future Headmaster of Gordounston, shrewdly appointed as Office Manager by Alan Tammadge to help maintain the ever increasing flow of ever more detailed paper-work and associated chores – correspondence with parents and with prep and primary school headmasters, absentee records, timetable cards, room allocation, private study arrangements, the School Calendar, the timing of exams, the prompt dispatch of reports, the booking of school mini-buses, the issue of bus passes, the parking of sixth formers' cars, supervision of the contract cleaners. . . . Fortunately, both men devoured all this work with positive zest, and though by 1982 Pyper was also Director of the Summer Festival (and in 1986 Registrar too, when Alcock became Estates Bursar), they seemed quite unperturbed by the Headmaster's apparently inexhaustible appetite for precise facts, figures and projections.

Though Barker did not always see eye to eye with Robert Froy, who as Vice-Chairman and then Chairman of Governors took an unusually close interest in almost every aspect of school life, the relationship between them, their mutual respect for each other's devotion to the school, tenacity in its defence and determination to safeguard its future, was in the end extremely beneficial. The Chairman fully supported his Headmaster's attempts to improve the School's academic standards and generally to enhance its attractiveness by financially bold projects: he knew that, in most cases, these projects were the result of a careful, realistic assessment of the "market", but also of a genuine belief that the visible pursuit of excellence was in the long run the proper duty of the School. For his part, Robert Froy had already done a great deal to rationalise the School's budgeting procedures: determined to shed the habit of financing every new project – and often much of the essential repairs and maintenance – by means of either an expensive bank loan (borrow first, then build) or an uncertain windfall gift, he convinced the Governing Body that "forward" financing (save first, then build) was the only realistic way to ensure the continued advance of the School. Certainly, fees would have to be raised, and despite a generous provision of Scholarships this would inevitably put the School beyond the reach of a few more of William Sevenoaks' local "poor children whatsoever coming thither to be taught," who once would have hoped for a free place. But there seemed no alternative, for parents, particularly parents of boarders, were becoming increasingly knowledgeable and perceptive when choosing a school for their children: a respectable record of success in public examinations was one thing, but they also cast a critical eye upon the school's ability to cater for every aspect of a child's development and happiness. How big were the classes? How close were the beds in dormitories? Were there individual study-bedrooms for older pupils? How much choice was there at meals? What weekend activities were organised? Could they see the changing-rooms and lavatories? If certain facilities were inadequate, what were the school's plans to improve them? Barker and the Governors knew that this last question was crucial not only to the satisfaction of parents but to the morale of the staff, and to the school's ability to attract teachers of the highest calibre.

Sennocke House and Other Prizes

Thus, since it was clear that if full co-education was to become a reality there had to be provision for girl boarders, not too much time was wasted in opting for a brand new "prestige" boarding house rather than for a less expensive alternative such as adapting the newly acquired Temple House or extending the Girls' International House Annexe. Sennocke House, formally opened by Lady Sackville in 1985, obviously made formidable inroads into the School's resources, already fully stretched by Barker's and the Governors' efforts to improve the facilities and amenities available to staff and to pupils: the new Daygirls' Centre above the Medical Centre, six new classrooms (including a Computer Room complete with a new Head of Computing), more staff houses and flats, an all-weather cricket strip on Duke's Meadow, improvements to boarding houses, and a new forge for the 1984 Craftsman Fellow, Tony Wooton.

Fortunately, meanwhile, Sevenoaks boys and girls continued to enhance the school's national reputation by remarkable individual or collective achievements: Neil Dickenson won the French Under 20 Chess Championship; Nicholas Booth and Richard Black each gained six Grade As at 'A' Level and two Distinctions at 'S' Level; Michael Punnett and Paul Roberts represented Great Britain in the European Science Championships in Copenhagen with their intelligent disc drive, and carried off the second prize of £1,000; the "Moonwriter" designed by Neil Darracott, Jon Harlow and Chris Berry was chosen as Britain's entry to a world design competition in Japan, and won the B.B.C. Award for "the individual, organisation or firm that, during the last year, developed an aid, or initiated a service, of the greatest benefit to visually handicapped people in Britain." That year, 1984, their great teacher, Gerd Somerhoff, retired at the age of 69, and was deservedly made a Member of the Order of the British Empire in recognition of his service to the teaching of technology in schools.

But 1984 was above all Emma Johnson's year. A fast growing and increasingly captivated nation-wide audience followed the progress of this modest, charming and immensely gifted young clarinettist, through the heats of the B.B.C.'s Young Musician of the Year competition, to her final triumph in the Free Trade Hall, Manchester, with an exquisite performance of Crusell's Clarinet Concerto; in the audience were her teacher, John Brightwell, Peter Woodward, the Director of Music at Sevenoaks, and Richard and Imogen

Barker. Within days the School was being bombarded with offers from Oxbridge colleges, eager to recruit this young phenomenon to read Music *or* English *or* French – or almost anything else.

That same year, Old Sennockian and Former Captain of Sailing Simon Donaldson (1969-75) became Wallis Professor of Mathematics at Oxford, the University's youngest ever professor at the age of 27. The School celebrated, at its own humbler level, with excellent exam results: a 92% pass rate at 'A' Level, with 72% "good grades"; 100% I.B. passes; 4 Oxbridge Awards and 18 places for 7th term candidates; 1 Award, 9 places and 9 conditional places for 4th term candidates.

In sport, too, things have gone well. One of Richard Barker's outstanding achievements so far has been his success in dramatically raising the standards of excellence aspired to and reached in sports previously involving relatively few pupils, but now enjoyed by many: tennis, sailing, squash and shooting among others. This he has done not only by the injection of money and the provision of better facilities, but by personal encouragement, and by an insistence that wherever possible skilled coaching should be available to all, not just to the elite practitioners (and additional talented coaches have sometimes been lured to Sevenoaks from overseas on temporary appointments, or on one year exchanges with members of staff). Under Charles Cunningham, Irene Rowley and now Andrew Penfold, our shooters have distinguished themselves at the highest competitive levels, while our sailors, tirelessly and skilfully coached by Bruce Hebbert at Bough Beech, capped a decade of truly remarkable success of carrying off, in 1991-92, the top titles in the International, World Schools and U.K. Championships at Burghfield. Not that the major games have been neglected: after a second successful world tour to Australia and Fiji in 1988, Mike Williams' 1st XV had an excellent season, the highlight of which was their victory over Palmerston North, a powerful touring team from New Zealand; cricket has flourished under Ian Walker and his colleagues: in 1990 the 1st XI Captain, Omar Iqbal, scoring 825 runs at an average of 63, came nearer than anyone else to Chris Tavare's 1,036 in 1973; in 1989, girls' hockey teams played a total of 60 matches: the 1st XI lost only twice in 18 matches.

The middle of the decade was darkened by the tragic deaths of three really exceptional schoolmasters. Willie Bleyberg, who went missing in the mountains of Yugoslavia, had been at the School for 27 years. Head of Chemistry, Head of Science, Housemaster, Divisional Headmaster, Common Room Minuting Secretary, coach of Fencing, organiser of an enthusiastic jazz group, officer in the C.C.F., ferryman for the V.S.U., passionate supporter of Amnesty International, he had also for some years taken upon himself, despite his seniority – and this is perhaps the clearest indication of his quality – the abhorred and thankless job of Master i/c Scavenging. Jim Nottidge died after a heart attack. A modest, wise and humane man, a great deflator of pomposity,

243

he had been an excellent Staff Tutor, Head of the Junior School, Housemaster of Johnson's, Middle School Divisional Headmaster, Head of Biology and Master i/c Digweed. No school could afford the unexpected loss of two such rarely experienced and devoted schoolmasters. Yet not long afterwards another was lost who surely would have been their equal: Mike Spear died of a heart attack in June, 1986, at the age of 41. A passionate believer in excellence – on the tennis court, on the rugby field, in Adventure Training or in a Classics class – he drove himself always a little harder than those who loved and strove to please him.

The *apologia* with which this chapter started must now come into effect. Despite the new pressures, exerted upon all schools by the introduction of the National Curriculum and a renewal of intense governmental and public interest in education, and upon independent schools by recession, the continued upward surge of the School in the last six or seven years has been impressive. It deserves, and no doubt one day will receive, the detailed yet discriminating praise whose objectivity greater distance will secure. For the purposes of this brief chronicle of the fortunes of Sevenoaks School over so many years, a few as yet unrefined comments must suffice.

Management of the School's financial affairs by Governors, Bursar and Headmaster has been calm and skilful, cautious but never defensive or fearful. The introduction of full co-education, though it has clearly resulted in a rise in the academic standard of pupils admitted, was bound to be very expensive if girls were to be provided with facilities at least the equal of those available to boys. Barker was keen to make a new Appeal for funds. Some Governors had misgivings, but allowed themselves to be convinced, and the 1986 Appeal for £750,000 was launched at a glittering candle-lit banquet in the Great Hall at Knole, where once Thomas Sackville, first Earl of Dorset and High Treasurer of England, had entertained his financial advisers and discussed ways of raising money for an impatient queen. Paying warm tribute to Kim Taylor and Alan Tammadge, and to the great generosity of previous benefactors, Barker argued that a great school must be sensitive to the changing needs of society: "As the awe-inspiring revolution in micro-electronics begins to influence all around us," he urged, new science laboratories were essential; increasing demand among boys and girls for more music facilities meant that a Music Centre must be added to the Aisher Hall; and growing enthusiasm for games previously thought of as "minor" at Sevenoaks, coupled with the immediate sporting needs of girls not yet numerous enough to field large competitive teams, rendered highly desirable the third major object of the appeal: a set of high quality indoor tennis courts. Before the evening was over, £79,000 had been raised, and two years later Robert Froy was able to announce that the original target had been reached.

As a result of the Appeal's success, of further generous gifts – notably from the ever supportive Aisher family – and of "good housekeeping" by our administrators – the School's facilities have been vastly extended and improved. Though the particular genius of Gerd Somerhoff proved irreplaceable, the new Science and Electronics Centre, opened in November, 1988, by Sir Geoffrey Howe, has greatly improved the effectiveness and broadened the range of our science and advanced technology teaching. The splendid Bailey Tennis Centre, also opened in 1988, was named after the Kent county tennis captain, Charles Bailey, who devoted an enormous amount of time and other resources to the project: with his invaluable help and expertise, a grant from the Sports Council and a loan on generous terms from the Lawn Tennis Association were obtained to help defray the final cost. Open throughout the year from early morning until late at night, it was immediately popular with Old Sennockians: applications from the public for club membership were welcomed, and Tennis Scholarships offered by the School to suitably qualified boys and girls. Only two years later Sevenoaks won its first national title, the Under 16 Public School Championships; since then, our senior teams have regularly figured honourably in all the major championships, confidently rubbing shoulders with the country's top tennis schools.

This is not the place – nor would there be room – to do full honour to the many staff involved, at all levels, in the School's multifarious sporting and other out-of-school activities. Already, in 1939, the Inspectors had praised the loyalty and enthusiasm of the small band of teachers who, despite "very full timetables . . . do not hesitate to take on . . . innumerable out-of-school activities." Did they work harder than today's staff? It seems unlikely, for "facilities" and "teaching aids" are deceptive terms, and it must seem to many teachers that, no sooner does a new building or machine arrive to "facilitate" the performance of one task, it is also found to facilitate the introduction of two more, in the shape of added opportunities offered to pupils.

Barker, like Taylor and Tammadge before him, expects a lot of his staff, and is himself extremely hard-working; he introduced staff "appraisal" long before it became official government policy, and urged staff to keep themselves up to date by attending refresher courses; but he has also, with the Governors' full support, done much to show his appreciation of their efforts. Departments increasingly teach in classrooms grouped about their own departmental offices or resource centres. The much improved Sevenoaks Salary Scale, negotiated in 1987, elicited a warm letter of appreciation from the dreadfully over-crowded Masters' Common Room. A few years later, the Common Room itself had been transformed into a spacious and comfortable haven of rest, conversation, preparation or marking. The dramatic consequences of the Governors' "Site Improvement Project", energetically conducted by Sir William Pile, with David

Bartleet, Kim Taylor and others, were at first viewed with some alarm when builders began to dig up the lawn behind School House and erect, to Richard Reid's specifications, an odd-looking pattern of brick pavilions and walls; however, when the work was finished, when the soothing "water feature" was flowing, and when the creative flair of our brilliant Head Gardener, Ian Harrington, had with lawns and trees and flowers softened the impact and brought harmony to the whole, few could deny the improvement. Similarly, between Reid's new Lodges topped by their airily floating cubes, the handsome Froy Gates, erected to honour twenty years of distinguished service by an exceptionally hard-working and devoted Chairman, convey something of the old School's present day pride, confidence and concern for style.

As early as 1983, Barker had fiercely supported the staff's plea that 'A' Level students should be taught separately from International Baccalaureate students, had obtained the Governors' agreement to take on extra staff, and thus not only removed a source of acute strain but laid the foundations for the remarkable pioneering success of the I.B. programme at Sevenoaks. His enthusiasm for internationalism in education has helped to encourage the extension and proliferation of our educational exchanges with schools in France, Germany Spain and more recently Russia, and to increase the number of ambitious departmental projects and cultural expeditions abroad during full or half-term holidays; he and Imogen have visited all our "twinned" schools, some of them frequently.

In 1986 Brian Scragg retired, having served as Deputy to four Headmasters. He was succeeded as Undermaster by Casey McCann, a physically and metaphorically larger than life bachelor passionately devoted to the School, and particularly to the International Centre where for thirteen years he had been a powerful Tutor; scourge of the lazy, the unmannerly, the untidy, the unpunctual – whether pupils or staff – yet generous friend to many of them, he had done a great deal during the permissive Seventies to maintain unfashionable standards of industry, behaviour and appearance in a 400-strong sixth form, giving as much time and attention to the removal of excessive hair and the confiscation of "illegal" ear-rings and bangles and scarves as he devoted (aided by the School Chaplain, Peter Hullah, later to be Headmaster of Chetham's) to rescuing victims of the "Moonies" from their fortress in San Francisco, or placing leavers in some of the good American universities he had visited. Like Willie Bleyberg a "complete" schoolmaster, he found no job beneath him: a hater of games, he was Master i/c Off Games; fearful of water, he regularly did shore duty for the Sailing Club. In 1988, when Barker was ill for a term, he "Acted Headmaster", as he put it, and apparently found the role to his taste, for two years later he accepted the post of Headmaster of St. Paul's School, Sao Paulo, Brazil. His old Housemaster at the International Centre, Old Sennockian John Guyatt, became Undermaster. That same year, Mark Pyper left to be Headmaster of Gordonstoun, handing over the now enormous Sevenoaks Summer Festival to Roger Woodward and his team, and the Registrarship to Hugh Pullan.

With many long-serving members of staff leaving or nearing retirement (and one, George Alcock, tragically becoming in 1990 the fourth "total schoolmaster" within five years to die in service), the Common Room has been getting younger. Some applicants for teaching posts, interviewed by the Headmaster and left in no doubt about the extent and intensity of the commitment required, have rapidly withdrawn. Many of those appointed were women: by 1991 there were 25 women teachers – including the popular and exuberant Imogen Barker – many of them in senior positions, and they have done much to ensure the now established success of co-education under the watchful eye of Senior Mistress Pat Johnson. Barker firmly resisted the temptation to imagine that co-education means denying the sometimes different needs of younger boys and girls: all Tutor Groups in the Junior and Middle Schools are single-sex, girls with a woman Tutor, boys with a man. Good pastoral care, already strong under Chaplain Nicholas Henshaw, is seen as vital, and is constantly under review: an independent Counsellor has been appointed to help boys or girls in need of special support.

Looking Forward

The future for the School looks bright. The Governing Body, under its new and very energetic Chairman, Robert Wilkinson, and strengthened by the recruitment over previous years of several distinguished women members, is determined that Sevenoaks School shall maintain and consolidate its hard-won reputation as a pace-setter among independent schools, and as an unashamed defender of the pursuit of excellence. Demand for admission is buoyant. The Headmaster's energy appears quite undiminished, as is his keenness to examine every new possibility of making the School a better place to grow up in – whether by the widespread introduction of computerisation or by the happy assimilation of two partially sighted girls from Dorton House. The handsome new wing to Park Grange, designed by Claude Kempton and opened in 1992, means more boarding places for girls at 13, while the arrangement negotiated by Barker with the Heads of certain co-educational prep schools enables us to offer, at 11, places or Scholarships to girls who will join us two years later. Academic standards are steadily rising, and though it is to be hoped that the appearance of League Tables will never make Sevenoaks forget that the passing of exams is but one part of education, the quality of the staff is unlikely to let those standards fall. Barker's successful application for Assisted Places – though only five were allowed us – supplemented a generous range of Scholarships in the attempt to make the School available to as many children as possible.

The Johnson Library, the Sackville Theatre, the Aisher Hall, the Swanzy Block, Lambardes, Boswell, Plender, Fryth, Fenton, Grote, Hardinge . . . in these names of buildings and pastoral groups are commemorated some of those who have guided, sustained or merely shared our fluctuating fortunes over the years. The little village grammar school is now a great independent school, determined to bring further honour to its Founder's memory by facing with enterprise and zest, as he would have done, the challenge of the future. Certainly, the School has never appeared more confident, nor more beautiful than it does today, looking out over the park to the great house of Knole, with whose history, as with that of the Town whose name it bears, its own is proudly interwoven.

APPENDIX 1

Headmasters

	Appointed
Hales, Thomas	1495*
Younge, William	1498*
Painter, William, Senr.	1560*
Painter, William, Jnr.	1560
Cotton, Edward	1576
Buckley, Richard (Revd)	1595*
Frank, Humfrie	1605*
Holdsworth, Robert	1610
Vincent, Nathaniel, B.A.	1618
Toller, John	1619
Bosse, Richard	1633*
Hilles, Francis, Jnr.	1648*
Hooper, John	1654
Turner,	1662
Wrentmore, Robert, M A.	1663
Weston, Andrew, M A	1674
Bloome,	1691
Lewis, George	1700
Fenton, Elijah M.A.	1708
Hussey, Christopher	1711
Simpson, John	1716
Holme, Edward	1750
Hardy, Edward, M.A. (Revd)	1770
Davis, George M.A.(Revd)	1771
Whitfield, Henry, M.A. (Dr.)	1771
Whitehead, Gervase, B.D., M.A. (Revd)	1778
Wilgress, John Thomas M.A. (Revd)	1813
Heawood, Edward M.A. (Revd)	1831
Wallace, James Lloyd M.A. (Revd)	1837
Presgrave, William, M.A.(Revd)	1843
Crofts, Christopher,M.A. (Revd)	1854
Chapman, David M.A.	1877
Birkett, Daniel Maule M.A.	1878
Heslop, George Henry M.A.	1898
Garrod, Geoffrey, M.A.	1919
Higgs-Walker, James Arthur, M.A.	1925
Taylor, Leonard Clive, M A	1954
Hinton, Michael George, M.A.	1968

Tammadge, Alan Richard, M.A.   1971
Barker, Richard Philip, M.A.   1981

Dates with an asterisk are known dates during tenure but where no precise dates of appointment or cessation of office are recorded.

APPENDIX 2

Recent Chairmen of Governors

–1908	Lionel, 2nd Lord Sackville
1908–1913	Col. J M Rodgers
1913–1926	Lionel Edward, 3rd Lord Sackville
1926–1938	Charles P Johnson
1938–1959	Charles John, 4th Lord Sackville
1959	Sir Charles Innes (father)
1959–1962	Sir Charles Innes (son)
1962–1981	Lionel, 6th Lord Sackville
1981–1991	Robert A D Froy
1991–	Robert P Wilkinson

APPENDIX 3

Family Service on Governing Body

1560–1682	Bosville and Boswell families
1663–1769	Lambarde family
1663–1782	Farnaby family
1742–1799	Dukes of Dorset
1790–1888	Lambarde family
1788–1924	Amherst family
1877–	Sackville family

Buildings

Nothing is known of the buildings in which the School first began its life. Thereafter the main additions or changes were as follows:

Date	Buildings	Source of Funds
1631	New Schoolroom and Master's House	John Blome
1732	Burlington's new School House and Almshouses	Sale of Sevenoak's London properties
1879	Dormitory floor added to School House	Governors
1890	Gymnasium/Assembly Hall	Governors
1900	Laboratories	Governors & Kent Education Committee
	Cottage Building (Sanitorium) and swimming bath	W F Thompson and Appeal
1910	Solefields Road playing fields(part)	Sale of School Lands
1925	New Buildings (Swanzy Block)	F Swanzy
1927	Johnson's Boarding House	C P Johnson
1930	Fives Court	E Johnson
1931	New Sanatorium	Governors
1934	Johnson Hall	CP and E Johnson
1947	Manor House	Governors
1948	Park Grange House and Estate	Johnson Trustees
1955	Red Lodge	Governors
	Park Grange Gardens	Governors
1957	New Science Block	Governors and Industrial Fund for Science
1960	7 and 9 High Street	Governors
1961	Headmaster's House	Governors
1962	International Sixth Form Centre	Governors
	Little Theatre (cinema/lecture hall)	Governors
1963	Technical Activities Centre (VISTA)	Governors
1965	Lambardes	Governors
1967	Art Room/Dining Hall Block	Governors
	Aisher Hall Music Centre	Eileen Aisher
	Orchards, Chaplain's House	Governors
1968	Post Office Tennis Courts	Governors
	Running Track	Governors
1970	Biology Laboratories	Governors
1972	Language Teaching Centre	Pipemakers Company and Elia Salzman
1976	Johnson Hall converted to Library	Governors
1977	Marley Sports Hall	J. Aisher & Marley Tile plc
	Girls' International House	Governors
	Two Squash Courts	Governors

1981	Sackville Theatre	Appeal
	Kirkella	Governors
	14 High Street	Governors
1983	Temple House	Governors
	38 High Street	Governors
1986	Sennocke Boarding House	Appeal
1988	Science, Electronics & Computer Centre	Appeal
	11 High Street	Governors
1989	Bailey Tennis Centre	Charles Bailey and Appeal
	2 High Street	Governors
1990	Site Improvement Scheme	Governors
	Staff Common Room Extension	Governors
1992	Claridge House	Governors

INDEX
Numbers set in **bold** refer to the plate sections.